Praise for

Rosemary

"In her engaging and compassionate *Rosemary: The Hidden Kennedy Daughter*, Kate Larson illuminates the poignant story of a resolute girl falling behind in a glamorous and competitive family. Rosemary's own story comes alive against the broader and often shocking background of twentieth-century attitudes toward the intellectually disabled, and sheds fascinating light on how the characters of Rose Kennedy, Joe Kennedy, and Rosemary's famous siblings were indelibly shaped by her determined yet tragic life."

— Will Swift, author of
The Kennedys Amidst the Gathering Storm

"A heartbreaking book that makes clear the pain and passion behind the Kennedy family's efforts on behalf of the disabled."

— BBC.com

"Kate Clifford Larson delivers an engrossing portrait of Rose and Joe Kennedy's tragic misunderstanding of their oldest daughter's capabilities, and of how her fate changed the Kennedy family forever. And yet it is Rosemary herself who shines from the pages of this profoundly revealing family story."

— Marya Hornbacher, author of
Madness: A Bipolar Life

Rosemary

Rosemary

The Hidden Kennedy Daughter

Kate Clifford Larson

MARINER BOOKS

HOUGHTON MIFFLIN HARCOURT

BOSTON   NEW YORK

First Mariner Books edition 2016

Copyright © 2015 by Kate Clifford Larson

For information about permission to reproduce selections from this book,
write to trade.permissions@hmhco.com or to Permissions, Houghton Mifflin Harcourt
Publishing Company, 3 Park Avenue, 19th Floor, New York, New York 10016.

www.hmhco.com

Library of Congress Cataloging-in-Publication Data
Larson, Kate Clifford, author.
Rosemary : the hidden Kennedy daughter / Kate Clifford Larson.
p. ; cm.
Includes bibliographical references and index.
ISBN 978-0-547-25025-0 (hardcover) — ISBN 978-0-547-61795-4 (ebook)
ISBN 978-0-544-81190-4 (pbk.)
I. Title.
[DNLM: 1. Kennedy, Rosemary, 1918–2005. 2. Kennedy family. 3. Intellectual
Disability—United States—Biography. 4. Family Relations—United States—
Biography. 5. History, 20th Century—United States—Biography.
6. Institutionalization—United States—Biography. 7. Mentally Disabled Persons—
United States—Biography. 8. Psychosurgery—United States—Biography. WM 302]
RC464.B56
362.196890092—dc23
[B]
2015028793

Book design by Victoria Hartman

Printed in the United States of America
DOC 10 9 8 7 6 5 4 3 2 1

*To those struggling
with disabilities and mental illness,
and the families who love them*

Contents

Rosemary

1

A Home Birth

Rose Kennedy, pregnant with her third child, felt her contractions beginning on Friday, September 13. The nurse hired to attend her during the last days of her pregnancy quickly sent for Dr. Frederick L. Good, Rose's personal obstetrician, to come to the Kennedy home at 83 Beals Street in the Boston suburb of Brookline. The first two Kennedy children, Joseph Jr., now three years old, and sixteen-month-old "Jack," had both been born at home, and Rose was electing to do the same with this baby. It had been an uneventful third pregnancy. The deeply devout Rose would have been acutely aware of the gift of such a healthy pregnancy in the midst of great danger.

During the war years of 1917 and 1918, Spanish influenza swept the globe, killing tens of millions worldwide and debilitating millions more. By the fall of 1918, the flu's deadly march was taking its toll on the citizens of Boston. By mid-September there were more than five thousand diagnosed cases of the Spanish flu in the city alone. Deaths mounted daily as the pandemic made its second of three deadly passes across the nation in less than a year. The closing of theaters, lyceums, halls, and churches became mandatory, and public gatherings were discouraged to avoid the spread of the disease. Local hospitals, clinics, and doctors' offices around Boston and its suburbs were overwhelmed. Unlike other flu epidemics, which claimed mostly the lives of the very young and the very old, this viral infection took the lives of healthy young men and women in the prime of their lives as well. Young soldiers who had survived the trenches and battlefields of Europe during World War I and returned home triumphant began dying by the thousands from pneumonia and respiratory failure. According to one nurse who worked day and night during the worst of the epidemic in Boston, "All the city was dying, in the homes serious illness, on the streets funeral processions." Nearly seven thousand residents died within a six-month period.

But the lethal virus did not infect the home of Joseph and Rose Kennedy and their young family. The nurse had been checking the unborn baby's and Rose's health daily, listening to both baby's and mother's heart rates, monitoring the baby's position vis-à-vis the birth canal and its in utero activity, noting the details in a ledger for the doctor to review when he arrived. With Rose's labor begun and Dr. Good sent for, she transformed Rose's room into a modified antiseptic hospital labor room, ordered the general maid or hired girl to heat water, and made sure that all instruments and equipment the doctor might need were within reach.

Trained in the latest obstetrical nursing practices, the nurse was responsible for two patients, as her nursing manual would have reminded her: the mother and the unborn child. "If during the absence of the doctor the mother should die," the *Obstetrical Nursing* guide warned ominously, "upon the physician's return the nurse . . . could hardly excuse herself to the physician or to the family." This directive put the nurse in an untenable position: she had been trained to deliver babies but also to wait for the doctor to arrive to deliver the baby. She could not give Rose an anesthetic as labor became more intense and painful, because only the physician and his anesthetist, in this case probably a Dr. Edward J. O'Brien, could administer anesthesia as a matter of course when they arrived.

But on this day, the doctor had not arrived once the baby began entering the birth canal, and Rose could not resist the need to push the baby with each more forceful contraction. The nurse tried to keep her calm, encouraging her to endure each contraction and to fight back the urge to push. Yet Rose's baby started crowning, a crucial point in the birthing process. It was well understood that preventing the movement of the baby through the birth canal could cause a lack of oxygen, exposing the baby to possible brain damage and physical disability.

The doctor was delayed, caught up in attending his many patients stricken by the deadly flu. The nurse demanded that Rose hold her legs together tightly in the hope of delaying the baby's birth. Despite her training as an obstetrical nurse, she opted not to deliver the baby herself.

"I had such confidence in my obstetrician," Rose wrote as a much older woman. "I put my faith in God . . . and tried to sublimate my discomfort in expectation of the happiness" she expected to feel once the baby was born. Dr. Good and his colleagues, however, may not have been driven wholly by the desire to provide the best care for their patients. Fees derived from supplying health services to Boston's social and economic elite provided a steady, and hefty, income in the days before medical insurance. If Dr. Good missed the birth of the baby, he could not charge his extremely high fee of $125 for prenatal care and delivery. When holding Rose's legs together failed to keep the baby from coming, the nurse resorted to another, more dangerous practice: holding the baby's head and forcing it back into the birth canal for two excruciating hours.

The doctor did finally appear at the Kennedys' home, and at seven in the evening he delivered Rose's seemingly healthy third child. The *Boston Globe* announced the birth: "A dainty girl was added to the nursery which previously sheltered two sturdy sons." Flowers and cards of congratulations poured in. The baby would be named for her mother. Little Rose Marie Kennedy—"Rosie" to the family, and later called Rosemary—would be loved and nurtured by both of her parents.

Rosemary was "sweet and peaceable and cried less than the first two," Rose would recall more than fifty years later. Rose spent several weeks "lying in," the length of time middle- and upper-class women took to recover from childbirth. New mothers, it was recommended, should rest and remain in bed for at least nine days and slowly begin daily activities, like walking, over a period of many more days, increasing activity gradually over several weeks. Six weeks was considered ideal. Rose enjoyed this time alone, nursing and doting on baby Rosemary. Full-time and part-time nursemaids and other household help took care of the boys, cleaned, and cooked. "The quiet and peace surrounding the mother and child at this period is good for both," Rose later wrote about this time alone with her newborn baby.

JOSEPH "JOE" P. KENNEDY SR., as the new assistant general manager of the Fore River Shipbuilding Company, a subsidiary of Bethlehem Steel in nearby Quincy, could afford such luxuries for his wife. Most men of his age—Joe was thirty years old when his first daughter was born—were now required to register for the wartime draft. But he was exempt from military service because of his role working for the shipyard and managing its multimillion-dollar government contracts and thousands of workers now building naval vessels destined for the war in Europe. Joe was brilliant at his job, and his business and management acumen spurred the expansion of not only the shipyard and its workforce but also the support systems required to shelter, feed, and transport the thousands of workers at the plant. Joe's workload increased "exponentially" at this time, keeping him working lengthy days and often not returning home for the night, establishing a work ethic that would persist for the rest of his life. This pace, however, earned Joe an ulcer, and just a month after Rosemary was born he checked himself into a sanitarium to recuperate. Persistent ulcers and other intestinal issues, too, would plague him until his death.

The 1914 marriage of Rose, the beautiful and intelligent eldest daughter of Boston's mayor, John "Honey Fitz" Fitzgerald, and his wife, Mary Josephine "Josie" Hannon, to Joe, the scion of a politically powerful East Boston family, had signified a strong political and economic union. It was a foundation from which the couple rapidly ascended to the pinnacle of Boston's newly established Irish social, political, and economic elite.

By the middle of the nineteenth century, two generations earlier, the North End of Boston had become a community of immigrants and the working poor whose interests and needs varied greatly from the native-born Brahmin and Yankee aristocracy. This group, whose ancestors had settled Boston centuries before, shaped New England culture and society. Its Puritan legacy informed the region's politics, education, social interactions and relationships, economics, and the very landscape of cities and towns where immigrants settled to build new lives. The historic neighborhoods of some of Boston's founding families included the Brahmin stronghold of Beacon Hill. The south side of the hill, dominated by the Massachusetts State House, faces the city's common and public garden. Powerful business, political, and literary leaders lived in the neighborhood mansions, forming a distinctly Protestant aristocracy. The mere one hundred acres of the North End, located on the northern reaches of the city and bordered by the Charles River and Boston Harbor to its north and east, respectively, was one of the most densely populated neighborhoods in the country. In 1860, nearly twenty-seven thousand people crowded its crooked streets and lanes. More than half were Irish immigrants. During the latter quarter of the century, however, a tidal wave of eastern European immigrants fleeing political, economic, and agricultural disasters and massive anti-Semitic pogroms in Russia and other nations provided a steady flow of desperate and hopeful people. In sharp contrast to Beacon Hill— a half mile away—the North End's tenements and sweatshops teeming with people spilled out onto streets and wharves.

The congestion in such a small area placed terrible stress on the entire city and its residents. In spite of the benefits of a bustling economy, sewage, garbage, and low-wage maritime, industrial, and textile businesses plagued the health and well-being of individuals and families in the crowded district. The economic and human costs were great. Classrooms were horribly overcrowded, filled with children from myriad ethnic and racial backgrounds who spoke dozens of distinct and different languages. The city scrambled to accommodate them; it was imperative that they be taught English and good work habits, and that they become "Americanized" as quickly as possible, native-born elites believed. Eager to impart white, middle-class Protestant confor-

mity, many city public schools were open eighteen hours a day to
provide programs not only for two shifts of daily classes for children of all ages but for their parents, too.

Such densely packed buildings and streets eventually drove
the young Fitzgerald family out of the North End, where Rose's
father, John Fitzgerald, had grown up as the fourth of twelve children. Rose's mother, Josie Hannon Fitzgerald, was from Acton, a
rural farming community twenty-five miles west of Boston. After the couple's marriage, they settled in the North End, but Josie
longed for the green grass and fresh air of the countryside. In
1892, when Rose was two years old, Fitzgerald yielded to his
wife's wishes and bought a large house for his family in West
Concord, three short miles from Acton but thirty miles from Boston. Like many of their Irish neighbors, the Fitzgeralds left behind the rickety wooden and dilapidated brick tenements of their
poorer neighbors for more space, inside and out, and more refine-
ment. Between the late 1890s and 1920, the West End of Boston,
Brighton, Roxbury, Dorchester, and Hyde Park experienced tremendous growth and development, prompting the annexation of
these communities by the city proper. The construction of an el-
evated railway and subway system in Boston in 1897 made these
areas more easily accessible to the city and to jobs.

Eager to take an active role in politics, Fitzgerald was elected
to Congress in 1895. He split his time between West Concord
and Washington, but the idyllic setting, close proximity to her
own Hannon family, good schools, and a large home with servants
were ample compensation to Josie for her husband's frequent absence. Honey Fitz, though, never forgot his love for the crowded
and vibrant culture of Boston. His decision to run for mayor of
Boston in 1905 was reason to move his family back to the city.

The compromise for taking Josie away from her rural home was a beautiful mansion on Welles Avenue in Dorchester, with an easy commute to the heart of the city.

By the time of Honey Fitz's run, the Boston Irish had become a powerful constituency, having demanded and won, over the course of several decades, a bigger role in the city's governance as well as in its economic and social institutions. Consolidating political power through the ward-boss system, a particularly effective organizing tool rooted in close-knit neighborhood organizations and committees, the Irish capitalized on their settlement in nearly all districts of the city, building strong and sophisticated political machines. This system enabled Fitzgerald to win a hotly contested mayoral race in December 1905, when Rose was fifteen years old. But he differed markedly from his immigrant Ireland-born predecessors: he was part of a younger, progressive generation of American Irish Catholics, campaigning for the poor, hungry, jobless, and downtrodden. Though Fitzgerald had already served in various city, state, and national offices, his election as the city's mayor was a milestone for Puritan Boston. He had run against Patrick Kennedy, Joe's father, and in spite of Kennedy's loss, the two men remained cordial friends and sometimes political allies. Their distinct political power bases were both valuable and representative of a diverse Irish community.

The alliance between Honey Fitz and Patrick Kennedy had its basis in political and social interactions over the years; their families had summered in Old Orchard Beach, Maine, since both Rose and Joe were toddlers. But it was not until the summer of 1906, after Rose graduated from Dorchester High School and Joe was looking toward a final year at the prestigious Boston Latin School, that the two teenagers became reacquainted. Their immediate attraction upon being reintroduced to each other in Old Orchard Beach through mutual friends blossomed into love.

Rose during this heady time was well positioned, as the newly elected mayor's daughter, to step into Boston Irish society. Not only was she considered beautiful, but also her intellect and outgoing personality rounded out her position as one of the aspiring new women of Irish Boston. She took courses in foreign languages, perfected piano at the New England Conservatory, volunteered at the Boston Public Library, and participated in German and French cultural associations in the city. She thrived in the spotlight.

Rose had become her father's companion on the campaign trail, appearing frequently with him, even as a high school senior, in place of her mother at Boston parades, luncheons, dinners, political rallies, and more. When she was born, in 1890, Rose filled a deep void in Fitzgerald's life. Two sisters and one brother had died in infancy, and his mother had died in 1880. When he married Josie Hannon of Acton and brought her to the North End home where he lived with his nine surviving brothers, she was the first woman to live in the house since their mother had died. He desperately wanted a baby girl, and his prayers were answered in Rose. A close family friend later told historian Doris Kearns Goodwin that "his love for her . . . was greater than any feeling he had ever known." Rose thrived as her father's eldest; beautiful and smart, she was his favorite among his three daughters. She returned his adoration: "To my mind," she later told Goodwin, "there was no one in the world like my father. Wherever he was, there was magic in the air." Outgoing and quick of wit like her father, Rose enjoyed the political and social world of her father as much as he did. She was an ideal stand-in for her mother, who preferred the privacy and cloistered life of her own home and family.

Fitzgerald had high expectations in suitors for his eldest daughter. "My father," Rose wrote many years later, "had extravagant notions of my beauty, grace, wit, and charm." As she grew older, "these delusions deepened. I suppose no father really thinks any man is good enough for his daughter." He was, she concluded, "a hopeless case." Rose complained that her father refused to allow her to attend school dances or to socialize with boys and young men. In her mind, her father was excessively conservative and overly protective. Once the family returned from Old Orchard Beach that fall of 1906, dating posed considerable challenges for Rose and Joe. Undaunted by Honey Fitz's rules, the young couple would remain committed to each other, finding ways to see each other without her father's knowing.

Rose at this time was determined to participate in the burgeoning freedoms available in the modernizing new century. Women were moving into the public sphere in droves; they were working in business, retail, health care, law, social work, education, the arts, and more. Educational opportunities for women were expanding, social mores were relaxing, and women's political power was growing. Though lacking the vote, women organized—often through women's clubs, unions, and progressive reform groups—to lobby for legislation affecting wages, working conditions, urban politics, education, and public health.

Rose's aspirations included college, and living in Boston made the pursuit of higher education a possibility. Home to several secular universities and colleges, Boston offered middle-class and some working-class women educational and professional training not available in many other parts of the country. At sixteen, however, Rose was a little young to enter college immediately after her graduation, so she decided to take a postgraduate year in preparatory classes at Dorchester High School to further groom her for the rigors of college.

By the time Rose was contemplating college, Catholic institutions of higher learning for women were still few. Convent schools had long been the standard, though most did not confer college degrees. The Catholic Church in the United States had just begun its commitment to establishing private Catholic colleges and universities, but they were for men exclusively. Secular, Protestant, and Methodist colleges in the Boston area, including Simmons, Harvard, Wellesley, and Boston University, all accepted women either directly or in annexed institutions, like Radcliffe at Harvard, educating women in mostly segregated classrooms.

Even a separate Catholic primary and secondary school system was slow in coming. Frustrated by the discrimination and bullying that Catholic students were facing every day in Boston's public schools, the local Catholic archbishop, John Williams, began establishing Catholic parochial schools throughout the region starting in the 1880s. Such bold maneuvers by the Catholic Church, Boston's Brahmins imagined, threatened the very foundations of civil society and undermined cherished Puritan values. Protestant denominations had long dominated private schools, but New England's Yankee and Protestant elite had also defined public-school education through well-delineated curriculum standards for more than two centuries. How could this elite control the Irish population if it could not control who was teaching Irish children?

Once the process started, however, mostly through small schools attached to local churches, the number of Catholic schools for children in Boston grew rapidly. The quality of these schools varied. Even so, dedicated nuns and a few lay teachers brought more than a few programs up to the high standards of other New England public and private schools. By 1900, Catholic schools in the large urban centers, where immigrants settled nearly exclusively, were considered a "safety valve for the public system" that was groaning under the weight of immigration and grossly overcrowded classrooms. Some diocesan schools offered the latest in manual and vocational training in addition to the usual academic subjects, providing a path to jobs and a way out of poverty.

Mayor Fitzgerald, even as a Catholic public figure, believed strongly in public education. The mayor's brother Henry recalled that Fitzgerald sent Rose and her brothers and sisters to Concord public schools because he believed that "public schools were training grounds for success in the world." This, although his choice conflicted with the wishes of the Archdiocese of Boston. Under the leadership of Archbishop William O'Connell, the archdiocese pressured Catholic families to send their children to Catholic schools, even if they were inferior, while influential Catholic theologians directed Catholics to invest in parochial schools. O'Connell's colleague Archbishop Ireland of Minnesota claimed, in 1906, that "the peril of the age, the peril of America is secularism in schools and colleges." Parents "should bend their energies to give their children a thoroughly Catholic education. There is no room for argument," he expounded. "Nothing but the daily drill in the teachings of the faith . . . will sink so deeply into the soul of the child that it must remain there through life unaltered and unwavering." Otherwise, he warned, the "losses to the faith will be immense." By 1910 nearly fifteen percent of all students in Massachusetts attended parochial schools.

The Catholic Church had taken a conservative tack at the turn of the century, and its separatist views fueled even more distrust and fear among non-Catholics. Anxiety over Catholic control of education, in combination with the rising tide of immigrants from southern and eastern Europe who did not speak English and who dressed oddly, practiced different religious customs, and ate strange foods, sparked raging nativism. Anti-Catholicism reached a fever pitch, at levels not seen since the decades prior to the Civil War.

Nevertheless, when his family moved to Dorchester and could easily attend one of Boston's many elementary and secondary Catholic schools, Fitzgerald enrolled his children in the public schools. He ignored the directive from the church, and as mayor he in fact supported expansion of the public-school system to accommodate the growing influx of immigrant children and their parents.

During Rose's postgraduate college-preparatory year at Dorchester High, she applied to Wellesley College, located on the shores of Lake Waban, twenty miles outside of Boston. One of the nation's premier colleges, Wellesley, founded in 1870, offered a rigorous liberal arts education exclusively for women. Its world-renowned faculty taught students who as graduates numbered among the most notable female social, scientific, political, literary, and economic pioneers and leaders of the day. Rose was eager to explore new intellectual pursuits, and when she and three of her friends, Ruth Evans, Vera Legg, and Marguerite O'Callaghan, were all accepted into the fall freshman class, she was ecstatic.

Rose and her friends would be among a very few young American women to graduate from high school and attend college at the time. Fifty-five percent of Boston's high school graduates were young women, but only 12 percent of all students of high school age graduated. From 1900 to 1920, the percentage of all women attending college in the United States rose steadily, from 3 percent of high school graduates to 7.6 percent—similar rates to those for men. Although women constituted nearly 40 percent of total college enrollments and 20 percent of graduates, the great majority attended teachers' colleges, or "normal schools," which were overwhelmingly female-centered, offered a relatively short period of study, and did not grant bachelor's degrees. Rose's decision, and financial ability, to attend a four-year women's college put her among the most elite of American women.

Wellesley was a secular college. In spite of the school's strong emphasis on church attendance and Christian values and beliefs, Catholic leaders were suspicious of its Protestant foundation. They feared the independence fostered at such institutions, preferring instead a strict, sex-segregated Catholic education featuring instruction in a far less progressive curriculum than that offered by colleges like Wellesley. In the general culture, too, concerns that a college education made a woman unattractive for marriage fueled deeply held fears about spinsterhood, keeping many women from achieving educational goals and self-supporting careers.

However, Rose's parents allowed her to make her own decision. She had received the blessing of her father to apply to Wellesley as a day student. Her Honey Fitz was a modern man, and his bright daughter would be a new woman of the age. Smart, cultured, sure of herself, Rose would be the perfect "Wellesley girl," or so she thought.

On the eve of her departure for college, in September 1907, Rose's parents sat her down and told her she would not, after all, be joining her friends and attending Wellesley. Rose was crushed. She begged her father—she knew the decision was her father's, not her mother's—but he was immovable. "There was screaming and yelling, absolute madness," Rose later told Kerry McCarthy, a close relative.

Though unaware of the details at the time, Rose came to understand that her father had chosen his politics over her future. Fitzgerald had been warned by Boston's Archbishop O'Connell that his days as mayor could be numbered if he did not embrace O'Connell's brand of Catholic conservatism. The mayor should, he was told, commit to shaping a new, separatist Catholic power structure within the city. Honey Fitz, well into his reelection campaign for mayor and in the throes of a crippling political-corruption and graft scandal that threatened to derail his administration and his candidacy, could not afford O'Connell's disfavor. The archbishop could easily throw his support in the upcoming election — and the Catholic vote — behind another candidate. When O'Connell learned that Rose was going to attend Wellesley, he warned Fitzgerald that Boston's Catholic voters would disapprove. The mayor's daughter was one of the leading young women in the city, O'Connell argued, whose example other young Catholic women sought to follow. If she went to Wellesley, O'Connell feared, these young women and their families would be "heeding the siren call of secularism," and the bishop would be forced publicly to condemn Rose.

Rose's confidence in her ability to shape her own future, along with her emotional alliance with her beloved father, was shattered. "I was furious at my parents for years. I was angry at the church. As much as I loved my father, I never really forgave him for not letting me go," she recalled years later.

Rose would learn to abide by her parents' wishes, however painful this was to her. There were no options for an accredited Catholic college education for women available in 1907 in Boston. The first accredited four-year Catholic college for women, Trinity College in Washington, D.C., had opened in 1900, but it was one of only ten Catholic institutions of higher learning for women in the United States, none of which were located in New

England. Rose enrolled in the Convent School of the Sacred Heart on Commonwealth Avenue that fall. It would not be the Wellesley education she'd yearned for, and it would never make up for her loss. Seventy years later, Rose still harbored the painful memory of her dreams of a college education dashed because her father had placed his own politics before her aspirations. "My greatest regret," she told Doris Kearns Goodwin, "is not having gone to Wellesley College. It is something I have felt a little sad about my whole life."

Established in 1880 by Mother Randall, one of the Sisters of Saint Joseph, the Convent of the Sacred Heart was a day school providing a classical education for girls and young women from the elementary level through two years of postgraduate work. Of French origin, Sacred Heart schools had been spreading across Europe and the United States for decades, their object "the propagation of the devotion to the Sacred Heart [of Jesus] and the education of the upper classes." A classical course of study similar to what Rose had experienced at Dorchester High School was augmented by intense religious instruction, medieval church history, and French, of which Rose was not very fond. "I knew Latin, Roman and Greek history and grammatical French," Rose told Goodwin, "but knew nothing of medieval history and literature, nor could I understand spoken French." Her public-school preparation had not readied her for the particular instructional demands familiar to students who had attended Sacred Heart during their formative years. These included "ethics, metaphysics and psychology, history . . . close reading of English classics and general history of foreign literatures; mathematics . . . Latin . . . [and] experimental study of the natural sciences." Modern languages other than French were optional. The lack of advanced classes in math, science, and modern literature prevented national accreditation, however. Rose's course of study also included a heavy dose of domestic science, preparing those young women not destined for a religious order to be model wives and mothers.

Religion and faith stood at the core of the Sacred Heart studies. "Let religion be at once the foundation and the crowning point of the education [that the Sacred Heart schools] intend to give and consequently the chief subject taught," the early constitution of the schools declared. At the time Rose entered the convent school in Boston, its curriculum had not changed materially since 1869. "Under such training," one sister Sacred Heart school boasted, "were formed those women who are now doing credit to their Alma Mater, as consecrated virgins, modest wives, consorts to whom are entrusted the mightiest cares of State, and the queenly mothers whom the Catholic Church delights to call her daughters." Archbishop O'Connell's demand that Fitzgerald and his daughter demonstrate their devotion to their faith as upperclass Irish Americans, and their fidelity to him as a rising power among Catholics in Massachusetts, would forever change Rose's future.

Joe would become Rose's touchstone over those years of disappointment. As she achieved the higher education available to her, whether at the convent school on Commonwealth Avenue or at the New England Conservatory in Boston, where she studied piano, her time with Joe soothed her wounded soul—and, given Honey Fitz's disapproval, was perhaps an outlet for rebellion. The young couple managed to see each other through subterfuge and clandestine meetings, often helped along by their friends. "It took teamwork and conspiracy," Rose remembered many years later. Her father pushed other suitors, but to no avail. Even Fitzgerald's chauffeur, who had a soft spot for Joe, would drive Rose to some of their rendezvous, without the mayor's knowledge.

Honey Fitz's specific objections to Joe aren't clear; certainly his background and drive would have felt familiar to the older man. The grandson of immigrants from County Wexford in Ireland, Joe grew up in East Boston, an urban center dominated by Irish immigrants across the harbor from Boston. A large neighborhood, East Boston differed from other immigrant enclaves in Boston, because it had developed well-established districts populated by middle- and upper-class families. Joe's father, Patrick Kennedy, lost his own father as an infant and was sent to work at an early age. His wages from toiling on the nearby wharves helped support his widowed mother, Mary Augusta Hickey, and two older sisters, Loretta and Margaret. Smart and hardworking, Patrick Kennedy made successful investments in small taverns and liquor importation that helped him move his family from its immigrant tenement to the wealthier East Boston neighborhood of Jeffries Point. His son Joseph "Joe" Patrick Kennedy, born in 1888, would have all the educational and economic advantages he did not as a child. Ambitious, articulate, and athletic, Joe would enter Harvard in 1908, a year after Rose began at the Convent of the Sacred Heart.

By that summer of 1908, with possible criminal charges pending against him, Fitzgerald decided to bring his wife and two eldest daughters — Rose, then eighteen years of age, and sixteen-year-old Agnes — to Europe for a lengthy tour, with the goal of leaving his daughters at the Blumenthal Academy of the Sacred Heart in Vaals, the Netherlands, for the year. Having lost his campaign for reelection to a second two-year term as mayor the year before — the campaign that cost Rose her college education — Honey Fitz and the whole family had receded from the public eye. Though he was out of office, a continuing investigation into corruption during his mayoral administration weighed heavily on him. Rose, highly sensitive to her father's disgrace, knew that it was a privilege to travel to the Continent for an education, but she also knew the tour meant not seeing Joe for a very long time.

At Blumenthal, Rose immersed herself in European cultures and languages. The school, she observed, was overtly focused on the "practical things of this world," including *"Kinder, Kirche, und Kuche"* — children, church, and cooking — and the necessity to prepare oneself for those domestic and religious obligations. It was assumed, Rose recalled, that once she and other young women at the convent were married, they would have hired help to cook, clean, and take care of the children. Therefore, their skills lay in their ability to manage household staffs and their proficiency in home economics.

Religion, however, remained the "foundation and the crowning point" at Blumenthal, just as it did at all other Sacred Heart schools. But Blumenthal was an especially strict and rigorous convent school, requiring fasting, silence, and meditation. It was here that Rose entered into sodality with other young women dedicated to living their lives like the mother of Jesus by becoming a Child of Mary. The Children of Mary was a specialized society advocating devotion to Mary, seeking commitment from young women to be "pure like Mary, humble like Mary, charitable like Mary, obedient like Mary, industrious like Mary," and to "apply themselves, then, to the constant imitation of Mary's virtues, and they will be her favored ones indeed." These essential virtues were "Purity, Humility, Obedience and Charity." Within two months of enrolling at Blumenthal, Rose had become an "aspirant," committing her to a six-month devotional and meditative experience preparing her to become a full-fledged Child of Mary. By the following winter, however, Rose realized that her infatuation with news from home and her love of travel had kept her from truly engaging in her course work and communing with other young women at the convent. "It came to me," she recalled, "that I must try harder to dedicate myself to the standards of the convent life, and that I must take more seriously my commitment to becoming a Child of Mary." Rising early every morning for meditation, Rose aspired to be "a model of perfection" so that she could attain "the highest honor a child of Sacred Heart can receive." In May, Rose wrote home to her parents that she had received her Child of Mary medal, one of only three issued that spring among 150 young women enrolled at the school, securing her place as a Sacred Heart role model and spiritual protector. The achievement required of Rose a remarkable self-discipline and commitment to her faith as a calling and a duty.

Once their studies were completed for the spring term of 1909, Rose and Agnes decided they had been away from home long enough. Though Fitzgerald's intention was to leave the girls at Blumenthal for two years, they missed America, their family — and, for Rose, Joe. Fortunately for the girls, Honey Fitz had decided to run a third time for mayor, and having his daughters home was probably better for his campaign than leaving them in Europe. His prospects were good, now that the taint of political corruption had passed and he had been cleared of wrongdoing. Rose would take her place, again, next to her father on the campaign trail. This time Fitzgerald would be successful, and with a change in the city charter that extended the mayor's tenure from two years to four, Honey Fitz looked forward to a long and productive run.

In the meantime, with Joe enrolled at Harvard and Rose — eager to continue her education but to be closer to home — now at the Sacred Heart School at Manhattanville in New York, they were not an ocean apart. During Joe's Harvard years, Rose later recalled, she fell "more and more in love." But her father was more determined in his steadfast refusal to allow Rose to spend time with Joe. His schemes to keep them apart—a trip to Palm Beach so that Rose could not attend Harvard's junior prom in 1911, arranging dates for her with other eligible young men, another summer tour of Europe—upset Rose and did little to dampen her passion for Joe. Once Joe graduated from Harvard, in the spring of 1912, Honey Fitz and Josie finally relented, becoming resigned to Rose's wishes and Joe's intentions. And so Fitzgerald gave his blessing to the young couple. Though Joe never met with the mayor's complete approval, his determined pursuit of Rose and his eventual hard-earned business success secured Honey Fitz's respect over time.

Gone were the secret and furtive meetings. The young couple could at last enjoy each other's company in public. The course of their courtship was now closely watched in the society columns of Boston's newspapers. Upon graduation from Harvard, Joe embarked on a career in finance. After a stint as a state bank examiner, he secured enough financing through family and business connections to save the Columbia Trust, a local East Boston bank that Joe's father, Patrick Kennedy, had helped found decades before and that was now under threat of takeover by larger Boston banking interests. After acquiring a majority-stock position in Columbia Trust, Joe named himself bank president, appointed sympathetic board members, and hired competent friends. Bank assets nearly tripled. His real estate investments flourished.

By 1914, this financial success had brought the economic and social status Joe needed, finally allowing him to marry Rose after an eight-year courtship. On a Wednesday morning in October, Joe and Rose were wed by Cardinal O'Connell in a private ceremony in front of family and close friends. Cardinal O'Connell's intervention and the resulting postgraduate years at Catholic schools had recast Rose, molding her into a more conservative and devout Catholic, a self-identity that would forever circumscribe her future with her husband and their children.

After a honeymoon traveling across the United States, the couple settled into their modest new home on Beals Street in Brookline. Joe and Rose's first child, a son named Joseph Patrick Kennedy II, arrived in July 1915. John "Jack" Kennedy was born in May 1917, adding to the busy household that now included a nurse, governess, and maid.

Baby Rosemary was christened in the Catholic Church within a week after her birth. Joe's sister Margaret Kennedy was the godmother, and Eddie Moore was chosen to be Rosemary's godfather. Moore had been a trusted friend and adviser to Rose's father, serving as Fitzgerald's secretary when he was mayor of Boston. In time, Moore became one of Joe's most relied-upon business associates, and he and his wife, Mary, became close friends to Joe and Rose both. As a devout Catholic, Eddie Moore took his role as godfather to Rosemary very seriously. As cosponsor, with Rosemary's parents, for the sacred Catholic rite of baptism, Moore made a commitment to the Catholic Church that he would remain devoted to Rosemary his entire life and be available to her whenever she needed him. His role, along with that of Rosemary's godmother, Margaret Kennedy, required that through his words and actions he would guide Rosemary's spiritual growth in the Catholic faith.

"We owe them so much for their unswerving devotion, their affection, their care and solicitude for our children," Rose later wrote of the Moores. Childless themselves, Eddie and Mary shared in almost daily interactions with all of Joe and Rose's children. "They derived vicarious pleasure from ours," Rose later remembered of the Moores' love for the Kennedy children, "rejoicing with us on the birth of a new son or daughter and later in life weeping and mourning over the poignant tragedies of war and death which came to us." The Moores were present at holidays, birthdays, and religious ceremonies. Mary Moore helped the children learn to shop for presents at Christmas and birthdays, often acting as godmother without the official title. Rose would later write that she and Joe trusted and loved them like cherished, older family members. Eddie would become even more than that to Joe. Gloria Swanson, who was to become one of Joe's more famous mistresses, remarked that Eddie was Joe's "shadow, his stand-in, his all-around private secretary and aide-de-camp," and his "chief brain, his auxiliary memory. He kept track of everything that went on." Wherever the Kennedys went, Eddie and Mary followed, nurturing special bonds with all of the Kennedy children. Their love and devotion to "Rosie" would be the most important bond of all.

2

The Making of a Mother

BY THE TIME the Kennedys were celebrating Rosemary's first birthday, Rose was pregnant again. "There were no signs," Rose observed, "that anything might be wrong." But as the months went by and she found herself closer to the birth of her fourth child, in February 1920, Rose started noticing that Rosemary's development was markedly different from her boys'. "She crawled, stood, took her first steps, said her first words late . . . She had problems managing a baby spoon." Rose tried to excuse the differences as being due to gender and temperament. Rosemary's failure to reach typical developmental milestones made her mother slightly anxious. Rose dismissed those concerns, however, "because of wishful thinking."

There were other serious strains. Rose was now a stay-at-home mother of three, soon to be four, children. It was a far different role from being Joe Kennedy's fiancée or Honey Fitz's escort and confidante. Rose's relative isolation compared to her premarriage life affected her sense of self and her youthful needs for independence and attention. The dreams she and Joe had talked about all those years while they were courting and he was having his first business success were playing out in a way she had not imagined.

Rose was deeply committed to the vows she had made as a Child of Mary at Blumenthal, vows she understood carried enormous expectations and requirements of selflessness. A Child of Mary would "bear with submission, humiliations, such as advice, reprehensions, punishments which she may deserve, but she will be glad to have occasion to practice the virtue of humility . . . True humility will render a Child of Mary full of deference for her Superiors, and even for her companions; she will gladly renounce her own will and judgment to submit to that of others." But the challenges of marriage and raising children tested Rose's commitment to self-sacrifice. Humility would be, for her, perhaps the most difficult of virtues.

Rose's private struggles with her commitment to being an ideal Catholic mother and wife were not made easier by the very public gains in liberties and advantages experienced by many American women as the 1920s dawned. The movement for universal suffrage was at fever pitch; in August 1920, the Nineteenth Amendment would give women the right to vote. The New Woman of the 1920s demanded more rights in the workplace and better access to education, jobs, and political power. Fashions were changing rapidly: hemlines were creeping up, corsets were thrown in the trash, and new, supple fabrics fit the curves of a woman's body less restrictively, allowing for greater flexibility and movement. There were sharp distinctions between attitudes of the nineteenth and the twentieth century toward smoking, drinking, sex, and independence, particularly for privileged white women. Women were experiencing, and enjoying, far fewer restrictions on their behavior and using their newly won freedoms to ensure greater autonomy and equality both at home and in public. Though women still endured second-class status in society—many professions remained closed to women or severely limited them, women's wages lagged behind those of men, and civil and legal equality would take decades more—the 1920s ushered in new choices and options redefining the lives of American women.

Publicly, Rose appeared apolitical on the question of woman suffrage; the years of acting as her father's helpmeet in the political sphere had been enough for her. She demurely suggested that she hadn't developed a solid "impression of the suffragettes" during a visit to England in 1911, when tens of thousands of them had marched on London. Her father ridiculed Boston suffragists, and a majority of Massachusetts politicians and certainly the Catholic leadership remained opposed to enfranchising women. Considering the near-constant reporting of the woman suffrage movement's gains and losses during her early married life in Boston, it is unlikely that Rose remained uninformed or that she lacked an opinion on the subject. Perhaps her Catholic friends did not talk about suffrage, but her suffragist mother-in-law, Mary Kennedy, certainly did.

Rose was yearning for active engagement in something important in the outside world—if not the politics of her father's world, then the business dealings of her husband's world. Her participation in the Ace of Clubs—a women's club that hosted guest speakers on history, culture, and contemporary issues which she had established with friends after she returned from school at Blumenthal, in 1911—provided some inspiration, but a monthly club meeting did not deliver the deeper stimulation she sought. Each evening that she was left alone by her husband, and each day that she spent focused on tending to her children's needs and managing her small staff—Mary O'Donohue, a thirty-year-old Irishwoman, and Alice Michelin, a twenty-six-year-old recent immigrant from France — was increasingly painful. The conflict between the vows she had taken as a Child of Mary and a wife and the personal freedoms evident in the modern world around her would plague Rose for the rest of her life.

Rose reached a breaking point near the end of her fourth pregnancy. She abruptly moved out of the Beals Street house, leaving Joe behind with the three children — Joe Jr., Jack, and Rosemary — and their nursemaids. She could no longer bear that "life was flowing past." The demands of children, marriage, and pregnancy threatened to swallow her up.

Separating from Joe and the children and leaving Beals Street was a personally extreme act, one that risked social exposure if others outside the family guessed that Rose's motives were more than to be near her mother as she approached her delivery. It seems likely that there was a precipitating event. Joe had always worked late, and now he traveled and spent more time out in the evenings with business associates. Rose would have known that he was enjoying some of his time away with young, liberated women; she might have taken in his "reputation for being a ladies' man." But now there was talk that Joe was having affairs, "and some of this gossip may have caught up with Rose." Resettling into her old room in her parents' home in Dorchester, Rose never spoke about what was going on, though her siblings and parents saw that she was unhappy and believed that Joe was at least part of the problem. Honey Fitz knew her future would be doomed if she left Joe permanently. Perhaps he stifled the urge to say he had warned Rose about him. She was married to Joe, married in the Catholic Church, and bound by vows that were ironclad in the minds of Catholics everywhere. Joe was not physically abusive, he was a good provider, and he was her husband. She was responsible for their children, whom Joe loved. And Honey Fitz's home was no longer her home. Rose paraphrased her father's response to the separation: "The old days are gone. Your children need you and your husband needs you. You *can* make things work out. I know you can . . . There isn't anything you can't do once you set your mind to it. So go now, Rosie, go back where you belong."

The Catholic education Rose's father had forced her to accept many years before would now become her solace. Reaching deep into that well of Catholic faith, and into her own resources of intellectual reasoning and determination, Rose left her parents' house and slipped away to a Catholic retreat. It was only a few short weeks before the birth of a second daughter, Kathleen. Through intensive prayer and meditation, and inspirational lectures by priests who counseled spiritual rededication and rejuvenation to help one face life's daily challenges, Rose found the strength to recommit herself to her marriage and to her role as a mother.

ROSE NOW SAW clearly that the only way she could have access to the public sphere was in the role of the wife of a successful Joseph P. Kennedy. Joe's financial success was a potential path to public office—always an undercurrent of his activity—and his wealth and public distinction would be her entrée back into the intellectual and social worlds that she missed and in which she thrived. Divorcing Joe and becoming an independent woman again was completely out of the question, but remaining at home, sequestered and miserable, was not an option either. She must get her husband to understand that she could be an asset to him, just as she had been to her father. Her role as wife was one defined by a rigid Catholic vision that regarded women as helpmeets to their husbands. She would take a back seat to Joe's needs and desires, then, in order to gain entrance to his world. She would raise their children to do the same thing: her daughters would learn to make sacrifices for their father, brothers, and husbands. Rose's newly hardened worldview required her silence, particularly in public: "The most successful luncheons or dinners to me are when there are from six to eight people and the men talk across the table brilliantly and the women for the most part keep silent . . . If a woman at the table insists on injecting an extraneous remark or a stupid one, often the men will cease and not consider it worth-while to prolong the discussion. I never talk very much as I think most people are interested in what Joe is doing and is thinking, not I."

Joe had long stopped discussing his business plans, ideas, and concerns with her. Later, Rose would reflect with some defensive-ness that even during their courtship and early years of marriage, "Joe's time was his own." His education had consumed his atten-tion during their early years together, and "now it was business that did so." The preservation of their marriage and mutual con-tentment now depended on accommodation and common goals. For the public, they would need to show a united front.

Writing about her early married life and the group of close friends she and Joe enjoyed, Rose recalled "the great new experi-ence we shared, which affected our thinking about everything else in life, was parenthood." Nevertheless, and in spite of the sense of commonality she claimed they all felt as young parents raising families together, Rose was clear that her social world did not in-clude constant discussions of children. "I don't recall that there was any great amount of conversation" about children or the daily chore of child rearing, "certainly not on my part, at least." Rose felt there was "always a multitude of things more interesting to talk about than . . . diaper rash." They and their friends, Rose re-called years later, felt incredibly blessed. Children, she believed, brought her closer to God and her husband. But she would not allow the daily rituals and requirements of caring for children to consume or define her in social situations.

Nor would she let herself be reduced to the role of a complaining, harried mother in the home. Rose looked to her mother as a model for managing the tenor of her child-filled household. "She believed," Rose noted of her mother, "that my father worked hard for her and for us children and that he should be made comfortable and happy at home." In this, Rose followed Josie's lead. She was determined to make sure Joe was comfortable and happy in their home, too. She would not bother him with small details of her day. She encouraged him to take vacations without her if she felt he was working too hard or not feeling well. When he traveled away from home, she did not worry him with the latest child's illness or mishap on the playground, nor did she complain about her own health or exhaustion. "Why worry him?" she later reflected. "How could a man work if he was concerned about me or a youngster, and what purpose would it serve?"

As a bonus for being an excellent administrator and manager, directing and overseeing everything in her home, Rose asked for and received whatever material support she wanted or needed from Joe. Her father had told her that if "you need more help in the household, then get it. If you need a bigger house, then ask for it. If you need more private time for yourself, take it." New homes, cars, furniture, jewelry, clothing, private schools for the children, trips abroad, vacations, and full-time staff to run the household and care for the children were never denied her, and they alleviated her feelings of isolation and loss of status, as well as relieved her of the many duties of a full-time mother. Rose and Joe reconciled their interior lives to each other's and came to an agreement: their deeply rooted intellectual and religious connection, their love of their children, and political expediency remained central to the survival of their marriage.

It is not clear how early in the marriage Rose's devotion to a very conservative version of Catholic womanhood became a barrier to sexual intimacy. The church deplored "deliberate cultivation of sexual union as an end in itself" and upheld "the primary purpose[s] for which marriage exists—namely, the continuation of the race through the gift and heritage of children; the other is the paramount importance in married life of deliberate and thoughtful self-control." One of Rose's friends from those years, Marie Green, later recalled that Joe found Rose's refusal to engage in sex for pleasure extremely frustrating. Green reported that Joe often teased Rose about her confined and restricted view of sex. "This idea of yours that there is no romance outside of procreation is simply wrong," Marie heard Joe saying to Rose during one of their Friday-night get-togethers playing cards. "It was not part of our contract at the altar, the priest never said that and the books don't argue that," Joe claimed. But Rose was resolute, and, in spite of what Joe argued and wanted, she had church teachings to support her. Green later recalled that after the birth of the Kennedys' ninth child, Edward "Teddy" Moore Kennedy, in 1932, Rose told Joe, "No more sex."

It probably mattered little by then. By the mid-1920s Joe had become a notorious womanizer, juggling affairs and illicit liaisons with starlets, intellectuals, and "party girls." Rose gave the impression that she was ignorant of his liaisons, but it is more likely she turned a blind eye. Deal making and the crafting and cementing of business relationships often required after-work hours devoted to socializing at restaurants, the theater, clubs, and speakeasies that filled the neighborhoods of Prohibition-era Boston. And Joe's entertainment of clients and potential investors in his expanding business interests often entailed the company of "the-ater girls" and others.

Rose attended occasional theatrical performances with Joe, where she met some of his theater friends and business associates. She later claimed that all this was "a completely new and differ-ent environment . . . gay, exciting and quite different and quite breathtaking to me." The familiarity and intimacy some of the women displayed toward Joe, and the frequency with which he spent time with them without her, would have been clear. Until she died, though, Rose argued that she trusted him completely. "I had heard that chorus girls were gay, but evil, and worst of all, husband snatchers. But nothing shocking happened," she claimed. Joe, Rose later wrote, "always liked to have someone gay around him, so he would have relief from his heavy cares and responsibilities." She and Joe "trusted one another implicitly," and he always told her when he was going out with "theatrical people." Just as Rose was quite assertive in her claims concern-ing her own enjoyment of Joe's theatrical world—so "new and different . . . gay [and] exciting"—so was she ardent in her de-fenses of his obvious infidelities. "There was never any deceit on his part and there was never any doubt in my mind about his mo-tives or behavior." Joe's extramarital activities and the public per-ception of her marriage were to be managed with intensity. Rita Dallas, a family nurse, observed that Rose's "formula for survival seemed to be based on: see what you want to see and hear only what you want to hear." This was a lesson Rose had learned from her politician father at the center of the many smear campaigns and slanderous newspaper articles that defined Boston's political gamesmanship. "Gossip and slander and denunciation and even vilification are part of the price one pays for being in public life,"

Rose later wrote. For the Kennedys, this maxim would hold true for generations to come.

But despite Rose's public sentiments, Joe's need for gaiety and his finding it in the theater district plagued her, feeding her insecurities and self-doubt. Rose was becoming less "gay" and more unhappy. This provided even more reason for Joe to find pleasure elsewhere.

IF ROSE'S CRISIS and retreat resulted in a reimagining of her marriage, it also led to a new conception of her role as mother, one that would affect none of her children, perhaps, more than Rosemary. Returning home to her children, Rose devoted herself to them, now convinced that the "challenge" and "joy" of her role was to "mold and to influence" every child. "On [a mother's] judgment [a child] relies and her words will influence him, not for a day or a month or a year, but for time and for eternity and perhaps for future generations." Rededicating herself to becoming the exemplary, consummate Catholic mother, Rose would eventually emerge in the public sphere—as Joe's life became more prominent—as the model for professional motherhood, an image she would cultivate and promote for the rest of her life. Her children, she believed, would be indebted to her forever.

The children, in a very profound way, would be Rose's security in the marriage, even if Joe found sexual and emotional fulfillment with other women. Through their children, she found ways to remain the center of attention and in control. Her children would become her career. She would not allow herself to become "an emaciated, worn out old hag" or "a fat, shapeless, happy go lucky" mother whose life was defined solely by "children, kitchen, and church." Instead, "I looked upon child rearing as a profession and decided it was just as interesting and just as challenging as anything else and it did not have to keep a mother tied down and make her dull or out of touch."

The Kennedys' fourth child and second girl, Kathleen, was born on February 20, 1920, when Rosemary was not yet eighteen months old. Beginning with the birth of Kathleen and after the birth of each child thereafter, Joe would send Rose on a vacation and take "responsibility of the family . . . It was a relief to know that the children were well supervised in case of an eruption of children's diseases, which often hit four or five of them at once."

Accommodating Rose had become a linchpin of the marriage. In April and May 1923, she took an extended vacation to California with her sister Agnes, leaving Joe behind to manage their household and children, all of whom were between the ages of eight and two and required constant supervision and care. While Rose was enjoying spa treatments, sightseeing, and the lovely beaches of California's south coast with her sister, the boys, ages eight and six, were taunting everyone with a charming song called "Bed Bugs and Cooties" and had started a boys' club, which required new members to be stuck with pins as their initiation. In frequent letters to Rose from Boston, Joe's initial confidence devolved into growing anxiety about her extended vacation. In a telegram sent on April 8, Joe was cheerful and optimistic. Though a governess, a cook, the Moores, and assorted Fitzgerald and Kennedy relatives shouldered the major portion of the child care, Joe painted a scene of himself commanding the helm of orderly bliss. "The children are fine," he assured Rose, and "Jack is sleeping every noon and is greatly improved . . . the Moores have been the busiest people in the world . . . and we are all doing nicely." Joe finished his telegram wishing Rose would have "a real good time because you richly deserve it please do not think too much about us and spoil your party . . . I am not lonesome because I find myself in happy thought that you are enjoying yourself . . . lots of love from us all, Joe." Shorter telegrams followed until five weeks later, on May 13, when Joe wrote rather desperately, "Dear Rosa Mother's Day finds us all looking forward to your return . . . we all realize now more than ever how important you are to the happiness of you [in] this home . . . we all love you and want you back . . ."

Rose's lengthy trips, especially those abroad, became more common during the late 1920s and 1930s, unsettling the children, who never seemed to adjust to her absences. Young Jack complained about his mother's repeated "holidays" away from her family. Before leaving for California in 1923, Rose noted in her diary that Jack told her, "Gee, you're a great mother to go away and leave your children all alone."

But these trips were only a respite from the constant demands of Rose's highly controlled mothering. At home, she set rigid rules for raising children, rules Joe tried to adhere to while she was away. As more children joined the family, this organization helped her maintain the order she needed and the singular purpose she craved. It was an era when the principles underlying industrial efficiency and time management were being promoted in the latest literature to American businessmen and mothers alike. Rose, always an avid reader, embraced the new ideology of modern motherhood. The "Home Manager . . . is the active partner in the business of running a home," a popular magazine of the day declared, "to make home life happy, healthful, and beautiful." Rose would apply the most current business and industrial-management techniques to the raising of her children and the running of her household.

She had strict guidelines for health and cleanliness, eating, reading, dinner conversations, playtime, education, and more.

In spite of all the full- and part-time help, Rose later insisted that she maintained an active role in the children's lives. Diapers needed changing, washing, and drying, and baby bottles needed cleaning, sterilizing, and refilling. Someone had to manage the hired help doing all that work. "The bottles for the babies had to be cleaned and sterilized at home on the kitchen stove and woe to the nursemaid if she put her bottles on the stove when the hired girl was preparing the lunch or cooking a cake. Words would fly and kettles would be pushed back and forth and diapers would stop boiling and there would be . . . a fight from the kitchen." While havoc swirled, Rose would take the youngest in a carriage, with "one or two others on each side," and up the street the family would go, stopping at the grocery store and visiting Saint Aiden's Catholic Church on the way back home.

Rose's index-card catalog for the children became legendary among members of the family. She chronicled medical records for each child, noting every illness, disease, vaccine, and surgery endured, as well as complications, medications taken, height, weight, doctors' names, allergies, physical exams, and eye-test results. She noted dates of each child's baptism, schools attended, First Communion, Confirmation, graduation, the names of godparents, and more. Not only did the file cards help her keep track and stay in charge of each child's medical history, but they also were available to Joe and to all the nannies, nursemaids, and other caretakers responsible for the children during Rose's absences. The British press would later marvel at this system, dubbing Rose the model of "American efficiency," but Rose called it "Kennedy desperation."

Rose's obsession with weight would become notorious, too. The Saturday-morning weigh-in was a ritual in the Kennedy household. Each child's weight was noted in Rose's card-catalog system. The children would not become "emaciated . . . fat . . . [or] shapeless" if she could help it. If a child's weight "showed a change, his program changed." Young Jack was often underweight, so for him "there would be less swimming and perhaps more fat in his diet." Alternatively, she would put her children on diets if they gained too much weight, and order them to get more exercise. Because Rose was constantly worried about her own figure, her fixation on weight would dominate nearly every letter passed between the children and their parents well into their adulthoods, even extending to Rose's grandchildren in the 1960s, 1970s, and 1980s.

Dinner conversations were always lessons of some sort. Rose drilled her children on the saints and martyrs of the church, famous men in history, and "great leaders in their country." The children, Rose wrote, were "taught to admire the leaders of Christendom who died for their faith . . . [and] to emulate the Pilgrim fathers . . . and [they] learned about Paul Revere and his famous ride." Leadership, Rose firmly believed, was the result of patient, deliberate efforts on the part of parents, who encouraged their children through solid instruction and example.

The children's upbringing included an emphasis on sports as well as on academic studies. "They learned to be winners, not losers in sports," Rose proudly claimed. Rose and Joe tried to attend as many school sports competitions as possible, spurring the children "on to victory" and providing a little sympathy—though no more than a "nod"—when they lost. When a child failed to win, "the reasons for this were analyzed." As each grew older, it fell to him or her to urge on the younger siblings, yet they were very competitive with one another, too. Rose liked that.

As the family disciplinarian, Rose believed in "good old fashioned spanking," though she did not allow family nurses, maids, or governesses to punish the children physically. Fully aware of debates about the efficacy of corporal punishment and the possible physical and psychological pain caused by it, Rose nevertheless believed it was vital in teaching young children the difference between right and wrong, particularly as a "means of preventing accidents and bad behavior." She prided herself that none of her children ever said no to her, though this seems highly unlikely to be true. Rose claimed she would not hesitate to hold a child's finger to a hot stove to show that he or she would get burned, or to prick a little finger with the point of a pair of scissors to emphasize the danger of running and falling or poking a sibling with them. A ruler was never far from reach. "After a few raps, the mere mention of the ruler would usually bring the desired results."

AFTER THE BIRTH of Kathleen, Rose realized her modest house on Beals Street was much too small for a growing family of little children, along with an expanding staff. Joe's career was flourishing; he had joined Hayden and Stone, a stock-brokerage firm, in 1919, had been buying and selling property through his own real estate investment company, and was maintaining his profitable interest in Columbia Trust. He and Rose sold the eight-room home to Eddie and Mary Moore and bought a larger and more formal twelve-room house around the corner, on Naples Road in Brookline. The school district—an exceptionally good one—remained the same, so Rose felt assured that her children's early education would be first-rate and uninterrupted. She could attend the same church and remain in a familiar neighborhood where the children had made friends, where they could take their daily walks and visit the local shops, and where they had long grown accustomed to playing. The Moores, who had been living with Mary's mother in an apartment in Charlestown, on the other side of the Charles River from Brookline and Boston, were now just a block away, available at a moment's notice when needed and in a house the children already loved.

After settling into their new Naples Road home, in October 1920, when Rosemary had just turned two and Kathleen eight months, Rose discovered she was pregnant again. The newest baby, Eunice, was born at Naples Road in July 1921 and named after Rose's youngest sister. Perhaps Rose knew that her sister did not have long to live. Eunice Fitzgerald had contracted tuberculosis while working for the Red Cross, nursing sick and wounded soldiers in Boston during and after World War I. Ten years younger than Rose, with a brilliant intellect and a soft beauty that some believed surpassed Rose's, Eunice had replaced Rose as Honey Fitz's most favored daughter. He showered her with the attention and affection that Rose had once enjoyed before she married Joe and moved out of the family home. Honey Fitz spared no expense trying to find a cure for his dying daughter. The new baby would carry not only Eunice's name but also the strong intellect of her Fitzgerald aunt and the political genius of her grandfather Honey Fitz.

The house on Naples Road had a large wraparound porch, which Rose and her staff would divide into sections for the children's play. Separating the children with folding child-safety gates allowed them to play in segregated sections according to age groupings. Rose felt that with so many children—two more followed Eunice over the next four years on Naples Road—having them all play together was problematic. "There I was with seven children and when they would play they would knock each other down, [and] gouge each other's eyes with toys." The older boys were rough, and the younger children were bound to get hurt. The divided porch solved the problem nicely. "They could see one another and still they could not push one another or stick some heavy thing on top of the baby carriage," Rose recalled years later. Neighbors, deliverymen, and police officers would stop by and chat with the children, distracting and entertaining them, Rose observed, allowing her to "read the papers inside or outside with an occasional look in the direction of the children."

Photographs from that time show Rosemary as a happy little girl seemingly as alert and able as her siblings. Yet soon after Kathleen, affectionately called "Kick," was born, when Rosemary was a year and a half old, her development became a serious cause of concern for her parents. First Kick and then Eunice quickly surpassed Rosemary in every measure of intellectual and physical skill. Rose noticed that Rosemary "could not steer a sled" nor easily master childhood sports nor write on paper easily. Rose could see that Rosemary was struggling when other children were not. "I realized," Rose reflected, "at an early age, that Rosemary was not like the others." Though Rosemary was still very young and a diagnosis had not yet been confirmed, the specter of having a child with disabilities was overwhelming for her parents.

In Rose's diaries of those early years, her sporadic entries are dominated by comments on the children and their activities. Busy with the everyday responsibilities of running her household, Rose could find only a few moments a month to record some of these childhood antics. Some years are missing entirely; either those diaries are lost or Rose failed to keep one. The pranks of the two oldest boys, Joe and Jack, litter her early entries, alongside notes about the children's health and vacations. Sickness overshadows entries for 1923, for example. One member or more of the family always seemed to have a cold, bronchitis, or worse. She also noted some of the precocious things the children did. Eunice, a toddler, was walking and talking in 1923, "the best little talker of all," Rose remarked. Rosemary is rarely mentioned, though Rose noted with some humor that four-year-old Rosemary stuck her tongue out during Easter dinner at her Kennedy grandparents' home in Winthrop. The lack of diary entries belies Rose's special attention to Rosemary's needs—attention, Rose later revealed, that she felt may have been a detriment to the other children. "I often wondered if Jack felt neglected . . . because when he was young, and of course, Rosemary was a year and a half younger than he was, I gave her a great deal of attention, thinking that I could circumvent this affliction she had, or I could have her so educated that it wouldn't be noticed at all or she could still go on with the other children in a normal way." A neighbor and a friend of the boys remembered that Rose "wasn't a bring-them-to-the-bosom kind of mother. There was a reserve between Mrs. Kennedy and her children, except for the case of Rosemary, who received most of her affection."

Rosemary could not compete, physically or intellectually, in the active Kennedy family. "When we have a number of children, we cannot understand why they are all not alike," Rose would later muse, "especially if the oldest ones are brilliant scholastically or outstanding in athletics. Then when the younger ones come along, we naturally expect the same thing and we become critical and impatient if this is not the case." But Rosemary's limitations were far more complicated than mere personality differences, and the pressure to mold her to expectations wore heavily on her parents. To Joe, being "different" meant being excluded from clubs, parties, and business deals. He had spent his life battling the discrimination that kept him from the inner sanctums dominated by the Protestant moneyed elite. He had felt the sting of rejection because of his ethnic and religious heritage, and he had long vowed never again to be subjected to outsider status — nor would his children be. They would excel in everything. He would spend his life grooming them to be accepted into those inner circles, and he would not risk having any of them falter.

3

Slipping Behind

In the fall of 1923, when Rosemary was five, she was enrolled in kindergarten in Brookline, at the Edward Devotion School, just as her brothers had been. Rosemary appeared "deficient," a label teachers and school systems were beginning to use to describe children who were lagging behind their peers in school. At that young age, there really were no other educational or therapeutic options for Rosemary, and Joe and Rose did what most other parents of intellectually disabled children did: they hoped that her teachers could help Rosemary catch up to the achievement levels of her classmates.

"I had never heard of a retarded child," Rose wrote. She had not been prepared to mother a child who was different or less than capable. In fact, Rose did not like people who lagged behind or who were different. Now she had a child who did not meet her standards, or Joe's, and who was indeed "different." Rose would reflect that "mental retardation was not a current expression in those days," though a growing body of research into mental and intellectual disabilities was beginning to use the term. On her own and with a passion that characterized her inner drive and determination, Rose began reading whatever she could find on the subject of retardation, trying to come to terms with its meaning and its implications for Rosemary's future.

Rose was determined to keep Rosemary enrolled in public school with her peers, augmenting daily school lessons with her own additional instruction. She feared that if Rosemary "went away to school where other children were slow," she would not be challenged to meet her greatest potential. In this, Rose was ahead of her time; there was little thought during that era that there could be any positive educational reason to include an intellectually delayed child in a public-school classroom. Rose would have to meet that challenge herself. Her later statement that "one [child] may be smart in studies, one dull — one may be overconfident, another shy — and so a different approach must be made" gives a sense perhaps of Rose's determination to transform disability into achievement.

Specialized and individualized instructional plans and activities in reading and writing, occupational therapy, and other therapeutic services supporting children's and adults' emotional, social, and intellectual needs, which are routinely offered today, were not available to Rosemary. Furthermore, Rose's own education had focused on classical literature, history, and languages, not, of course, on the latest educational methods for children with disabilities. Finding time to work with Rosemary at home, with many other small children demanding her attention, was not easy.

In the spring of 1924, Rosemary's kindergarten teachers Betsy Beau and Cordelia Gould refused to promote her to first grade. "I did not know . . . how to cope with the situation," Rose would write years later. "I talked to our family doctor, to the head of the psychology department at Harvard, to a Catholic psychologist who was head of a school in Washington. Each of them told me she was retarded." Mental "retardation" and "arrested growth" were not well-defined diagnostic terms then, and were used broadly and carelessly by doctors and other educational professionals to describe a variety of intellectual and physical conditions. The diagnosis provided little direction for educational or therapeutic options, and it offered scant hope for what Rosemary's future would hold. "What to do about her, where to send her, how to help her seemed to be an unanswered question." Rosemary would repeat kindergarten the following year.

While the particular needs and requirements of children like Rosemary were not yet considered worthy of specialized treatment in public-school systems, the Brookline schools did deliver a determination of Rosemary's impairments in the form of an IQ test. IQ, or intelligence quotient, testing was in its infancy when Rosemary was evaluated in school, probably when she was six or seven years old. Brookline was one of the first school systems in the country to adopt intelligence testing for its students, in the form of the Otis Intelligence Test, developed for young children by psychologist and statistician Arthur Sinton Otis. Though Rosemary's specific results are unknown, Rose wrote, "I was told that her IQ was low," meaning that Rosemary's mental age was lower than expected for her chronological age as compared to other children. How low the actual score was remains an important question. Today, an IQ test score of 70 or below denotes significant intellectual impairment, although we now know that with specialized therapy, education, and stimulation, some individuals may improve their scores and achieve the skills important for leading independent, productive lives. Since the test was so new in the 1920s, however, what Rosemary's score meant for her future was unknowable. Even with test scores in hand, few school systems were equipped to deal with the information, leaving parents to struggle at home either to provide resources for their children so that they might reach their full potential or to choose institutionalization, where the child could be housed with other physically and mentally disabled children and adults.

The family endured other unhappy times during Rosemary's early childhood. In May 1923, Joe's mother, Mary, died at the age of sixty-five from cancer. The following fall, on September 19, just as Rosemary had started kindergarten, Rose's sister Eunice finally succumbed to tuberculosis. It was a devastating loss to the entire family. Rose spent months formally mourning her sister's passing, declining invitations to the theater, events, and dinners with friends well into the new year.

The time of deep mourning ended in May 1924, when Rose gave birth to the Kennedys' fourth daughter and sixth child, Patricia. Baby Pat arrived just as Joe, who had left the successful brokerage firm Hayden and Stone in 1923 to form his own investment partnership, was embarking on a career path that would ensure a new level of financial achievement. A smart, detail-oriented analyst, Kennedy parlayed his skills and tolerance for risk into extraordinarily profitable investments. Investing advantageously, and using insider information and shrewd exploitation of the unregulated markets in certain stocks — all legal in the 1920s — Kennedy made an enormous amount of money. In fact, as Rose was going into labor with Pat, Joe was engaged in a ruthless plan to repel corporate raiders who were driving down the stock price of Yellow Cab, a company in which a Kennedy associate had invested heavily, in an attempt to ruin Yellow Cab's plan to enter the New York City taxi business. Holed up in the city's Waldorf Hotel, in a room transformed into an office, Joe successfully thwarted the raiders' attempts through clever manipulation of the company's stock during April and May, saving his friend and other investors millions of dollars. Rewarded well with cash and stocks, Joe had finally earned a reputation as a bold and brilliant market strategist on the biggest financial stage in the world. It would be nearly a month, Joe later recalled, before he met his newest baby. Such hard-driving work habits brought Joe to exhaustion — a common occurrence that worried Rose and Joe both — but his success in New York demanded that he spend ever more time there.

Traveling to Wall Street from Brookline every week started to take its toll on Joe. He and Eddie Moore, whose role as Kennedy's closest adviser carried him to New York as well, would leave their homes on Sunday night and take the five-hour or longer train ride to New York City, then return home on Friday or Saturday night, leaving few hours for family time. It was during this stressful period that Joe set up trust funds for all the children so that, should his health fail him, they would be provided for.

Rose would occasionally travel to New York to spend the weekend with Joe, but she preferred to have him come home to spend some time with the children. The arrangement was not ideal, so discussions about leaving Boston, and the family home in Brookline, began in earnest. As the couple debated the family's move to New York, a process that played out over two years, Joe became interested in the movie business. He believed that Hollywood, on the eve of technological advances that would soon give rise to talking films, promised to be a gold mine of remarkable returns. When Bobby, the couple's seventh child, was born, in November 1925, Joe was on the verge of embarking on his first big Hollywood venture with the purchase of a film production company called FBO, or Film Booking Office. As the owner of a chain of movie houses in New England, Joe had been trying for years to engage in the business of financing films. His offer for FBO, in the summer of 1925, was at first rebuffed, and Kennedy returned his attention to the world of stocks and bonds. In a surprising change of direction, however, FBO executives abruptly and eagerly accepted Joe's months-old offer early in the winter of 1926. The Kennedys were now in the film business.

The new venture required Joe to travel not only to New York but to California as well. Joe and Rose had come to the definite realization that they could no longer live in Boston. Access to New York City, physically and financially, improved Joe's prospects for success. The family must move to New York so Joe could have his business and family closer together, at least some of the time.

Moving for business was not the sole driving force behind the Kennedys' departure from Boston. By 1927 Joe was fed up with the old Yankee elite's denying him membership in the leading social clubs that would prove he had finally succeeded in New England's Protestant-controlled society. As difficult as it was to leave extended family behind, business and social success trumped familial comfort. New York was a more diverse and tolerant place, full of brilliant, successful people on the move. The older children could still attend choice private high schools and, later, college, and the younger ones could attend high-quality local public and private schools. The family, Joe believed, would thrive in New York amid greater diversity and less prejudice.

On September 26, 1927, the Kennedys boarded a private railroad car that Joe had hired to transport his large family to Riverdale, an affluent neighborhood situated on the Hudson River in the northwest corner of the Bronx. The Kennedys settled into a rented, thirteen-room stucco home that could accommodate the family of nine and an expanding number of nurses, governesses, housekeepers, and other staff. The large Riverdale estates and smaller mansions of the city's business and professional elite benefited from the highest elevation in New York City, featuring rolling hills, fields, and forests, with spectacular views of the river and the skyscrapers of Manhattan, ten miles away. The Kennedys' new home in Riverdale was larger than the family's suburban home in Brookline, and their new neighborhood was less densely populated, featuring large lawns and abundant green spaces. Rose had decided on Riverdale because there was an "excellent boys school there with supervised play" for Joe and Jack, then twelve and ten years old, respectively, one of her few requirements in a new community. Riverdale Country School offered programs for girls, too, and the children could take the bus every day together. The youngest children enrolled in the local elementary school; they could walk back and forth to school and "get some fresh air and exercise." They would be home every day, where Rose would continue to contribute to their early development.

Though Rosemary had repeated kindergarten at Edward Devotion and then moved up to first grade in the fall of 1925, her learning disabilities forced her to repeat that grade as well, in 1926. When the family moved to Riverdale, Rosemary was enrolled in second grade at Riverdale Country School along with her younger sister Kick, while Eunice entered first grade. Other girls of Rosemary's age, nine, were entering the fourth grade.

Joe was wrong about New York's being more tolerant. Riverdale had one small Catholic church, but most of its residents resembled the Brahmins he resented so much. Rose, who spent far more time in Riverdale than Joe, would remain an outsider. Joe's absence from school and community functions isolated Rose even further. Neighbors viewed Rose's devotion to Rosemary, and to the rest of her children, as a curiosity. Reserved and cloistered with her family at home—child number eight, Jean, was born five months after the move to Riverdale—Rose rarely interacted with her neighbors. Though she "was one hundred percent mother, absolutely one hundred percent," a neighbor recalled, Rose "had very little to do with local social activities." Another neighbor, a childhood friend of Jack's, recalled that the Kennedys "were like fish out of water" in Riverdale "because of their life-style, their close-knit family of eight children, their father's non-participation in neighborhood activities, and the mother's Catholic activities, which few if any of the neighborhood families shared." The neighborhood children cared little for these issues, but the Kennedy children drew them anyway. For them, the Kennedy home was the go-to place for outdoor sports and indoor games, dances, and roughhousing.

The financial indicators predicting the Great Depression—a financial collapse that devastated the economies of not only the United States but nations around the globe—were merely glowing embers in 1927 when the Kennedys moved to Riverdale. By 1929, when the stock market crashed, Joe was playing the market brilliantly and taking advantage of broad and unregulated practices that in fact helped cause the collapse. Through risky speculation and manipulation of prices, Joe produced huge gains for his portfolio. He masterfully shorted many stocks ahead of the collapse, cashing in on his bet that the market would decline. Rather than enduring tremendous losses like most other investors, Joe made a fortune for himself and his investors. Yet the new wealth of the Kennedys did not help them bridge any social distance in Riverdale.

By 1927, before the Kennedys' enormous wealth was so fully secured, Rose had every material household support to settle the family into their new home. Rosemary, however, was not easy to settle. Her transition to school in Riverdale was fraught with frustration and anxiety. Already labeled "slow" and "delayed," Rosemary needed ever more demanding educational support. Rose struggled to accommodate her while also helping the rest of the children adjust to their new home, school, and neighborhood. This was a fresh opportunity for Rosemary, and no doubt Rose hoped the new environment would spur her on to do better in school.

To those outside the family, Rosemary seemed much shier and less polished and coordinated than her hyperactive, outgoing, and competitive brothers and sisters. Her soft-featured prettiness, seemingly happy disposition, and carefully disguised intellectual disabilities masked the seriousness of her condition. Rose made sure of that. In spite of Rosemary's disabilities and the extra attention she required, Rose and Joe were determined that Rosemary be treated just like the other children. Expectations that she meet the social, academic, and physical demands placed before her as best she could became the hallmark of the Kennedy family's determination to keep Rosemary from being viewed as "different."

Once settled in Riverdale, though, it was quickly apparent that Riverdale Country School would not be the hoped-for fresh start for Rosemary. She struggled with the simplest of elementary studies while her younger sister and classmates were readily mastering reading, writing, and math. She had a tendency to write from right to left, rather than left to right—often called mirror writing—a clear indicator of developmental disorders. She struggled to shape her letters, and as she grew older she would fail to master writing in longhand. Her spelling was hit or miss. Sentences were often deficient and incomplete, and she could not write in a straight line unless using lined paper as a guide. A Riverdale classmate of Kick's recalled that even though she'd been placed at least two grades behind her age group at the school, "Rosemary just plugged along with the rest of us."

Placement in the Riverdale classroom with younger children did not help, so Rose and Joe removed her from school. "Her lack of coordination was apparent and . . . she could not keep up with the work," Rose recalled years later. Rose organized scores of private lessons and tutors to work with Rosemary at home so that she could, they hoped, advance with her age group through school.

By the age of ten, Rosemary could not row a dinghy on the bay at the Kennedys' new summer home, in Hyannis Port on Cape Cod, acquired the year after they moved to Riverdale. She could not steer a sailboat in the many races in which her siblings competed at the same age. Though Rose spent hours playing tennis with Rosemary to help her sharpen her skills, she could not play with her physically more able siblings, even the younger ones. Years of dance lessons made little difference, and her poor coordination left her still "heavy on her feet." She could not cut meat on her dinner plate; her food was served to her already sliced.

Rosemary's inability to decode the difference between left and right may have been a sign of dyslexia. This developmental disability may also explain her limited capacity to spell, to correctly form letters, and to master directions. These skills require levels of concentration and dexterity that were beyond her capabilities no matter how much tutoring she received. A diagnosis of dyslexia at that time was improbable. Treatment and educational resources that might have helped her cope with that particular disability were years away from being developed. Dyslexia, however, does not explain Rosemary's other difficulties and limitations, indicating more severe but undiagnosed impairments and developmental problems. Rose took her to "experts in mental deficiency," but their assessments and recommendations left Rose discouraged. The specialists told her that Rosemary had suffered from an unspecified "'genetic accident,' 'uterine accident,' 'birth accident,' and so forth."

Some of Rosemary's siblings believed that she also suffered from intermittent epileptic seizures. Eunice remembered sudden and hurried calls to the doctor, who would rush to the house and administer injections and medications to Rosemary. "I think she was partly epileptic as well as retarded," Eunice recalled. "I can remember at the Cape the doctors coming in and giving her shots and then disappearing." Whenever one of these episodes occurred, the children were whisked away to another room or sent outside to wait until the doctor left, and only then were allowed to resume their activities. None of them dared ask what was wrong with Rosemary.

Gloria Swanson recalled Joe's rage when she asked about Rosemary's condition. Joe had met Swanson not long after the family's move to Riverdale. At that time, she was one of the most famous movie stars in the world. Smart, ambitious, and hard-driving, Swanson had made some bad investment decisions and contractual commitments that threatened her financial solvency. Through mutual business associates, Kennedy was introduced to her as the man who could straighten out her disordered finances and take over the management of her production company. Joe's experience with theaters, and now with FBO, enabled him to talk to Swanson with an expert's understanding of the movie industry and a banker's eye to financing and running a business profitably. They embarked on an illicit affair that lasted several years. Early in their liaison, Swanson overheard Joe talking on the phone with someone regarding the then ten-year-old Rosemary. He was "agitated" and annoyed with the person on the other end of the line.

Apparently, Joe was trying to get an unidentified doctor to treat Rosemary and "cure" her. He offered to purchase a new ambulance for the hospital if the doctor would take Rosemary as a patient. The telephone call ended abruptly. Swanson suggested that Joe bring Rosemary to meet with her personal physician in California, Dr. Henry G. Bieler. Bieler advocated a therapeutic diet as an alternative to drug therapies to cure a variety of illnesses. Swanson, like many other Hollywood stars, had followed his regimen and believed he held the key to lasting good health and mental well-being.

"I had seen him [Joe] angry with other people, but now, for the first time, he directed his anger against me," Swanson wrote in her autobiography. "It was frightening. His blue eyes turned to ice and then to steel. He said they had taken Rosemary to the best specialists in the East. He didn't want to hear about some three-dollar doctor in Pasadena who recommended zucchini and string beans for everything." Swanson persisted, encouraging him to consider Bieler. Joe reacted even more harshly: "I don't want to hear about it! Do you understand me? *Do you understand me?*" She knew never to ask Joe about Rosemary a second time, and Joe never mentioned her again, either. Later, Swanson approached Eddie Moore about the scene. He warned her that Rosemary was "a very sore subject with the boss." Tapping the side of his head, he looked at Swanson and said of Rosemary, "She's . . . not quite right."

Educating Rosemary at home was not ideal. The lack of social interaction with other children outside of home denied her a typical childhood experience. Watching her siblings now go off to school every day was difficult for her. In spite of Rose and Joe's efforts to treat her as if she were unimpaired, Rosemary had difficulty understanding why she was treated differently than other children.

With Rosemary's disabilities becoming more evident and the gap between her and other girls her age ever widening, Rose and Joe reconsidered advice to place their daughter in an institution.

During Rosemary's childhood, the distinction between the intellectually disabled and the mentally ill was rarely made. Instead, according to psychological definitions of the day, "idiots" were the most severely disabled, classified as those with the intellectual capacity of a two-year-old or younger; "imbeciles" as those with a three- to eight-year-old mental capacity; and "morons" as those with an eight- to twelve-year-old capacity. These labels limited society's understanding of people with intellectual and physical disabilities, and lacked nuanced interpretation of the causes and conditions of various disabilities, including the many types of simple and complex learning disorders. Within this limiting framework, mentally disabled and learning-disabled children and adults had few options and bleak prospects for education and for leading autonomous or semi-independent lives.

Many institutions, both private and public, became warehouses for the insane, the disabled, and the addicted. There were hundreds of state and private hospitals and homes for the mentally ill and the mentally and physically disabled across the country. Wealthier families, like the Kennedys, could afford private institutions, whereas those with fewer financial resources often turned to state-run or private charitable or church-owned facilities. Regardless of who ran these institutions, many of them were houses of horror. One former inmate of the Fernald School, a notorious Massachusetts state hospital, described the facility as "purgatory."

Dark, dirty, and disease- and rodent-infested, many institutions for the insane and disabled provided little more than shelter and some food. Medical care was spotty; occupational therapy and educational and vocational training were nonexistent. Patients and residents would sometimes spend their days and nights caked in their own excrement. Orderlies, doctors, and guards sometimes raped women residents, while others were forced into prostitution businesses organized on institution grounds. The intellectually disabled were often housed side by side with the mentally ill, the suicidal, the alcoholic, the drug-addicted, and those adjudged "criminally insane." Cries for attention or relief from suffering and pain usually went unanswered. Physical and emotional abuse were rampant, dehumanization and intimidation commonplace.

Rose's consultations with a variety of doctors, psychologists, psychiatrists, academic specialists, and religious leaders took on a new urgency. None offered Rose what she thought was best for Rosemary, making her "terribly frustrated and heartbroken." Rose was accustomed to controlling her children's social and intellectual lives, and she was determined that Rosemary would not be separated from the family. Joe Sr. believed, too, that keeping Rosemary at home or enrolled in nearby private schools provided her with more benefits than an institution for the mentally disabled would.

Both of them clearly understood that in the socially elite circles of Boston, New York, Europe, and elsewhere the pressure to institutionalize Rosemary, a choice many of their similarly situated wealthy counterparts made for their disabled children, would be great. Rose and Joe's peers had been influenced by the powerful eugenics movement that swept Western societies during the latter part of the nineteenth and early twentieth centuries. Eugenics was fueled by pseudoscientific claims that the human race consisted of "two classes, the eugenic and the cacogenic (or poorly born)." The cacogenic, eugenicists claimed, "inherited bad germ plasm, and thus as a group . . . at the very least, should not breed." African Americans, immigrants, the poor, and criminals were often deemed cacogenics; fears of the "immigrant hordes" streaming into American cities and the migration of African Americans out of the Deep South into northern and western cities led some native-born white Americans to embrace these beliefs.

The intellectually and physically disabled were another category of "defectives." Eugenics scientists and their followers believed that these individuals were also the products of inherited bad genes and should be treated much the same way as the mentally ill, criminals, and the chronically poor. Forced sterilization, they argued, was society's cure. Some believed that spending money on insane asylums, poorhouses, and other charitable and social institutions and programs serving the mentally ill and disabled only encouraged the propagation of "bad seeds." The parents of "defectives" carried these bad genes—an idea that placed the blame and shame squarely on families. Some of the most prominent industrialists, scientists, and political leaders of the late nineteenth and early twentieth centuries, including President Teddy Roosevelt, supported these views. Wealthy industrialists John D. Rockefeller, Andrew Carnegie, John Kellogg, Mary Williamson Harriman, and early feminist Victoria Woodhull became advocates of eugenics, funding spurious research promoting racial and ethnic discrimination through false claims of genetic deviance in nonwhite and ethnic minorities.

Labels such as "moron" and "mental defective" further complicated an already difficult life for Rosemary and her family. For Rose, reading eugenics literature and hearing such words describing her lovely daughter were stressful and heartbreaking.

Christian beliefs and biblical tenets were no more helpful. These overtly blamed parents for the physical, mental, and intellectual shortcomings and disabilities of their children, warning believers who failed to follow the Ten Commandments and the teachings of the Old Testament that God would punish them by "visiting the iniquity of the fathers upon the children unto the third and fourth generation." At that time the Roman Catholic Church routinely refused the sacraments of Holy Communion and Confirmation to intellectually disabled children, especially those with Down syndrome. Even today some local churches still refuse the sacrament to those with intellectual impairments, in spite of a directive from the church during the latter part of the twentieth century that clergy should offer the sacraments to them. Did Rose question a religion that would have excluded her child from some of the most holy of Catholic sacraments?

If Rose and Joe were to reveal that their daughter was a "defective," they and their children risked being ostracized and shunned. To survive spiritually and emotionally, Rose and Joe had to mold Rosemary into the likeness of themselves and her siblings, an impulse that fed their constant pursuit of a potential "cure" for Rosemary. "My parents, strong believers in family loyalty, rejected suggestions that Rosemary be sent away to an institution," Eunice later recalled. She remembered her father arguing, "What can they do for her that her family can't do better? . . . We will keep her at home." But keeping her at home had become increasingly exhausting and difficult.

Struggling to come to terms with Rosemary's limitations and the stigma surrounding them, Rose and Joe reached a crisis point. By the time Rosemary was eleven, and after a year of private instruction at home, they decided to send her to a private boarding school. Her daughter's young age must have made Rose hesitate; developmentally immature, Rosemary always had difficulty adjusting to new situations and demands. Living away from her home and family would be quite destabilizing for her, but the Kennedys felt they had no other acceptable alternatives. Her persistent lack of academic progress and the rising tension and frustrations facing the Kennedy household as it tried to accommodate her at home drove the decision to send her away sooner than they would their other girls. In contrast, Rose would wait until Kick turned thirteen before sending her to boarding school; Eunice went even later.

4

Five Schools

THE KENNEDYS CHOSE the Devereux School in Devon-Berwyn, Pennsylvania, for Rosemary. Founded in 1912 by Helena Trafford Devereux, a former Philadelphia public-school teacher, the school provided specialized and individualized lesson plans for a wide range of intellectually challenged students. As a young teacher in Philadelphia, Devereux had observed that children who learned differently or were "slow," developmentally delayed, or disabled were often kept from advancing to higher grade levels with their age-group peers. Educational instruction for these students consisted at the time of pared-down or "slowed-down" instruction and repetitive drilling of lessons in separate classrooms or in a segregated area in mainstream classrooms. Many of these children received little stimulation, lacking the varied curricula their peers experienced. Given this, coupled with low expectations, their futures were bleak. In Philadelphia, Devereux began creating special curricula for individual students. The Philadelphia school system nearly immediately assigned more children to her classroom, recognizing that through her carefully crafted and individualized programs tailored to each child, these students thrived rather than failed.

Devereux was frustrated, however. She could not pursue further research and engage in more intensive curriculum development under the constraints of a public-school system, in spite of Philadelphia's adoption of her program. Though her exceptional work with disabled children earned her an appointment as director of special-needs education for Philadelphia's public schools, she declined the position so that she could start her own school. She wanted the freedom to explore her belief, as David Brind puts it, that "disabilities need not cause feelings of difference and isolation but instead had the power to create strength of character, bringing each child closer instead of farther away from a sense of belonging to the larger humanity to which each child longed to be a part." With a small amount of money, she started a private school in her parents' home, developing the foundation for a residential educational and therapeutic program for disabled children.

Rosemary experienced a rough transition to Devereux that fall, but she finally settled in. In a November 1929 letter, Joe compliments her on improvements in her report card during her early months at Devereux while also gently challenging her: "I am sure that within the next couple of months it will be even better." In time, according to her teachers, Rosemary "made the necessary social adjustments" to boarding school, showed "excellent social poise," and was "quite charming at times." Her course work included drills in spelling and math, grammar, and reading comprehension, as well as more hands-on, developmentally appropriate work in handicrafts, art, music, sewing, and drama. Her struggles to achieve academic success, however, fueled anxiety that manifested itself in "outbursts of impatience." Rosemary's problem, the teachers believed, was rooted in low self-esteem and self-confidence, requiring continual encouragement and positive reinforcement.

Rosemary could not have felt her foundations were firm that fall of 1929. Her parents had gone off to promote Joe's latest film, *The Trespasser,* starring Gloria Swanson, in London and Paris, leaving Eddie and Mary Moore to substitute as parents and to settle her into her new home at Devereux. Rose, in addition to providing care and supervision for eighteen-month-old baby Jean (born the winter before), four-year-old Bobby, five-year-old Pat, and the older children, was also, that summer and fall, busy settling the children into a new family home, a large brick mansion Joe had bought in the tony New York City suburb of Bronxville. Rose had never felt comfortable in the rented house in Riverdale, and by 1929 she and Joe knew that the move to New York City would be permanent and that the family of ten plus six staff members needed more space. Joe's success shorting the market had so enriched him that he was able to purchase the magnificent new Bronxville home just a few months before the stock-market crash in October. The estate was purchased for a then incredible $250,000, and Joe would add tens of thousands of dollars in choice furnishings and decorations.

Bronxville was in Westchester County, just a few miles northeast of Riverdale. Nestled on six acres of land, the house, at 294 Pondfield Road, boasted modern appliances and systems rare for those days. The bathrooms had showers, supplied with hot water from a large oil-burning heater. The entrance hallway was graced with a grand staircase, balconies, and Ionic columns. The basement featured a billiards table, and there was a garage for five cars with a chauffeur's quarters. The third floor contained "an elaborate, always-growing train system," lorded over by Joe Jr. and

Jack. But Rosemary had left for boarding school shortly before the family settled into the Bronxville home; it was home to her, from then on, only for occasional school vacations.

The move to Devereux would be the beginning of a series of physical and emotional transitions for Rosemary that would define her life and struggles for the next decade and more. It would also mark a somewhat new stage in her relationship with her father, who assumed increasing responsibility for Rosemary's formation now that she was essentially away from home and on the verge of being in the world. Eunice later told her mother, "You were in charge of us and raised and trained us while we were children. And then, when we began turning into young people, Dad took charge the rest of the way." Rose, Eunice believed, had become exhausted by the responsibility of taking Rosemary to "doctors, educators, and psychologists." Joe, though supportive, was "easily upset by Rosemary's lack of progress, [and] her inabilities to use opportunities for self-development." This would remain a constant theme in the family, one that Rosemary must have sensed as Joe took over the management of his daughter's care and education: the Kennedy children were expected to take full advantage of the opportunities afforded them by their rich and demanding parents.

Rosemary's first year away coincided with the great stock-market crash of October 24, 1929. Within days, billions of dollars in private capital evaporated. The country spiraled into a deep economic recession, then depression. Four years later, the monetary value of all goods and services manufactured and produced in the country had declined by fifty percent. Millions of American workers—over twenty-five percent of the nation's workforce—lost their jobs and income. Thousands of banks failed. Lacking the federally insured bank deposits that are common today, Americans' savings disappeared. Unemployment insurance, Social Security, Medicaid and Medicare, and other social and economic safety-net programs had not yet been created. Poverty, homelessness, and hunger spread across the country. The collapse of agricultural prices and of the farm economy in the 1920s—an early indicator of an impending economic depression—compounded by a devastating drought in the plains and the Southwest during the 1930s, ruined the lives of millions more.

While capitalism had helped turn America into the world's industrial and financial leader, its excesses and unregulated banking and investment practices played a leading role in the greatest financial crisis the world had ever seen. The grinding poverty and widening wealth gap between the poor and the rich, many of whom were weathering the crisis with some of their assets intact, became more pronounced with each year of the Depression. Some of the very wealthy, like the Kennedys, were faring better than ever, taking advantage of deeply discounted prices to acquire real estate, businesses, and other assets. The market crash and subsequent economic decline had little effect on them, and by 1935 the Kennedys were ranked among the richest families in the country. This disparity between the very rich and nearly all other Americans threatened the stability of the nation and its democracy.

Unlike so many families, the Kennedys could continue to pay for private boarding school for Rosemary and their other children. By the end of the first year, Rosemary had finally made the essential "social adjustments" required to successfully live away from home. She had "written several very good stories about the robin and her trip to Washington" and had performed well enough in math and other subjects, the school reported to Rose at the end of Rosemary's first year. Her low self-esteem and low confidence, however, remained a major stumbling block to her success, and episodes of irritability reflected her frustration and anxiety when she could not perform.

Rosemary returned to Devereux in the fall of 1930. The staff had spent a year working with her strengths and weaknesses, but Rosemary's teachers soon discovered their progress with her had faded over the summer. They found her even more resistant to completing reading and writing assignments, and math continued to pose a significant challenge. In a November progress report, her teachers complained to Joe that Rosemary "dislikes exerting the effort necessary to accomplish acceptable results" in math. Reading comprehension suffered, they wrote, because she "skips a good deal and fills in from her imagination." Though she still suffered from a lack of confidence, the teachers found that Rosemary did not care about "making the effort necessary to attain good results." Her short attention span frustrated the teachers' attempts to teach her to "persevere." They believed she was capable of more, but how to prove that remained elusive. "Rose's achievements in class work are seldom commensurate with her ability, and an effort is being made to bring her work up to the standard she is really capable of. This is a difficult task, as she has so definitely acquired the idea that her abilities are negligible and that her work cannot reach [any higher] standard."

Rosemary, unaware of what the school was telling Joe and Rose, tried to convey to her parents that she was doing extremely well academically. In a carefully printed letter to her mother just four days before the report from the school was sent home, she reported, "I am working-hard-Mother Because I Get 100 in Arithmetic-all-the-time. I am wonderful in spelling."

Devereux had strict rules and guidelines determining rewards and the earning of special allowances. The staff preferred few interruptions in a child's education, discouraging frequent visits from family members and trips home. Earning a few days' vacation at home for Thanksgiving could have been an incentive to get Rosemary to work harder. Rosemary may have suspected something was amiss when, in the same letter, she pleaded with her mother to let her come home for Thanksgiving: "Did you ask Miss Devereux if I could go home on Thanksgiving? You said you were going to do it. Please do." Only twelve years old, Rosemary still suffered from the separation from her family. "I miss you very much," she wrote her mother. "Give everybody my love, please. When you go up to see Joe and Jack [now at Choate School, in Connecticut] give them my love please . . . Write me a long long long letter."

With Rosemary now boarding away from home, Kick, a year younger, blossomed. Kick was doing well in school, was tremendously popular, and was becoming the family's substitute older sister. Eunice, nearly three years younger than her oldest sister, became Rosemary's closest sibling; her temperament and emotional age were better matched to Rosemary than to Kick. Their closeness would last for more than seventy years.

After a visit home for the Easter holiday in April 1931, Rosemary wrote to Eunice, pouring out her disappointment at having to leave the family so soon after the holiday:

Dear Eunice, I miss you very much, Didn't we have fun together when I was home? I was so sorry I had to leave all of you. so soon. Tell the girls to write me as much as they can . . . I will see you quite soon, sweetheart. I'm dying to hear frm [sic] Mother and Daddy. Tell Mother to send me my box of candy that she gave me Easter. I feel very upset when I don't hear from Mother tell her that. Write me a long long letter and make it as long as you can, darling. I know you will dear, love Rose.

When Rosemary returned to Devereux in the fall of 1931 for a third year, she was thirteen. The Kennedy girls' teenage years posed a particular dilemma, apparently, for Rose. When Kick turned thirteen, in 1933, Rose shipped her off to boarding school. "She was tremendously popular with the boys," Rose later wrote, "who were always telephoning her and asking her on dates . . . So boarding school was the answer, no phone calls or distractions from study, with girls her own age and whose families we all know." Keeping her girls under control was a significant priority. There is no explicit record of Rose's thoughts on Rosemary's sexual maturation. She had read the literature of the era, however, on female "defectives"—how they were more likely to become promiscuous, to have children with similar disorders or worse, and to create a more dangerous "class" of criminals, prostitutes, and "feebleminded" offspring.

During the spring of Rosemary's third year at Devereux, after the horrific kidnapping and murder of the baby son of aviator and national hero Charles Lindbergh, the country witnessed a sickening rise in kidnapping-for-ransom cases. Rose began to worry that the teenage Rosemary "would run away from home someday and get lost, or that she would meet with an accident, or that she would go off with someone who would flatter her or kidnap her." Given the Kennedy family's modest fame but enormous wealth during the depths of the Great Depression, Rose's kidnapping concerns were not unfounded. Rosemary or any of the younger

Kennedy children could have been easy targets of ruthless kid-nappers. But her use of the phrase "flatter her" suggests that Rose feared sexual as well as financial exploitation.

That spring, Rose was busy again with a new baby. Edward Moore Kennedy, named after Eddie Moore, was born in February 1932. "Teddy" would be Rose and Joe's ninth, and last, child. Even with Joe Jr. and Jack at Choate, Rosemary at Devereux, and Kick off to boarding school in the fall, there were still five children at home. A bus from the private boys' day school in Riverdale brought Bobby back and forth every day, and Eunice, Pat, and Jean were now ensconced in new schools in Bronxville.

When Rosemary was home, however briefly, during the school year, Rose made sure that she was watched and that she stayed occupied as much as possible. Rosemary continued to test her parents' patience, and her actions played on their fears. She resented having a companion join her when she traveled by train, and she would occasionally deliberately run away from caretakers. Sometimes she delayed returning home after doing an errand for her mother, setting Rose on edge until she finally appeared in the doorway. Rose was still devoting her own time and care to Rosemary. Neighbors in Bronxville remember Rose taking long walks with Rosemary alone. Paul Morgan, a teenager when the Kennedys moved into the upper-class neighborhood, recalled that whenever Rose and Rosemary walked by, his family's Great Danes would run out to greet them. Rose would wait patiently while Rosemary, then fourteen, would play with the giant dogs.

Believing that the special education Rosemary was receiving at Devereux was no longer benefiting her in ways they had hoped, and perhaps with the encouragement of Devereux's staff, Rosemary's parents transferred her to Elmhurst, the Convent of the Sacred Heart school in Providence, Rhode Island, in the fall of 1932. Their expectations were clear: they wanted Rosemary to progress in school as though her intellectual limitations were something easily overcome. A school such as Devereux, for "slow" children, had never been their permanent plan for Rosemary. Rosemary seemed high-functioning in many ways; her teachers at Devereux had assured her parents of her social skills. These attributes lent credence, in Rose's and Joe's minds, to their belief that she could achieve academically. Rose and Joe may have given Margaret McCusker, the director of Elmhurst, the same kind of initial impression. By the end of her two years at Elmhurst, however, Rosemary's handwriting seemed no better than when she had left Devereux. In a letter written to her parents in June 1934, Rosemary's poor penmanship, spelling, and grammar remained similar to that of a ten-year-old, though she was fifteen years old at the time:

Dear Mother and Daddy,

Thank you very much for the lovely letter you sent me. I got three bottles of perfume, but it is allright. I am satisfied. I like the handkerchief lot. Thank you very much for everything I appreciated it so much. EveryBody thought the Picture was grand.

I cannot thank you enough for everything you have done to make Elmhurst so happy. Thanking you again for your kindness.

. . . I gave a birthday party for Alice Reddy. We had eight Children to the Party . . .

. . . Latin test I had. Pray very hard that I will get some place. I tried as hard as I could.

History Doctrine are the last.

I went to the First and Second Elementary prizes. They were as Darling as they could be.

I will be so happy to see you all.

lots of kisses,

Rosemary

By the fall of 1934, Rosemary, at age sixteen, was enrolled in another private school, this time in Brookline, the suburb of Boston in which she had been born and had spent her early childhood years. A letter from Elmhurst's Margaret McCusker to Rose that October gives few clues as to what may have prompted the move to yet another school. It is clear only that Rosemary's lack of achievement at Elmhurst had once again undermined Rose and Joe's hopes for her advancement. After thanking Rose for a subscription to *Illustrated London News* and for the roses she believed Rosemary had sent to the convent school's Mother Superior, McCusker expresses regret that the students and sisters had not heard from Rosemary: "Of course we are deeply interested in her progress—and any item of news about her arouses attention. Mother Forbes still grieves—and *all* regret her absence. So do send her back if at any time, you think a return would spur her on."

The new school in Brookline was housed in a large mansion on Powell Street and run by Helen Newton and her mother, Adeline Newton. Rosemary's progress beyond the third- or fourth-grade level was frustrating, unnerving, and wearisome. The Kennedys were now pinning their hopes on Miss Newton's School, which offered a rigorous but supportive educational program that Rosemary's parents believed was more suited to her need for individual attention and encouragement. The Newtons provided instruction to gifted students as well as those who struggled with meeting scholastic challenges.

Each new school—this one was her third in five years—meant weeks of adjustment for Rosemary. A new living and learning situation posed anxieties that manifested in moodiness, uncooperativeness, and emotional instability. This pattern emerged early in Rosemary's childhood, yet her parents continued to move her from school to school with regularity. Barely a month into the first semester, Joe wrote Rose, who was then vacationing in Paris, that Rosemary "raised Cain first week but Miss Newton and her mother have both written me saying you would never know the child." But Joe was hiding the entire truth. A little more than a week later, he was reassuring Helen Newton: "I had a very firm talk with Rosemary and told her that something must be done, and I am sure she really wants to do it. It is something else besides herself that must be blamed for her attitude. By that I mean, it is her inherent backwardness, rather than a bad disposition."

Helen Newton had spent time exploring the latest techniques to teach "retarded children," she told Rose. In a letter to her father, Rosemary excitedly revealed that she was enjoying a challenging academic program with a more varied curriculum than at Elmhurst. She was taking French, and by October she was showing her father her latest homework in French vocabulary and phrase exercises. Such gains may seem remarkable, but it was with a great deal of help and supervision that Rosemary was able to perform. Newton observed that Rosemary could not concentrate on her studies for more than two and a half hours. Her limited attention span thwarted attempts to educate her, and in spite of Rosemary's frequent claims that she was working harder and performing better, the truth was she couldn't really do any better.

At sixteen, she remained far behind the academic achievements
of her peer group in regular classrooms, clearly evidenced by her
simple letters from Brookline to her parents—letters, given their
misspellings and other errors, that were likely composed with
some help from the Newtons:

October 1, 1934

Darling Daddy,

J'ai beaucoup trvaille a vous donner plaisir.

I have a travel book about Europe, and I am looking up
and answering all the questions.

I have a French book, called, 'que Fait Gaston?' I am
sending you a few lines from it.
The book is written all in French, and I have to translate it.

I am learning some History way back in the beginning
when men lived in caves, and did not even know how to
cook . . .

Did you receive my postcards and my letter? I am going to take some dancing lessons to get ready for the first
Dance.

I hope soon to send you a letter in French. give my love
to all the family.

Rosemary

Rosemary's placement in a school in Brookline had its advantages. Her being near family members—including Rose's parents,
Honey Fitz and Josie, and aunts and uncles—and close family
friends, who checked in on her and helped entertain her on weekends, relieved some of the anxiety her parents felt and the lone-
liness she experienced. Ruth Evans O'Keefe, a childhood friend
of Rose's, and O'Keefe's daughter Mary, who also attended Miss

Newton's School as a regular student, frequently hosted Rosemary in their home in Lynn, Massachusetts. The O'Keefe family included her in family outings, such as trips to the theater, movies, and skating, and in cookouts. She enjoyed the O'Keefes' game nights, playing cards and Monopoly with Mary's siblings, and she attended dances and other social events with them.

Joe asked Jack and Joe Jr. to keep in touch with Rosemary. Joe was a freshman at nearby Harvard College during Rosemary's first year at Miss Newton's School, and was able to take her on outings. "I think it is fine the way you are contacting Rose because it gives her a little more confidence," her father wrote to Joe Jr. "Keep suggesting to her that she should work very hard in order to get all she can . . . She must not feel she is there for social purposes and nothing else." Suggesting that the Kennedy men were now keenly concerned with whether Rosemary could "pass" in elite social situations, Joe Jr. reported that one of his classmates had met Rosemary and "thought she was very nice. Bob Downes also thought she was good looking, as did Francis Shea, so I think she is coming along finely. All these came from a clear sky, so they were not meant to be the old bunk."

Oddly, given his closeness to Rosemary, Joe Jr. held quite conservative views about the disabled. After graduating from Choate, in 1933, he spent a year studying in London rather than immediately enrolling at Harvard, where he had been accepted that spring. His father arranged for him to travel extensively and to meet some of the leading financial, literary, political, religious, and academic leaders of the day. Unrest was brewing abroad as the effects of the Great Depression destabilized economies and financial institutions across Europe even more deeply than in the United States. By the time Joe Jr. arrived in Europe, Adolf Hitler had come to power in Germany, and persecution of the Jews was on the rise. After visiting Germany, Joe wrote to his father that he had heard much "condemnation of Hitler and his party" while in London, but that he believed Hitler should be given a chance. As a consequence of economic devastation following World War I, Germans were "scattered, despondent, and . . . divorced from hope." Hitler gave them hope, and a common enemy, the Jews. "It was excellent psychology," Joe Jr. wrote, "and it was too bad that it had to be done to the Jews. This dislike of Jews, however, was well founded." Spewing Nazi propaganda like a fresh convert, Joe went on to claim that the "brutality . . . must have been necessary . . . to secure the whole hearted support of the people . . . In every revolution you have to expect some kind of bloodshed." Perhaps more shockingly, Joe also believed that Hitler's sterilization program was "a great thing. I don't know how the Church feels about it, but it will do away with many of the disgusting specimens of men which inhabit this earth." Hitler's sterilization program was deeply rooted in bigoted eugenics ideology that sought forcibly to sterilize anyone suffering from a number of physical and mental diseases, including "1. Congenital mental deficiency, 2. Schizophrenia, 3. Manic-depression, 4. Hereditary epilepsy, 5. Hereditary St. Vitus' Dance (Huntington's Chorea), 6. Hereditary blindness, 7. Hereditary deafness, 8. Serious hereditary physical deformity . . . [and] anyone suffering from chronic alcoholism." Between July 1933, when Hitler signed the "Law for the Prevention of Offspring with Hereditary Diseases," and 1945, when World War II ended, four hundred thousand people had been sterilized.

Joe Sr. responded to Joe Jr.'s letter quickly, praising his oldest son's powers of observation. He cautioned his son, though, arguing that Hitler had gone "far beyond his necessary requirements in his attitudes towards [the Jews], the evidence of which may be very well covered up from the observer who goes there at this time." Joe Sr. would later advocate for appeasement instead of war with Hitler, an argument that would eventually ruin his own political career aspirations. At this particular moment, however, he was eager to teach his son to be curious and to judge fairly when given all the facts. Interestingly, Joe Sr. did not address young Joe's comments about Hitler's sterilization program, nor did he explore his son's anti-Semitism. The fact of Rosemary's disability and the struggles the family had faced for years over her care did not prompt either man to draw a connection to the persecution of the mentally ill and the disabled in Germany. The plight of Catholics, also under attack by the Nazis, drew Joe Sr.'s interest instead.

In mid-October 1934, Joe Sr. traveled to Boston to visit with Rosemary. They attended a Harvard football game together and then visited with Joe Jr. While Rosemary craved and was excited by her father's attention, she remained vigilant against incurring his disapproval. She campaigned hard for his esteem. After her father's visit, Rosemary wrote to reassure him of her devotion and commitment to doing well at school:

October 15, 1934

Dear Daddy

I had a lovely time on Saturday.

Thank you ever so much for coming down to see me.

Sunday I also had a good time.

I would do anything to make you so happy.

I hate to Disppoint [*sic*] you in anyway.

Come to see me very soon. I get very lonesome everyday.

See you soon I hope. It was raining to-day. So We could not play hockey. So we went to Franklin Park. We had lots of Fun. I bought a New Hockey Stick for $4.35. Most Sticks cost $6.00. I got a very good one.

. . . looking forward to seeing you again some time soon. lots of love kisses, your loving daughter,

Rosemary

Rosemary's father would continually encourage her, using a softly chiding style to urge her on. "Mother sent me your letter and I was delighted to hear from you," Joe wrote in early December. "It showed a lovely spirit for you to write and pleased both Mother and me very much to think you are so appreciative and also that you feel that you are studying as hard as I know you can and are doing." He noted her efforts to learn skating—a difficult endeavor considering Rosemary's problems with complex coordination and athletic activities—with positive humor, a hallmark of Joe's parenting style. "I hope skating turns out to be lots of fun . . . Be sure to wear a big pillow where you sit down so that when you sit on the ice (and I know you will) you won't get too black and blue."

Jack, whose own boarding-school antics and lack of attention to his studies generated more than a few patient but scolding letters from his father, was encouraged by Joe Sr. to cheer Rosemary on, too: "It would do Rose[mary] good if you would write her . . . You know it is very important that we have a good job done up there this year." Jack, like his brother Joe, could be counted on to help Rosemary feel important. At one point, Rose wrote the headmaster of Choate, asking him to let Jack leave school briefly to attend a dance that Rosemary had asked him to: "The reason I am making this seemingly absurd request is because the young lady who is inviting him is his sister, and she has an inferiority complex. I know it would help if he went with her."

Rosemary's best friend in Brookline, Mary O'Keefe, is mentioned frequently in Rosemary's letters to her parents. The two went to dances, movies, and plays together. They played badminton, hockey, and other sports. They did other things that teenage girls did: go shopping, have their hair and nails done, compare tips on girdles, dresses, and shoes. Rosemary reported that she played bridge with Mary and her family. Her degree of success at the complicated game is unknown, but clearly the O'Keefes were offering her a variety of challenges she seemed to enjoy outside of the classroom. Her family paid for extra lessons in badminton, and private companions accompanied her to museums and other outside events, enhancing her academic lessons. And yet Rosemary attended Girl Scout meetings where "learning the names of trees," she reported to her mother, was a task she was finding a bit difficult.

Rosemary's persistent chatter about social activities caused her parents great concern. She reported in January that she had purchased a cosmetic compact for $1.50, and had had her hair waved and her nails manicured for an upcoming dance that Jack and Mary's brother John O'Keefe were accompanying the girls to. She delighted in her "blue evening dress, silver slippers," and a silver hair clip. No matter what event she reported to her parents, she was sure to describe what she wore. Rosemary cherished clothes and pretty things, encouraged, perhaps, by her mother and others. Even as a small child she was drawn to the latest fashions featured in shop windows at Coolidge Corner, near the Kennedy home in Brookline. Eddie Moore, as her godfather, delighted in buying her a new dress every year. "My dear Rosemary," Moore wrote during the spring of 1923, when Rosemary was four years old, "This season they are showing such wonderful and pretty little frocks for little women that I regretted not having you along with me to help me choose. I feel if you had been along we both would have decided on this little party dress so I am sending it to you with love and Easter greeting."

If Rosemary exhibited her mother's fashion consciousness and attention to her looks, she also shared her father's love of socializing. In a typical letter, her animation over social news overshadows any reporting of academic achievements:

Darling Mother and Daddy,

The Chauffer drove Mary O Keefe and I to Adams House on Friday night. thats Where we met Joe [Kennedy] and John O Keefe at ten past eight. Then Mary went with Joe in his car to the dance. I went with John O Keefe. He told the Chauffer how to go. It was a Costume party. but we diddn't know it. I wore my red evening dress, red shoes, 2 red bows on my hair, black evening coat. Mary wore her red evening dress, red evening coat. And we both had our nails polished . . .

[John] O Keefe did a backward Somersault at the dance . . . Saturday, Babe Kaughlin, a friend of Mary went down on the Beach and cooked sausages and put it in a sandwich, cooked steak and bacon, and brought gingerbread to eat. We made a fire, and got wood for it. Paper too. And we came home . . . I played Christine in ping pong, and Mary and babe also. We also played three handered bridge. At night Mary and I played Monopoly with Christine. Sunday, Aunt Agnas envite Joe and I to lunch. I stayed overnight . . .

. . . I am going to study Napoleon, Mary O Keefe has a new red and white bathing suit, new white shorts, new blue evening dress. I tried the bathing suit on me, also the

new silk dress she bought. I tried it on me. I get 3 dollars
allowance a week. I have had my hair waved and my eye-
brows plucked . . .

lots of love and kisses to the best Mother and father in
the world. Your loving daughter.

Rosemary

Loving new clothes or a pretty haircut and watching her weight
made Rosemary no different from other teenage girls. "Every time
I would say, 'Rosemary, you have the best teeth and smile in the
family,'" Eunice reported, "she would smile for hours." During
an interview for *Catholic Digest* in 1976, Rose remembered that
even the slightest attention or compliment directed toward Rosemary resulted in hours of happiness: "If I said to her no more than
'Rosemary, that's the most beautiful hair ribbon,' she would be
thrilled."

But there were other aspects to Rosemary's life that did under-
score her difference. In letters she wrote while still at Miss Newton's, she several times mentioned "Dr. Lawrence" giving her "injections" and "red pills." This was Charles Lawrence, a new doctor
engaged by the Kennedys to treat Rosemary. The injections were
part of an experimental regimen developed by Dr. Lawrence to
treat perceived hormonal or "gland" imbalances. Lawrence, a re-
nowned endocrinologist in Boston and chief of endocrinology at
the New England Medical Center, believed that disruptions in
sexual development due to dysfunctional hormonal levels produced by the pituitary gland were at the root of many developmental and emotional problems in teenagers and adults. Dysfunc-
tion of the pituitary gland was already linked to dwarfism and
gigantism, arrested or slow development of sexual organs, poor
sperm production, and irregular or nonexistent menstrual peri-

ods. But Lawrence, who was not a psychologist or a psychiatrist, focused exclusively on the endocrine system and the functioning of the pituitary gland in the normal and abnormal function of the human body and its effects on "nervous impulses" and intellectual development. Rosemary may have been treated for allergies as well, an ailment affecting young Jack and Kick most severely but afflicting almost all of the Kennedy children. It's possible that the "red pills" that Rosemary took may have been some type of antihistamine. Interestingly, Luminal, dispensed in a red-pill form, was a highly touted and newly developed phenobarbital-based barbiturate used at that time to relieve anxiety, to sedate violent patients, and in some cases to alleviate epileptic convulsions. Without further information, however, the specific purpose of Rosemary's red pills remains a mystery.

Helen Newton had recommended Dr. Lawrence to the Kennedys within the first few weeks of Rosemary's enrollment, in the fall of 1934. Joe was receptive; on October 15 — the same day Rosemary wrote to him to thank him for coming to see her and to say, "I would do anything to make you so happy"—he wrote Frederick Good, Rose's obstetrician and the children's pediatrician when they lived in Brookline:

> Some years ago when you came down to Hyannis Port we discussed the gland theory as affecting Rosemary. She is . . . still suffering from backwardness. Miss Newton told me yesterday that Dr. Charles H. Lawrence . . . had done wonders for a couple of her pupils, and I wondered if it would be too much trouble to . . . check up to see whether her suggestion is of any value and whether Dr. Lawrence is the one to start with . . . We do not want to leave a stone unturned if there is anything possible to be done.

Three days later, Good cabled Joe that he had "spent [a] very pleasant visit with Rosemary and Miss Newton." He thought Rosemary was "in excellent hands" with Miss Newton, and that the idea to refer her to Dr. Lawrence was an "excellent" idea. Good reported that Dr. Lawrence's "standing is one hundred percent" and that he was a "very capable man." Joe cabled back, directing Good to make an appointment with Lawrence as soon as possible. Dr. Good's assistance in helping Joe and Rose find a solution to Rosemary's "backwardness" suggests his culpability in Rosemary's delayed birth, though its consequences remained unmentioned.

Good and Lawrence met with Rosemary at Miss Newton's on October 20. They found her "in pretty good spirits" and kept the visit a "social one." The doctors and Miss Newton may have felt that a casual introductory visit with Rosemary was the right tack. "We had a very pleasant chat about football, school work, etc.," Good reported to Joe. Within a couple of days, Rosemary met with Lawrence in his office for a "complete physical examination and was found to be in perfect condition." Good continued to be impressed by Lawrence. "I am quite hopeful that a systematic treatment with Endocrines will do considerable good," Good reported, "[and] in fact, I will make it even stronger and say that I am very, very hopeful that within a few years, as a result of these Endocrine treatments, Rosemary will be 100% all right." He promised to see Rosemary on a regular basis, "to help her to keep up her spirits." Joe was thrilled, and after a later visit with Rosemary, in mid-November, he believed he was already seeing "considerable improvement," though he tempered his enthusiasm by noting it may have been his "imagination."

Given the state of medical science concerning women's health at the time, it is not surprising that Lawrence's methods were welcomed as potentially pathbreaking insights into the role of the endocrine system and its relation to human developmental abnormalities. But his medications, supplements, and injections proved ineffective, in spite of Joe's sense that Rosemary was better. No hormone injections were going to "cure" Rosemary of her intellectual disabilities. More important, the injections would not have helped even if she had suffered from more serious mental health problems, like depression or other mood disorders.

Joe was managing the situation himself that fall of 1934. Rose was away in Europe, celebrating her twentieth wedding anniversary alone, enjoying an extended vacation. Joe wanted Rosemary treated before Rose returned home, and Rosemary, always eager to please her father and to do as he asked, submitted to the thrice-weekly injections without complaint. By late January 1935, Good reported that he had seen Rosemary and that "she is 100% O.K. I am pleased to report, too, that I noticed marked improvement . . . and am quite hopeful that within the next eight to ten months everything will be perfect."

During the spring of 1935, with no significant improvement in sight, Rose — focused on educational rather than medical intervention for Rosemary — engaged Walter F. Dearborn, a specialist at the Psycho-Educational Clinic at Harvard University's Graduate School of Education, to work with her daughter. Dr. Dearborn's pioneering work on reading disabilities and human development was helping advance society's understanding of different learning styles and abilities in children. Dearborn had conducted decades of important research on learning disabilities, specifically on children with average and above-average intelligence. He proved that some children, even highly intelligent ones, could have difficulty learning to read, and that new alternative methods were available to teach these children. Dearborn was a strong advocate of intelligence testing and had written extensively on its useful application in schools and work environments as a basis for developing varied curriculum materials for disabled students and workers. He strongly advocated individualized teaching for most students. His chief complaint focused on the one-size-fits-all method of teaching groups of students in American classrooms; it was a serious obstacle to individual success, he believed.

But Rosemary was intellectually disabled, of below-average intelligence, an affliction distinct from those of certain learning-delayed or -disabled individuals. Dearborn's theories and ideas certainly had applicability for a child with intellectual limitations, but Joe and Rose were still hoping for a *cure* for Rosemary's disabilities. They hoped and believed that Rosemary had learning delays, not intellectual disabilities. Dearborn recommended an individualized course of instruction in arithmetic and reading. Rosemary should, for instance, have an account at a "department store," he told them, where she would have a budget, keep careful records, and pay bills on time.

Rosemary remained at Miss Newton's through the rest of that school year and returned in the fall of 1935 for another full academic year. Dr. Dearborn met with her in October 1935, reporting to Rose that "Rosemary seems to be very happy. She also appeared to me to have profited by the summer and to be more alert." Miss Newton's School was "an excellent arrangement," he told Rose, possibly because Helen Newton's program matched his research on the benefits of individualized teaching. Perhaps Rosemary's alertness stemmed from the close attention and encouragement she received there. The O'Keefes were still actively involved in Rosemary's life, and Dearborn was impressed by the affection between Ruth O'Keefe and Rosemary. "Mrs. O'Keefe is already attached to Rosemary and Rosemary to her. The relations with the other members of the family seem to be excellent, too," he assured Rose, "and Miss Newton reports that Rosemary has taken hold of her studies with more interest and vim, and she is very hopeful of further progress this year." Their meeting took place on a good day for Rosemary. She seemed compliant and eager to please the doctor: "We gave Rosemary a couple of tests . . . because she wanted to have a try at them. I was able to accomplish more in the short time that we worked with Rosemary than I had been able to on any previous occasion. I hope this all augurs, as I am sure it does, an even more profitable year than last year."

Rosemary was maturing into a lovely young woman, full-figured, poised, and sociable with her friends. Her academic progress remained negligible, however. Her letters to her parents during that year reveal a busy social life with the O'Keefes, as well as with family and other friends in the Boston area, but little about her academics. Rosemary's handwriting, though she was now seventeen years old, still appeared more like that of an eight- or ten-year-old, with incomplete and sometimes incoherent sentences, misspelled words, faulty punctuation, and poorly structured paragraphs. Writing was clearly arduous for her.

Even as Dr. Dearborn's efforts were not yet showing clear academic results, Dr. Lawrence's injections continued. "Sorry to say I have to take Injections 3 times a week," Rosemary reported to her parents in January 1936. Helen Newton went on experimenting with various techniques and strategies to help Rosemary learn. In the spring of 1936, Newton reported that Rosemary's writing was improving. She included a sample of Rosemary's homework in a letter to Rose: "Please show it to her father for it is a practically perfect paper, which we have been aiming for." She had been drilling Rosemary on famous European explorers and leaders, and she hoped that the Kennedys would ask Rosemary questions about the historical figures to observe how much she could recall. But Newton doubted that Rosemary remembered much about Renaissance painters, "as we hadn't drilled quite long enough here."

Helen Newton's mother, Adeline, was teaching Rosemary to weave, because the two educators realized that Rosemary could not tolerate academic lessons beyond lunchtime. Helen Newton found that breaking up Rosemary's day between academic lessons and craft activities helped with her concentration and gave Rosemary opportunities to talk about her academic work with Adeline: "I received this idea from visiting several schools for retarded children when they found this plan of procedure gives the best results, as 9–11:30 or longer is too long for her to concentrate on school subjects." Helen spent lunchtime showing Rosemary how to use her lessons as launching points for polite conversation. Adeline monitored Rosemary when she did her homework, and Helen noted, "She gets a great deal from my mother's personality."

Math continued to frustrate Rosemary. "There are days when change seems very hard," Helen Newton told Rose, "and of course she longs to do algebra as Mary [O'Keefe] does — but I've told her she needed the plain use of money more. If you can help me out here I'd be most appreciative." Newton co-opted Rosemary's Easter holiday trip to Palm Beach, where the Kennedy family had recently purchased a winter vacation home, to demonstrate the importance and usefulness of math: "I had her [make] up mythical prices going to Palm Beach and taking someone with her — using certain amounts to cover meals, berth, tickets etc."

Newton alluded to other issues. An early April letter to Rose reads, "I wrote thanking you for your cooperation in the other matter, but probably you've been too busy to write." What Newton was referring to is a mystery, because the next two sentences have been blocked out with opaque tape, purposefully redacted under the terms in the donor's gift of deed to the John F. Kennedy Library. But Newton was clearly expecting a response from Rose, a response that had yet to come. She closes the letter by reminding Rose, and the family governess, Alice Cahill, to let her know if Rosemary had retained any of her lessons as the Easter vacation proceeded, "because what I am trying to do and the results may not come as quickly as we all desire."

The tone of discouragement is palpable. By the time of Newton's letter, Rose had been in contact with another consultant, Mary Baker, a teacher who worked with "special children" in New York. During March, Rose engaged Baker to go to Boston and make an assessment of Rosemary, with an eye toward Baker's taking on Rosemary as a private student in her home on Long Island. After Baker's visit to Boston, she wrote to Rose and Joe on March 27:

> She is not only attractive but has possibilities exceedingly worth developing. It would make me most happy to have the opportunity to help Rosemary train those capacities in real happiness for herself and in increasing ability to deal with life and people. In all my work with special children I have found an entirely new environment away from things which they have been accustomed, a real necessity. In other words, if she were here with me I would handle the situation exactly as I have always done in my private school.

Baker suggested that Rosemary come to her immediately and begin "a period of intensive study of her interests, abilities, and special needs, and an intensive tutoring of her most needed and practical abilities and skills." Her daily program would include a "simple study of balanced diets and foods . . . making of simple candy, cakes, cookies, salads, etc. This furnishes excellent opportunity for gaining dexterity in the use of her hands; the practical arithmetic of measurements, simple fractions, temperatures, and telling time," Baker suggested. Reading, writing, and vocabulary drills would be promoted through lessons in history, geography, civics, and science, interspersed with "athletics," "music," "shopping," and leisure activities.

Baker would ensure that Rosemary had ample social interactions: picnics and parties during the day, and in the evenings, dances, the theater, concerts, movies, special dinners, and games with other students. "An occasional evening with a young man escort of fineness and understanding" would be part of the social development Baker envisioned. "Special emphasis would be placed on the matter of companions. I am in close touch with a number of exceptionally fine and understanding young people who would furnish excellent opportunity for happy companionship. All activities would be planned in the amounts best adapted to Rosemary's physical health as well as happiness and education." Those social activities would have to be balanced, Baker noted, with the Kennedys' need for privacy: "The people with whom I deal would in no way come in contact with your acquaintances and she would visit you only at times planned by you."

Baker met with Drs. Dearborn and Lawrence, too, going over "definite instructions as to [Rosemary's] care." Baker did not discuss the Newtons or Rosemary's studies with them but complimented Ruth O'Keefe instead: "Mrs. O'Keefe has made a wonderful contribution to Rosemary and I am hoping that I may have the opportunity to continue the excellent work she has done."

The Newtons were apparently unaware that Rose was inves-

tigating an alternative program for Rosemary. All the arrangements for Baker's meeting with Rosemary and her doctors were
coordinated through Ruth O'Keefe and her husband, Dr. Edward
S. O'Keefe, not the Newtons.

In any case, Baker's assessment and her plans to tutor Rosemary on Long Island were not acted upon. The Kennedys decided
to keep their daughter at the Newtons' school. Yet in August
1936, just before another fall semester was to begin, Helen Newton wrote Rose, telling her, "I have had from 15 to 20 years experience with retarded children, and Rose[mary] is the most difficult child to teach so that she may retain knowledge that I have
ever encountered." Now, after two years, Helen Newton said she
could do no more, denying Rosemary readmission for a third year
of instruction.

Immediately after Newton's letter was received, Rose found
another program, enrolling Rosemary at Miss Hourigan's Residence School. The school, located in Manhattan, had been established in 1920 by Mollie Hourigan. It occupied a spacious mansion at 37 East 83rd Street, offering instruction for young women,
ages seventeen to twenty-one, in "Music, French, Advanced English, Social Service, Journalism, Fine Art, Designing, Graduate
Medical Assistant, Law Assistant, Homemaking and Household
Management, Business," and "Bride's School." The bridal course
offered social skills and training for rich young debutantes of the
day. Miss Hourigan's did offer a rigorous high school and postgraduate program for young women, but it was far more demanding than what Rosemary would have been capable of handling.
She was able to enroll in classes outside of Miss Hourigan's, too,
receiving private daily instruction, for instance, at the Universal
School of Handicrafts at Rockefeller Center. To ease the move to
New York City and a new school, Rose hired a Radcliffe College

graduate, Amanda Rohde, to be both tutor and companion for Rosemary.

In the midst of this transition, tragedy struck the family. Rose's remaining sister, Agnes, suddenly died in September 1936, a devastating and unexpected blow. Agnes, who had married late but at the age of forty-three was enjoying life with her husband, Joe Gargan, in Boston, was a seemingly perfectly healthy and happy mother of three young children. An undetected embolism took her during her sleep, in just the way her grandmother had died from an embolism fifty years before. Her six-year-old son, Joey, discovered his mother dead in her bed the following morning.

Rosemary had spent a great deal of time with Agnes during her two years at the Newtons' school in Brookline, especially during the spring and summer of 1936. Agnes was fun and patient, a disposition Rosemary loved. Her aunt's death must have hit Rosemary exceptionally hard, as she was trying to adjust to a new environment and routine as well as to the frenetic pace of a big city. Rose, for her part, spiraled into depression. Her brother Frederick had died in February 1935, and now Agnes was gone. Rose later wrote, "A sister is a most wonderful asset, I believe, as a brother is to a boy. From my own personal experience and from watching my own children at all ages, I believe sisterly devotion is one of life's choicest blessings." Now, she had no more sisters.

Within a few weeks' time, Amanda Rohde was discovering how difficult working with Rosemary could be. Years of instruction, both individually and in classrooms, had advanced Rosemary only to the fourth- or fifth-grade level in math and English, in spite of her age of eighteen. Dance classes became a struggle of wills, as did many of her other lessons. Rohde echoed the concerns of teachers from the past seven years. "It appears to me that she has taken advantage of her weakness and has used it as a weapon to have her way too much," the twenty-one-year-old Rohde wrote to Rose in October. Not only was Rosemary a challenging student for the young woman, but also Rosemary's "attitude towards her work, and consequently towards me" made daily interactions with her exhausting. "Now she makes herself unpleasant when she finds herself in a situation in which she has to think. If she is allowed to continue with this, she will become more and more difficult to live with," Rohde cautioned. "Daydreaming" was her problem, Rohde believed, causing Rosemary to "brood too much about herself." Rohde asserted that "Rosemary has been allowed to escape too much for her own welfare. She has found it more pleasant to day-dream . . . Little by little she must be brought to face reality. It will be a long siege, but it can be done."

The Kennedys, as always, were hopeful that this new situation would work better than the last. They instructed Rohde to incorporate a curriculum developed by Walter Dearborn into Rosemary's daily studies at Miss Hourigan's. By this time Dearborn had been working with Rosemary for more than two years, but he was now more cautious concerning his expectations for her success. He observed not only that Rosemary was socially awkward but also that her anxiety and fears in public seemed to be the result of "intellectual blocking as a result of . . . tense social settings," where her clumsiness and incompetence raised "the concerned looks of all concerned," embarrassing and frustrating her even more. Just how this problem could be addressed was a question left unanswered.

Again, Rosemary would not progress as her parents had planned. By the end of the school year at Miss Hourigan's, Rosemary had achieved little. Rohde was taking the summer off to travel home to Sioux City, Iowa, and new exercises and assignments for Rosemary, especially the "handicraft" classes that Rose believed "would develop her fingers," would have to wait until the fall and a new academic year. That July, the Kennedys sent Rosemary to Wyonegonic Camp for Girls in Denmark, Maine—the first summer-camp experience for her—for the month of July. She was accompanied by Elaine Dearborn, Walter Dearborn's seventeen-year-old daughter.

Determined to provide Rosemary with all the advantages her sisters and brothers shared, Rose and Joe sent Rosemary and Eunice on a European tour at the end of the summer. The Moores and governess Alice Cahill accompanied the girls, who were then almost nineteen and fifteen, respectively, on their trip. Europe was struggling with economic stress and political upheaval, but the girls traveled extensively. They visited many historic sites, and Rosemary dutifully wrote home to her parents at Hyannis Port. In her disjointed writing style, she tried to convey as much of her trip as possible on the backs of postcards: "We took a boat to Drock. Next to Edam, the Process of Cheese Place. A boat to Volerdam where the shops were. Took a boat to Bland of Markeh, Where we saw the Dutch custumes. Monday we went to the Museum of Paintings of Rombrant, Rubens, Van Dyck. The Peace Palace, The Queens House and her sisters." They traveled through Switzerland, Paris, London, Austria, the Netherlands, and Germany. Rosemary wrote to all her siblings, telling Bobby and Teddy about the boat she sailed on, and Kick about monuments, natural landscape features, and the beautiful hotels in which they stayed. She also told her sister that "the boys over here are not bad. We saw some Swiss boys. A boy from the Lafayette [boat] was going to take me out at the Contineal [Continental Hotel in] Paris. He was 24 years old. I played Ping Pong, Ring Toss, in the gym every day [with] Jonny Admour."

Rosemary would not return to Miss Hourigan's for a second

year in the fall of 1937, in spite of Rose's expectation that she would do so. Though Rose had thought about sending Rosemary to the Sacred Heart Convent Academy at Manhattanville—and Rosemary believed she was going there—so that she could be with more young women closer to her own age of nineteen, Rose had ultimately decided that another year at Miss Hourigan's would better prepare her for Manhattanville the following year. On July 9, however, Mollie Hourigan wrote to Rose that she thought it best for Rosemary to enroll at the Sacred Heart school. "When I last talked with you, you mentioned that you would like to make an arrangement for Rosemary at Manhattanville . . . and, when Rosemary told us she was going . . . I surmised you had made the arrangement." Hourigan had already spoken with Mother Superior Damman of Manhattanville and had told her that "Rosemary's programme of study [would be] completely taken care of with Miss Rhode [sic]." She assured Damman how "fond everyone had grown of Rosemary, and how, definitely, the child seems to bring out the best in everyone." Manhattanville, Hourigan urged Rose, would be a much more suitable school, because Rosemary could "participate in many more group activities in the afternoon, such as, athletics, games, choral singing, with a much larger group than with us, and [because in] meeting college students at meals, she would have so much more opportunity for acquiring an easy give and take." Manhattanville also had a nursery school, where "Rosemary might find some interest in doing some work with little children." Hourigan assured Rose that Rosemary could, on occasion, join the students at Miss Hourigan's for the opera or the theater, but, she concluded, the convent school "may lead to something that would be happy for Rosemary and a comfort for you."

A few days later Rose responded: "I read your letter with great interest and I want to thank you for your thoughtful suggestions. I believe it would be better for Rosemary to continue along the lines which she started last year, as it takes considerable time for her to make new adjustments . . . Possibly Rosemary might go to Manhattanville occasionally next year to visit. I have already engaged Miss Rohde," Rose assured Hourigan, "who plans to live near Rosemary in order that the child may go back and forth to her studies in a less conspicuous manner." (It is unclear what a "less conspicuous manner" meant.)

But Hourigan had already decided that Rosemary could not reenroll for the fall term, and her tone and words in a follow-up letter on July 23 reveal a deeper annoyance with Rose. "I shall always be interested in her," Hourigan wrote, but, "quite frankly, the responsibility was much greater for me, last year, than I anticipated. Having accepted the child, and agreed upon the arrangements with you, it was only a short time before I realized that Rosemary needed continual protection or supervision." In what had been, and would continue to be, a constant theme for caregivers and teachers alike, Hourigan expressed frustration with the deep chasm between what Rose had told her about Rosemary's abilities and the reality of life with her. Rose kept the most problematic and difficult aspects of Rosemary's situation to herself, leaving tutors, aides, and teachers to discover the extent of Rosemary's disabilities and emotional challenges on their own. Hourigan felt betrayed. Her school was for young women who were intellectually and emotionally prepared for its rigorous academic program. Rosemary was not. Given the Kennedys' stature, it was no doubt difficult and complicated to confront them about the matter. Yet with the prospect of another year of a teaching task beyond the means and skills of her staff looming, Hourigan felt compelled to intervene. The continuous supervision of Rosemary "entailed a constant checking, which was a responsibility that could never be let down. I do not think we have ever had a more loveable girl, Mrs. Kennedy, but frankly, I have never before carried as great a responsibility, both for your child, and for my school." Hourigan believed that Rosemary would be safer within Manhattanville's cloistered convent grounds while still benefiting from a learning environment, "because, in that large group there would be more contacts of every kind without ever leaving the convent grounds."

With no other choices available on such short notice, Rosemary was sent to Sacred Heart Convent Academy in Manhattanville for the 1937–38 academic term. What Rose arranged with the nuns can only be surmised. It would, however, be another turbulent year.

5

Brief Haven in England

THOUGH JOE HAD taken over the primary responsibility of
Rosemary's placements during the early 1930s, by the time Rosemary entered Miss Hourigan's, in 1936, Rose was once again
managing Rosemary's educational and medical needs almost exclusively. Joe's thriving professional life had opened up high-pro-
file opportunities in President Franklin Delano Roosevelt's administration in Washington, D.C., where Joe had now settled
himself in a rented house away from his family in New York.
President Roosevelt had appointed Kennedy chairman of the Se-
curities and Exchange Commission during the summer of 1934.
The SEC was a newly created federal agency authorized by Congress and championed by Roosevelt as part of his Depression-
era New Deal programs to reform government, industry, and the
economy. The SEC was charged with regulating and reforming
trading practices on Wall Street. The chairmanship was a highly
coveted and important position, and Roosevelt knew he needed
a strong commissioner who was not likely to bend to pressures
exerted by powerful investment and banking interests. Initially,

because of Kennedy's own history on Wall Street and his past trading and financial dealings, through which he had made a fortune, many Roosevelt supporters were furious. A "grotesque appointment," one editor called it. Joe was responsible for crafting and overseeing the implementation of some of the most important regulations and reforms the industry had ever seen and badly needed. Roosevelt knew Kennedy was a perfect choice: who better to change the way Wall Street worked than a man who had taken advantage of its unregulated environment, making millions while others lost them? Joe's appointment was a reward for his campaign support during Roosevelt's successful 1932 run for the Oval Office. Roosevelt was confident and determined that this new agency, with Joe at the helm, would effectively regulate the financial industry, help rebuild market confidence and stability, and bolster positive public opinion.

After a successful three years as SEC chairman, Kennedy was offered the chairmanship of the Maritime Commission, another first of its kind; it was an appointment that Kennedy desired. Confirmed by Congress in March 1937, Kennedy immediately turned to reorganizing and expanding America's aging and inadequate merchant marine fleet. This job suited Kennedy well: he could tap into the broad and deep management skills he had acquired while operating the Fore River shipyard in Quincy, Massachusetts, during World War I. Government service was a natural segue into a political career, Kennedy had always believed. Eddie Moore would remain Joe's assistant, following him to Washington as his secretary and chief of staff.

War was looming in Europe, and the U.S. fleet—both naval and merchant marine—was in terribly poor condition to meet the needs of protecting America's commercial shipping interests and the nation itself. There was much work to be done, and Kennedy set about hiring the best and brightest talent he could find. He immediately ordered new ships, and also established minimum standards for wages, hours, and safety. The decrepit condition of many merchant vessels was not the only problem Kennedy faced. Morale in the fleet was extremely low, and order among merchant sailors had been deteriorating for years, so much so that some sailors had started ignoring orders from their captains while in foreign ports. Merchant seamen were not members of the United States Navy, but their services at home and abroad were vital both to commerce and as support for the navy during wartime. Kennedy threatened to incarcerate any sailor who refused to obey the orders of his captain, invoking a mutiny law enacted in 1790. Though enforcement of the law proved unpopular with the maritime unions and their supporters, Kennedy stood firm.

The economy steadily improved between 1934 and 1937, but, after Roosevelt's second inauguration, he and Congress suddenly halted and disbanded many government-funded New Deal jobs programs that had been helping fuel economic growth. The response was dramatic and swift. The stock market fell rapidly, plummeting nearly two-thirds in value in a matter of months. The ripple effects were predictable and painful in a struggling economy: corporate profits slumped, incomes dropped, and unemployment climbed back to twenty percent, up from fourteen percent. Prospects for the world economy were no better. The aggressive movements of belligerent nations stifled fledgling economic stability around the world. Japan was marching through southeastern China, Spain was embroiled in a full-fledged civil war, Mussolini was pursuing Italian imperialist ambitions in Africa, and, after conquering the Rhineland, Adolf Hitler had set his sights on annexing Austria and Czechoslovakia.

Kennedy and his staff completed an in-depth study of the status of the U.S. Navy and merchant marine, and sent his recommendations for a new, modern naval fleet to the president. Kennedy rewrote costly shipping contracts to the benefit of the U.S. government and recommended binding and compulsory arbitration of labor disputes, a move that again enraged seamen, their unions, and some industrial interests. New ships were useless if the country faced work stoppages and slowdowns at the hands of powerful unions, Kennedy believed. Interruptions in commerce because of seamen's strikes were already costing the country money and jobs. During weak economic times, striking unions and recalcitrant management, Kennedy argued, must be forced to negotiate and accept the terms of mandatory arbitration. Roosevelt's secretary of labor, Frances Perkins, forcefully disagreed with Kennedy, but Kennedy successfully persuaded Congress to act favorably on his recommendations.

By the end of 1937, having successfully executed a second presidential appointment, Kennedy was eager for an even more challenging and prestigious position in Roosevelt's administration. He was also looking for something that would boost the career aspirations of his sons. Roosevelt, grateful again for Kennedy's successful service to the administration, rewarded him in January 1938 with a much-coveted appointment as ambassador to the Court of Saint James's in Britain. Kennedy was thrilled. His appointment was an extraordinary professional accomplishment for an Irish American. He cared little when critics charged that he was anything but a diplomat.

Rose, too, realized that the ambassadorship would be a brilliant social achievement and an enriching opportunity for the entire family. With great delight she imagined the lasting benefits that would accrue to the children from living in a foreign country

and having access to some of the most important social and political figures of the day. With Joe's diplomatic position also came
tremendous social obligations, which Rose would be required to
orchestrate. Her performance while hosting and attending state
dinners and social events would be a critical piece of Joe's success
on the world stage. Finally, she had a role at Joe's side worthy of
her political and social accomplishment, and she intended to play
it perfectly.

Part of the performance included parading the children out in
public, offering hungry journalists and photographers carefully
choreographed opportunities to record the large family's activities and to keep the Kennedys on the society pages. The whole
Kennedy family bore the responsibility for navigating stereotypes
about Catholics. Rose wore her role as mother to a large brood
of children with great pride, while Joe delighted in his powerful
political, economic, and social position as confirmation of his triumph over his second-class Irish American roots.

Rose used her large family as a kind of prop, featuring and
promoting herself as a smart, efficient mother and wife, refashion-
ing the image of Catholic womanhood in the modern era. With
this she would capture the British public's imagination. Though
her orchestration of the family's appeal was rooted in a genuinely
deep faith and pride in her family, Rose's social acumen, attention
to detail, flair for the dramatic, and never-ending stories about
the children's activities would feed an international press keen for
stories about Americans and the rich and famous. Features about
the Kennedys' unconventional lives in traditional British society
would grace not only the society pages in America and abroad
but also the international news pages. Because of Rose, the whole
family, once in England, would be treated like Hollywood stars

and American royalty. Perhaps most important, Rose could finally share in the limelight that was so often reserved for her husband. This would be her moment of triumph, too.

The children already had significant training and preparation for the spotlight. Stars in the entertainment industry, social and cultural icons, literary figures, journalists, and business leaders were already regular fixtures of their lives. The older children had traveled abroad, as well, and had been groomed for the cultural and social adjustments and responsibilities expected of them. When Joe first entered government service, the children never thought twice about it. Intermittent news stories over the years about the family had also partially prepared them for the onslaught of attention they would receive in England and Europe. Rose would later explain that the children "were used to seeing their grandfather's picture in the paper," and public discussions involving their grandfather and father had long seasoned them to the benefits and disadvantages of press attention.

Children made for good stories that sold newspapers and magazines. During the Great Depression, the media promoted feel-good ideals of home and family and triumphant efforts to weather the economic storms that threatened social and family stability. Sentimental feature-length news stories about children and childhood belied the tension in a society filled with families living on the edge. The Dionne quintuplets, born in 1934 in Ontario, Canada, became a popular craze. A medical miracle, the birth of five babies without the aid of fertility drugs was unheard of. Taken away from their parents as toddlers, the five girls were raised by a doctor and several nurses in a specially built home where tourists and the media could watch their every move. Their daily routines, playtime, and education captivated a fascinated public weary of economic uncertainty and despair. As a tourist attraction, the quintuplets brought nearly half a billion dollars into the Canadian province.

Hollywood movies tapped into this phenomenon, too: child stars Shirley Temple, Mickey Rooney, and Judy Garland delighted moviegoers, offering an escape from daily worries and hopelessness. Portrayed as spontaneous, innocent, and charming, these youngsters were among the movie industry's biggest box-office draws. Shirley Temple, for instance, appeared in numerous films as, typically, an orphaned but incredibly resourceful, optimistic, and cute little girl who could charm millionaires, defend the defenseless, and "dispense moral advice" to adults who had somehow lost their way. Such movies and themes drew attention away from the stark realities of the thousands of children who were abandoned by poor and destitute parents who could no longer provide for them, crowding orphanages that once catered to truly parentless children. One in five children in New York City suffered from malnutrition, while nine in ten in the coal-mining regions of the country suffered starvation. The commercial exploitation and marketing of children—whether through film, magazine, or news coverage—satisfied adult needs to sentimentalize children, helping them avoid the realities of the Depression's effects on society's most vulnerable. The Kennedy children—well fed, well dressed, attractive, charming, and rich—offered a hopeful and idyllic view of family life.

Newspapers eagerly covered the Kennedys' move to London. Rose and Joe had determined that the family would travel in small groups rather than as one big family. Joe set sail on the USS *Manhattan* on February 23, 1938, after delaying his trip for two weeks to be with Rose, who had suffered a sudden attack of appendicitis and had to be hospitalized. Bidding farewell to his family and friends attending his departure from New York, Kennedy was besieged by the press. In spite of his successes as SEC chairman and chairman of the Maritime Commission, it was the incredible novelty of an Irish Catholic ambassador—a job that had previously been held only by elite Protestant Americans—that so excited the press.

In March, Rose set sail from New York on the USS *Washington* with Kick and the younger children—Pat, Bobby, Jean, and Teddy—along with the family's new nurse, Luella Hennessey, and governess, Elizabeth Dunn. Kathryn "Kiko" Conboy, the full-time nurse Rose had depended upon for nearly eighteen years, stayed behind, disappointing some of the children, who loved her and considered her a member of the family. Rosemary would keenly miss Kiko—an Irishwoman who loved all the Kennedy children and served as a surrogate mother—whom she had known nearly her entire life as a constant, nurturing presence. Dunn had already replaced former governess Alice Cahill, so that transition was less jarring, benefiting the younger children especially. Rose insisted the family cook, Margaret Ambrose, be brought along, ensuring that the family did not experience an interruption in their "regular family fare and our favorite American desserts, like strawberry shortcake and Boston cream pie." Joe Jr. and Jack would follow once their studies at Harvard had concluded, later that spring.

Kick had already graduated from the Convent of the Sacred Heart in Noroton, Connecticut, and had been taking courses in interior design at the New York School of Fine and Applied Art. The interruption in her studies apparently did not worry Rose or Joe, nor did any concern over the pause in the four youngest children's education prevent them from pulling those children from their classes. Eddie and Mary Moore, it was decided, would accompany Eunice and Rosemary to London later, in April. Sixteen-year-old Eunice was boarding at Sacred Heart in Noroton, and the delay in traveling to London with Rosemary and the Moores enabled her to finish her sophomore year there.

Preparing Rosemary for yet another transition required help. The *Boston Globe* reported on April 6 that Rosemary had been admitted to New England Baptist Hospital in Boston, with the family clarifying that Rosemary was there merely for a physical checkup, "following the example of her distinguished father who came to Boston for a physical examination at the Lahey Clinic before his departure for London." The hospital told reporters that she was not ill but would remain under observation for about a week. In fact, Rosemary had been in the hospital since the third week in March. "Rosemary has been in Boston," Eddie Moore wrote to Joe in London on March 23, "and all reports are most encouraging." Dr. Dearborn was sending the latest information on Rosemary, Eddie told Joe, and another physician, Dr. Jordan, had suggested that Rosemary "could take off 6 to 8 pounds in ten days" if she stayed at Baptist Hospital. By April 6, Amanda Rohde had arrived in Boston and reported to Eddie Moore in New York that Rosemary was "very well and happy." Rosemary had been "rather uncomfortable for a couple of days," but the cold she was "also" suffering from was responding to medicine. She did not leave the hospital until April 13. The specifics of Rosemary's health issues at that moment remain a mystery, though it is possible that anxiety regarding the upcoming trip abroad may have exacerbated preexisting physical or mental conditions. The loss of "6 to 8 pounds in ten days" seems very likely to have been a secondary, if not a primary, goal of the hospitalization.

Though the *Boston Globe* reported that Rosemary was "a graduate of Sacred Heart Academy, Manhattanville, N.Y., [and] is at present a student at Marymount Convent, Tarrytown, N.Y.," Rosemary had never officially graduated from Manhattanville;

and it is likely that she was simply living at the convent, where the Sacred Heart sisters lived, rather than taking college-level courses at their New York City campus, on Fifth Avenue. The nuns had asked for a private showing of the latest Disney animated film, *Snow White,* and Eddie Moore was eager to oblige them, he told Joe, because "they have been so sweet about Rosemary."

Rosemary went directly to New York City after leaving the hospital, moving in with the Moores at the Chatham Hotel until Eunice could join them and they could all leave together on the USS *Manhattan,* on April 20. Rosemary's adjustment to the new surroundings was bound to be difficult and slow, and this was probably why her arrival in London was scheduled to occur after the majority of the family had already settled in: the delay helped Rose, the personal family staff, and the embassy personnel to plan for Rosemary's needs and to accommodate them once she arrived.

Located at 14 Princess Gate, on Grosvenor Square, the embassy had been donated to the United States by the industrialist J. P. Morgan. The kitchen occupied the basement level, whereas the first floor was used as public space: a large, long dining room, two smaller reception rooms, another reception room for larger teas, and a small study for more private meetings and gatherings. The second and third floors contained eight bedrooms for the family, and the top two floors held the living quarters for embassy and family staff. Six-year-old Teddy enjoyed riding up and down the elevator for hours playing "department store," much to the chagrin of the embassy staff. Rose described the embassy as "simple" in decoration, though newspaper baron William Randolph Hearst loaned some of his art collection to grace its walls. Aside from commenting on the Lenox china bearing the seal of the United States, Rose had little to say about her surroundings.

With the help of governesses and secretaries on the ambassador's staff, Rose managed the busy schedules for all the children, whether they were in school, attending public functions with their parents, or traveling.

Astonishingly, the presentation of Rosemary and Kick at the British court a mere two weeks after Rosemary's arrival in London was a Kennedy priority. Presentation at court to Britain's king and queen was the apogee of the ritual London debutante "season" for elite young women of Britain's highest society. Weeks of parties, balls, formal dinners, and sporting events littered their calendars. The season served as the official "coming out" of eligible young women to a social world in keeping with a family's elite lineage and social status. It also offered an opportunity for the formal and public recognition of marriageable young women whose families hoped to pair them with socially and economically suitable young men. Such marriages often cemented social and financial alliances between Great Britain's and Europe's aristocratic families. The purpose of the season and the events it spawned over several months were taken very seriously. A tradition dating back hundreds of years, presentation to the king and queen at the royal court was reserved for the wealthiest and most politically powerful of British society. Not all debutantes were presented, however, and some wealthy married women coveted the invitation for themselves. The honor conveyed lifetime status, making them eligible to attend the many social functions hosted by the royals for the rest of their lives. This was what Rose aspired to: social status both in the United States and abroad for herself and her daughters. Although marriage for her daughters to aristocratic British heirs sounded appealing, the fact was that most eligible men were Protestant. Interfaith marriages were frowned upon by both Catholics and Protestants, and Rose would be no exception. The social cachet and privilege that emanated from a formal presentation at court were what Rose wanted, not necessarily husbands for her daughters.

The presentation would mark the first time that Rosemary would be in almost constant public view. The social pressure would be enormous. Her family and close friends, like the Moores, worried that she might do or say something inappropriate or reveal her intellectual limitations. The British aristocracy had long shunned their own mentally disabled and mentally ill family members, hiding them away in sanitariums, mental hospitals, country farms and cottages, and—a favorite of British novelists—attic rooms. To present Rosemary, an intellectually disabled adult, to the monarchy at Buckingham Palace during the debutante season was more than a bold act; a debutante with intellectual disabilities would have stirred long-held prejudices about passing along "defective" traits to the next generation. Joe and Rose were determined to keep the family secret, making sure that Rosemary was treated just like all the other eligible young women presented at court that year.

The formal presentation at court was "very rich in pageantry and very elaborate," Rose would write years later. Most eligible young women and their families spent months planning for the presentation, but the Kennedys' late arrival that spring had given Rose and the two girls little time to prepare. Rose privately complained that having such an event, with all the parties, balls, and social gatherings leading up to it, during springtime interrupted opportunities to travel. The social season in the United States traditionally took place during the fall or winter months, when the nights were longer and there was less to do and when fewer vacations were planned. Spring, with its "lovely days when one could go to the country," seemed less sensible to Rose. Hunting season dominated the fall and winter social scene in Britain, she later learned, leaving the spring to be the domain of the debutantes.

Young women who had been presented to the court in the years before the current one were called upon to help prepare the next group. Their mothers, often titled Englishwomen or wives of diplomats or military officers, coached the new group of debutante mothers on the rigid protocols, procedures, and rules that each woman was required to follow. Strict fashion guidelines were respected: dress designs were governed more by conservative court prescriptions than by fashion trends; lace trains and long gloves were uniform; and headdress styles were carefully regulated. The distance between each girl in the procession had to be the same so that the equally measured trains would not be stepped on. Two girls would approach the king and queen at the same time; months of collective curtsy practice were crucial so as "not to have one lady bobbing up while the other was stooping down."

Rose had long been a devotee of Paris fashion houses, and she was eager to make the trip from London to Paris to buy Kick's and Rosemary's dresses. She was warned, however, that buying from an English designer was expected. English designers "knew the type to be worn at Court, understood the importance of the train, etc." This was frustrating for Rose, who always wanted the latest and finest for herself and her daughters. Though she did not appreciate being told how to dress, Rose would not completely abandon British standards. For Rosemary and herself, she found a compromise in dresses designed by Edward H. Molyneux, a British-born designer who had established a successful fashion house in Paris decades before. Molyneux ran a smaller shop in London in the early 1930s to serve his British clients, but it was at his Paris salon that Rose chose her own and Rosemary's dresses. In a bit of nonconformity, Rose decided on a couture gown for Kick from the French fashion designer Lucien Lelong.

Traditionally, elite young women from America whose families could afford to send them to England for the season, or who were living in Europe or in London at the time, were eligible for presentation. Such an arrangement led to status-hungry citizens pressuring the American ambassador to allow their daughters to be presented at court. Joe, perhaps taking the opportunity to spoil things for a class of people who had long shunned him because of his working-class upbringing and Irish Catholic heritage, decided that only the wives and daughters of the U.S. diplomatic mission who were actually living in England could participate. The uproar was deafening. In spite of the negative press, but with President Roosevelt's support, Joe refused to acquiesce. The prior year had seen twenty American women presented at court. This year it would be only seven, three of whom were Kennedys: Rose, Rosemary, and Kick.

On the evening of the presentation, Rose claimed she felt like "Cinderella," dressed in her silver-embroidered Molyneux gown with matching tulle train. She wore long white gloves over which "jewels were added." A Molyneux dressmaker, who had come to the embassy to help Rose get dressed, secured three white feathers "at the proper angle" on her hair, and a jewel-encrusted tiara, purchased for the occasion, completed the look. Rose later wrote that she "ran into my husband's room to show him my elegance . . . His blue eyes lit up, and he grinned in the most loving way and said—as he *would* say—'You're a real knockout,' which was the highest compliment I could ever want."

Rosemary was resplendent in her "picture dress of white tulle embroidered with silver paillettes and worn over white satin," and she was a specific favorite of both the American and the British papers. Kathleen radiated in her French gown of "white and silver rosettes scattered" on white tulle over satin, with a matching embroidered train. Eunice would later remember that leading up to her presentation at court the following year, "more excitement and joy seized me than ever before in my life." Rosemary and Kick felt the same thing. The girls carried "Victorian posie" bouquets, while Rose, like the rest of the matrons attending, carried an ostrich-feather fan.

After the group gathered on the first floor of the embassy and posed for photographs, Ambassador Kennedy led his wife and daughters to a waiting limousine. Following a procession past thousands of spectators who lined the streets approaching Buckingham Palace, the Kennedys exited the car at a diplomatic entrance and were ushered along red carpets through the palace's opulent galleries via "a special route for the diplomats who head off the court's list." At 9:30 sharp, to the sounds of the national anthem, King George VI and Queen Elizabeth entered the ballroom and were guided to their thrones. The queen was wearing the famous Koh-i-Noor diamond in her crown. Weighing 105 carats, the diamond had been taken as war spoils from India a century before. The king, only a year past his coronation, wore the deep scarlet uniform of a field marshal. The debutantes, already lined up, began moving in perfect tandem toward the royal couple. The ballroom, decorated in gold, silver, and white, sparkled from the crystals twinkling in the giant chandeliers hanging above, which enhanced the jewel-studded tiaras, necklaces, earrings, and bracelets worn by the guests.

Rosemary was stunning, more beautiful than her sister. A few weeks of practicing the perfect "Saint James bow," smiles, handshakes, and ballroom dancing had paid off — almost. Much to everyone's embarrassment, Rosemary tripped and stumbled in front of the king and queen. Quickly catching herself and avoiding a reputation-shattering fall to the floor, Rosemary accomplished her curtsy and followed her sister Kick into the ballroom. Fortunately for Rosemary, she did not take the embarrassment as seriously as others in the room, and her evening was a success. She danced and chatted graciously like many of the other debutantes. According to the gossip columns, Rosemary and Kick both danced with "Prince Frederick of Prussia, Earl of Chichester, Earl of Craven, Viscount Duncannon, Viscount Newport, and Baron von Florow." Years of training and the close supervision that Rosemary received helped mask her intellectual challenges so successfully that no one seemed to suspect how profoundly different she was. Many assumed that the older, prettier sister was just a little more reserved or more shy than the younger and more outgoing Kathleen. But it was Rosemary, in her beautiful Molyneux gown, who received the most attention from the British press. Rose would later complain that the London papers reported on Rosemary's dress to the exclusion of Kathleen's. She believed the British prejudice against Paris fashions jaded the reporting, but she could not deny that her eldest daughter's great beauty had captivated the society-column pages. The *New York Times* noted, perhaps rather cattishly, "Court observers noticed that Mrs. Kennedy wore a white gown, the same as her daughters, a color formerly reserved for debutantes." Apparently, Rose committed nearly as bad a faux pas as her husband, who refused to wear the traditional formal British knickers and instead wore "ordinary full evening dress."

Rose planned for the girls to share in a coming-out party in June. She deftly orchestrated a dinner for eighty and a reception for one hundred more to celebrate the two sisters' coming of age and entrance into elite society. The embassy dining room glowed in shades of yellow, and guests sat at beautifully appointed tables topped with silver candelabras surrounded by rings of roses and sweet peas. Kathleen and Rosemary wore "severe gowns of white, relieved only by necklaces of pearls." The stunningly handsome sisters danced in the embassy ballroom, which was exquisitely decorated in "pink and mauve flowers." The event was called "one of the best of recent dances for debutantes" in London that season.

Becoming increasingly beautiful as she aged, and with a little extra weight adding to her voluptuousness (much to her parents' dismay), Rosemary attracted a tremendous amount of attention, including that of the men she met. Given Rosemary's easy sheltering at convent schools, it would take concerted, coordinated efforts by Rose, Joe, and Rosemary's siblings to monitor and guide Rosemary through social situations outside of school. She was now flirting freely and unabashedly. In July, after the presentation at court, Kathleen wrote that she and Rosemary and two other girls had gone out with "about six midshipmen after a movie." After singing some songs at a restaurant, they discovered their bill had been reduced by half by the owners of the establishment, who were honored to have the ambassador's daughters as customers. Kathleen would not mention Rosemary again in her diary for the rest of the year. With so many young servicemen eager for female company, and the sons of British aristocracy inviting her to parties and outings, Kick was eager to have a vibrant social life. She may have begun chafing at the responsibility of monitoring and chaperoning Rosemary.

Though invitations for both Rosemary and Kick continued to arrive at the ambassador's residence throughout the summer and fall, Rosemary was increasingly accompanied by other family members, the Moores, or hired companions. Kick, by contrast, was experiencing more liberty and freedom. In fact, eighteen-year-old Kick quickly became the darling of British society.

Finding it easy to socialize with Britain's nobility and politicians alike, she quickly won many friends. She danced at clubs all night and spent weekends at the country estates of Britain's social and economic elite, independently of her family. This may have deeply annoyed Rosemary, who was not allowed to live such an independent life.

By the end of June, the debutante season had run its course. Rose's parents, Josie and Honey Fitz, arrived in London on the Fourth of July and stayed for nearly three weeks. They visited historic sites; attended social and sporting events with political dignitaries, including the country's prime minister, Neville Chamberlain; and were treated to an audience with the dowager queen Mary. After they left, at the end of July, Rose gathered the children and headed to the south of France for a few weeks' vacation before the start of school, in late September.

Joe had rented a villa at Cap d'Antibes, near Cannes, for the entire family. When Rose saw the dirty pool at the villa, she complained, and Joe immediately secured a cabana at the nearby exclusive Hôtel du Cap, where the family could spend their days swimming, playing tennis, and enjoying other outdoor activities. Elizabeth Dunn and Luella Hennessey joined them, allowing Rose some freedom to travel to Paris and other places, with or without Joe. Movie star Marlene Dietrich and other American and European celebrities and dignitaries vacationed at Cap d'Antibes, too, delighting the girls in particular. Rose's focus on the children's weight had become a family obsession, one that did not lessen on vacations. "Almost go mad listening to discussion of diets . . . Jack is fattening, Joe, Jr. is slimming, Pat is on or off, and Rosemary (who has gained about eight pounds) and Kathleen and Eunice are all trying to lose."

Rosemary spent much of her time with Dietrich's thirteen-year-old daughter, Maria. An only child, Maria loved the Kennedys, preferring to be with a large family of siblings who were fun and constantly on the move than with her mother. Maria knew about her mother's infidelities—Marlene's affairs were common knowledge—and she soon realized that Joe Kennedy was becoming a frequent visitor to their cabana. "The Ambassador to the Court of St. James was kind of rakish," Maria later wrote. "For a man with such a patient wife, who had borne him so many children, I thought he flirted a bit too much." But she thought the Kennedy children were so much fun that, she later recalled, "I would have gladly given up my right arm, the left, and any remaining limb, to be one of them."

Maria noticed that Kick had "assumed the role of the official eldest sister" and that Eunice, at seventeen, was "opinionated, not to be crossed, the sharp mind of an intellectual achiever." Joe Jr. was "a handsome football player with an Irish grin and kind eyes," while Jack, "the glamour boy," was every "maiden's dream" and her "secret hero." Though Pat, "a vivacious girl," was nearest in age, Maria found herself more often paired with twenty-year-old Rosemary. Rosemary was "the damaged child amidst these effervescent and quick witted children, [but] she was my friend," Maria recalled fondly. "Perhaps being two misfits, we felt comfortable in each other's company. We would sit in the shade, watching the calm sea, holding hands."

A little afraid Rose might be angry about the affair between her mother and Joe Sr. and might possibly banish her from the family's daily activities, Maria was shocked to discover that Rose remained warm and inclusive in the midst of what Maria perceived as an obvious and brazen affair, as if nothing unusual was happening. Eventually, however, the guilt and embarrassment over her mother's affair with the ambassador forced Maria to stop spending her time with the Kennedys. She suspected, though, that they "were as used to their father disappearing as I was my mother."

During the latter part of the summer of 1938, Eunice, Pat, Bobby, and Rosemary traveled with the Moores and Elizabeth Dunn to Scotland and Ireland. Maria Dietrich joined them and found herself paired with Rosemary again, in spite of the large age difference. Eunice reported that the girls were getting "plenty of attention" as the daughters of the ambassador and that they had had several requests for interviews and autographs.

With the children all taken care of, Rose had stayed in Cannes by herself. Joe was by then attending to diplomatic duties in Paris. But by the middle of September, he was urging Rose to return to London. "When Joe phoned last night, he said things were terribly agitated in London and perhaps I should leave in the morning," she wrote in her diary on September 13.

Rose's absence was in fact causing her husband professional concern. Standard protocol for a newly arrived ambassador would have been to host scores of formal teas, diplomatic luncheons and dinners, and private social gatherings, and Rose was supposed to be the official hostess for these events. But Rose had been focused on organizing and settling her children and staff when they arrived in London in the spring, and then the court presentation and debutante parties for Rosemary and Kick took precedence. "I had to settle their problems without the aid of protocol," she later noted to her biographer. Nearly two months of vacationing on the French Riviera afterward had not endeared the Kennedys to a British public anxious about inevitable war. Rose's ambitions as ambassador's wife were in fact remarkably different from those of her husband.

Settling the children in school would be Rose's first priority upon her return to London. Catholic schools were preferable, of course. Rosemary was at first sent to a Sacred Heart school in the London borough of Wandsworth, about six miles from the embassy at Princess Gate. The Convent of the Sacred Heart Finishing School for Girls enrolled young women ages seventeen and older, "on the verge of womanhood," "to face the responsibilities of life, to control their own larger independence, and thus fit themselves to take with ease and dignity their place in the home and in society." Teddy and Bobby attended Gibbs Preparatory School, a London boys' school, while the younger girls, Pat, Jean, and Eunice, enrolled in the Sacred Heart Convent School in nearby Roehampton. Rose considered enrolling Kick in college in London, but after researching potential programs, she realized that college education for young British women was not as common as it was for American women, so that plan was abandoned. Perhaps with Kick's encouragement, Rose decided instead that she would help "a bit with my duties as hostess." Now, of the children, only Kick, the two youngest boys, and Rosemary lived at the embassy, but everyone was home for weekends as often as possible, ensuring their engagement in the cultural, political, and social life of their parents.

The educational program at Rosemary's Sacred Heart Finishing School was an advanced one. Diplomats and other foreign business leaders sent their daughters to this school, which specialized in educating students from across Europe, Asia, and America. Courses in literature, foreign languages, history, and art were part of the advanced and postgraduate high school curriculum. Domestic, social, and job-skills training was also offered, including dressmaking, cooking, typewriting, shorthand, elocution, singing, and dancing. Rosemary's skill levels would not have been adequate to compete or even participate in many of these classes. It is likely Rose arranged for a personal aide to work with her.

Whatever arrangements were made, Rosemary was soon transferred to another convent school, the Convent of the Assumption School, in Kensington Square, just across Hyde Park from the embassy and opposite Kensington Palace. Mother Eugenie Isabel, the Mother Superior, who directed the various schools run by the convent for children in elementary grades through high school, soon proved especially sympathetic to Rosemary and her needs. By the spring of 1939, Rosemary was making "remarkable progress." Mother Isabel (as she was known) assured Rose and Joe that there had been "a great change in her lately," relieving Rose and Joe's anxiety over yet another school transition. At the time, the schoolboy antics of baby brother Teddy, then seven years old, seemed to be much more of a concern to the sisters at the convent's boys' school than Rosemary's progress.

Tension over Hitler's aggression in Europe was escalating, but Joe was adamant that America remain neutral. He believed that the United States' interests would not be served by supporting Great Britain and other European nations in another war against Germany, but the British keenly felt their vulnerability in the face of an aggressive German army. In November 1938, Joe recommended that the United States refuse settlement of German Jewish refugees fleeing the Nazis. Britain had requested help with resettlement by suggesting that the "American government apply the unused portion of the sixty-thousand quota for British immigrants" to German Jews. Kennedy, without approval from Washington, suggested that the British open their own colonies for resettlement instead. His isolationist views tarnished his reputation among the British, who were actively preparing for eventual war with Germany. Kennedy firmly believed that England and France would be defeated by the Germans. To avoid war, negotiations to surrender their vast colonial possessions around the world to Japan, Germany, and Italy would be necessary, leading to the "collapse of the British Empire," Kennedy argued. Some of his arguments, as some officials in Washington believed, came dangerously close to accommodation rather than opposition to Hitler. By the end of November 1938, Joe was called to Washington by Roosevelt to defend his views regarding the situation in Europe. By this time, Roosevelt did not care much for Kennedy or his views, and the men met only briefly. Frustrated and defeated, Joe joined Jack—who had returned to Harvard—for a six-week stay in Palm Beach. Rose and the rest of the children spent Christmas in Saint Moritz.

Rosemary and her siblings went skiing, skating, and sleigh riding. "Everything is so beautiful . . . I wish I could stay for a month," Rosemary wrote her father. She was once again on a diet, eating her meals at the "diet table." Desperately wanting Joe to approve of her, she told him, "I don't want to be [fat]. I will. surprise you," she wrote in her usual poor scrawl. She assured him that she would try not to worry her mother.

Back in London after the New Year, the Kennedy children all returned to school. The Assumption Convent school had adopted the educational methods of Italian physician and educator Dr. Maria Montessori. Rosemary reported to her parents that she was extremely busy working on an "Album for Dr. Montessori when she comes in March," and she was finding it an "awful lot of work." She was taking elocution, and contemplating her next set of courses once the current term was over. She was working toward a "diploma," which, she believed, would qualify her to be a kindergarten schoolteacher. The entire school community probably shared Rosemary's excitement over Dr. Montessori's visit to the school.

The Montessori program at the Assumption school seemed to be a good fit for Rosemary. The Montessori method of education emphasized hands-on, individualized learning strategies and methods of teaching in multiage group settings. Children of varying intellectual abilities and levels worked side by side, learning at their own pace in open classroom settings. Dr. Montessori's methods spread quickly throughout Europe and then the United States, mostly in private schools, although some public schools embraced her ideas, too. Mother Isabel had been trained personally by Montessori and had become one of the method's most innovative and active adherents.

Born in 1870, Maria Montessori was a precocious child whose well-educated parents encouraged her sharp mind. She was awarded a medical degree in 1896, becoming one of Italy's first female doctors. Her medical training had taken her into the slums and orphanages of Rome, where she witnessed the ravaging effects of poverty and the lack of education on the city's most vulnerable children. She became particularly interested in disabled children—those with intellectual disabilities and emotional problems who were destined to live in empty, lifeless rooms. She opened a day-care center in the slums, the Casa dei Bambini, through which she developed theories about childhood development and learning. Montessori required that teachers and caregivers speak to the children with respect and caring, recognizing that in spite of their disabilities, ill health, neglect, and poverty, these children had an innate desire to learn.

Montessori believed that if children were exposed to a safe, experiential learning environment (as opposed to a structured classroom), with access to specific learning materials and supplies, and if they were supervised by a gentle and attentive teacher, they would become self-motivated to learn. She discovered that, in this environment, older children readily worked with younger children, helping them to learn from, and cooperate with, each other. Montessori advocated teaching practical skills, like cooking, carpentry, and domestic arts, as an integrated part of a classical education in literature, science, and math. To her surprise, teenagers seemed to benefit from this approach the most; it built confidence, and the students became less resistant to traditional educational goals. Through this method, each child could reach his or her potential, regardless of age and intellectual ability.

The Montessori method arrived in the United States just a few years before Rosemary's birth, in 1915, and it would be years before it was widely accepted. Although Rosemary might have benefited from such instruction as a young child, as it was, she would not be exposed to it until she enrolled at the Assumption school in London. For the Assumption Sisters, Montessori's ideas on good and evil also fit with their Catholic theology: "The first idea that the child must acquire, in order to be actively disciplined, is that of the difference between *good* and *evil;* and the task of the educator lies in seeing that the child does not confound *good* with *immobility,* and *evil* with *activity,* as often happens in the case of old time discipline."

Rosemary was hoping to please her parents when she reported in February 1939 that she had earned her "diploma for being a child of Mary." Rosemary would have known how important this was to her mother, who had become a Child of Mary herself at the Convent of the Sacred Heart school at Blumenthal, in the Netherlands, thirty years before. Rosemary also assured her father, again, that she was keeping faithful to her diet. "This diet of Elizabeth Arden is very good. I have gone down between 5 and 7 pounds already living on salads, egg at night, meat once a day, fish if I want, spinach and soup. Wait to [*sic*] you see me. I will be thin when Jack sees me." In spite of the pressure from home to conform both physically and intellectually, Rosemary flourished under the Assumption school's individual instruction, constant reinforcement, repetitious exercises, and emotional support, a program better suited to Rosemary's needs than that of any other institution she had attended.

During early February, Pope Pius XI died at the Vatican. Cardinal Eugenio Pacelli, the Vatican secretary of state, was elected his successor. Pacelli had met Joe Kennedy in November 1936, after Joe had successfully facilitated a meeting for Pacelli with President Roosevelt to discuss reestablishing long-severed diplomatic relations between Washington and the Vatican. The success of that meeting—a private luncheon hosted by the president at Springwood, Roosevelt's family home in Hyde Park, New York, two days after his second, landslide election that November—endeared Kennedy to Pacelli. The Kennedys later entertained the cardinal in their home in Bronxville before he returned to the Vatican, an event that thrilled both Joe and Rose. Now, with Pacelli's selection as the new pope, Kennedy requested the honor of attending the coronation as the president's representative. Joe was overjoyed when Roosevelt agreed.

Pacelli was crowned Pope Pius XII in the balcony of Saint Peter's Basilica looking over Saint Peter's Square, where thousands of people watched. It was the first coronation to be filmed and broadcast live on radio. Millions of devoted Catholics around the world shared in the holy and joyous occasion. The Kennedy girls were dressed in conservative dresses and black veils, and the boys in suits and ties. Their parents' excitement must have heightened their own anticipation and sense of honor.

Rose would remember this as one of the most important days of her life. The Kennedys were seated on the balcony with other dignitaries, causing an unexpected stir when it was discovered that the Vatican had planned seating only for Joe and Rose, not their children, the Moores, Luella Hennessey, and Elizabeth Dunn, all of whom were present. Either Joe had neglected to get permission to bring his entire family with him, or he had not sought such permission, knowing that such a large entourage would have been discouraged. Regardless, he proceeded with the entire family. Gian Galeazzo Ciano, Benito Mussolini's son-in-law and the Italian minister of foreign affairs under Mussolini's fascist dictatorship, arrived for the coronation to discover a Kennedy child sitting in his seat. A loud tirade ensued, punctuated by threats from Ciano that he would storm off the balcony and leave before the ceremony could start, insinuating that this would imperil the relationship between the Vatican and Mussolini. The seating arrangements were quickly resolved, and the ceremony proceeded without further unscripted drama. The Kennedy children got more of a performance than they had expected. The next day, the family arrived back at the Vatican for a private audience with the new pope, who individually presented them with specially blessed rosary beads. Two days later, young Teddy, age seven, received his First Communion in the pope's private chapel. Mother Isabel had personally seen to Teddy's preparation as the first American to receive the sacrament directly from a pope. This was an extraordinary moment for the Kennedy family.

That summer the family vacationed again on the French Riviera, staying at the Domaine de Ranguin, near Cannes. The usual stars and dignitaries were there, including Marlene Dietrich. Parties, luncheons, dances, and beach bathing occupied everyone for weeks. Though banned in fascist Spain, two-piece bathing suits were becoming increasingly popular, and Joe enjoyed the "leg show." Rose, however, objected to the "little brassiere[s]," bare midriffs, and "abbreviated" shorts, and would not allow her girls to wear "such a costume," so they stuck to the traditional one-piece suits she had purchased in New York.

Such gaiety and revelry on the Riviera belied the threat of war darkening the Continent. Germany's aggression and demands were escalating. Joe, still arguing for patience and appeasement, found himself mostly isolated by the growing sentiment that Germany needed to be stopped. France and England finally declared war on Germany on September 3, 1939. With the start of war, the Kennedys decided the children would be safer back in the States. Kick, Bobby, and Eunice sailed on September 14 on the *Washington;* it was Joe and Rose's preference that the large family never travel together so that, in the event of an accident, not all would be lost. German submarines had been patrolling the Atlantic and had sunk several British ships already, so the fear was quite real. Four days later, Joe Jr. left for Harvard on the RMS *Mauretania,* followed by Jack, who flew to New York the following day. Teddy, Pat, and Jean, accompanied by the family nurse Luella Hennessey, sailed on the *Manhattan* the next day.

Rosemary, it was decided, would stay behind, safely ensconced, it was believed, at the Assumption school. The school had transferred its students earlier that summer to Belmont House, on the grounds of a large Catholic estate at Boxmoor in Hertfordshire, thirty miles northwest of London, presumably safe from pending German airstrikes targeting the city. Rosemary thrived here—perhaps more so without the pressures of the family, embassy life, the press, and the city. Dorothy Gibbs, a young woman hired as her companion, reported that on her birthday, September 13, Rosemary "toasted Belmont in her tea-cup at her Birthday tea party saying 'It is the most "wonderfulest" place I've been to.' Everyone clapped her tremendously & she looked so very charming." At Belmont House, Rosemary would be constantly attended by at least one aide or teacher, and sometimes two. Weekly transitions between school and home, with weekends spent at the embassy—including the demands of numerous social functions and the high-level activity typical of the Kennedy family—had caused exceptional stress for her, because she was constantly controlled by her parents. Now, less would be asked of her and she could feel more relaxed.

Dorothy Gibbs was her constant companion and assisted her with her studies, social engagements, and any excursions away from the school. The sheltered environment and busy days kept Rosemary content and happy; but here, too, she would lose her temper and lash out at her new friends, nuns and teachers, and even younger students. The Assumption Sisters' letters to Joe and Rose suggest that they were very aware of Rosemary's disabilities, consistently remarking on the twenty-year-old's "marked improvement" in her studies and attitude since her arrival. But the sisters also reported that on occasion she needed to be reminded not to be so "fierce" in front of the children.

Joe made sure the convent school had a working telephone—a wartime luxury the ambassador could deliver immediately, putting his own mind at ease, as well as the minds of the Assumption Sisters and the students living there. He provided many other niceties for the school, including access to private transportation and a fire-extinguishing system, "to fight incendiary bombs." The Moores, who had remained behind in London, checked in on Rosemary, spending weekends with her and taking her on short trips off school grounds, just as they had always done. Joe sometimes spent weekends at Wall Hall, a Hertfordshire estate owned by J. P. Morgan and on loan to the United States government for use by the American ambassador as a retreat from the city and from the embassy. Joe flattered Rosemary, telling her "she was going to be the one to keep me company," since the rest of the family had returned home. He assured her that because he would be so close on weekends, he would be able to invite her and some of her friends from the school to private showings of movies. "That tickled her to no end," he wrote Rose, now back in New York. Joe also arranged to hire another young woman to work with Rosemary, to give Dorothy Gibbs some time off each week. Rosemary clearly enjoyed her time with her father and excursions for shopping and entertainment nearby.

The rest of the family may have been happier with this arrangement for Rosemary, too. Eunice later revealed that her parents were not the only ones concerned about Rosemary. "No one could watch out for Rose[mary] all the time, and now she was a grown-up girl," Eunice later remembered. She and her brothers and sisters all had worried that Rosemary might "accidently do something dangerous while mother was occupied with some unavoidable official function. Would she get confused taking a bus and get lost among London's intricate streets? Would someone attack her? Could she protect herself if she were out of the eye of the governess?" Even seven-year-old Teddy had observed Rosemary's intellectual shortcomings and called her an "empty head." But he "looked out for her, too," he later wrote in his memoir, "when I could, though I was fourteen years younger."

Joe wrote that Mary Moore "had never seen such a change in her life" after Rosemary had spent just a few weeks at Belmont House. Joe, revealing a profound sense of relief, told Rose that it was "apparent now that this is the ideal life for Rose[mary]."

Perhaps finally they had been successful in finding a good placement for her. Dorothy Gibbs felt hopeful as well. "Please God," she prayed, "that some day he will grant [the Kennedys] the joy of a perfect healing for her." What had started out as a wartime accommodation — a move safely away from the cacophony of air-raid sirens and drills in London — had become a blessing for Rosemary. The particularly beautiful, pastoral landscapes of Belmont House's extensive estate holdings, the Assumption Sisters' and Dorothy Gibbs's devotion to her, and the Montessori educational methods all worked in tandem to make Rosemary's day-to-day life brighter and happier.

A passionate and innovative educator, Mother Isabel seemed to hold "a magical key to learning." She believed that the Montessori method built "confidence not undermined by the wrong set of competition which often promotes envy and feelings of inferiority." The day-to-day operations of the school in Hertfordshire — now a full-time boarding school made necessary by the evacuation from London — required more of Mother Isabel's attention. Noted for her selfless devotion by those who trained with her, Mother Isabel possessed a warm yet assertive demeanor that smoothed the potentially disruptive transition for all the school's children, not just Rosemary. "She [Rosemary] is contented completely to be teaching with Mother Isabel. She is happy, looks better than she ever did in her life, is not the slightest bit lonesome, and loves to get letters from [her siblings] telling her how lucky she is to be over here, (tell them to keep writing that way)," Joe wrote enthusiastically to Rose that October. "She loves being the boss here and is no bother or strain at all . . . I'm not sure she isn't better staying over here indefinitely with all of us making our regular trips, as we will be doing, and seeing her then. I have given her a lot of time and thought and I'm convinced that's the answer." And then, a rather stark statement: "She must never be at home for her sake as well as everyone else's."

There was another accommodation Joe found necessary. Censors read every letter sent back and forth between the United States and Great Britain. Joe worried that Rosemary's childlike penmanship and the content of her letters might be leaked, causing embarrassment for the family. To avoid gossip, he began forwarding her letters to the family via his legally protected diplomatic pouch of official government correspondence. "I don't see any point in having any of her letters go to America and be talked about," he wrote. "Over here it doesn't make any difference."

The first test of whether it was better to keep Rosemary separated from the rest of her family would come at Christmas. Joe had received permission to travel back to the States for the holiday to meet with the president and other State Department officials. Writing to Rose before he set sail for America, Joe explained why Rosemary should stay in England:

> Now as to Rosie for Christmas. I think she should stay here, by all means. First she would not be able to come back once she got over there. No passports being granted. Second she is so much happier here than she could possibly be in the United States that it would be doing her a disservice rather than helping her. She had another nice girl with her yesterday for the weekend. The girls are very nice and fit in with her limitations without anyone being the wiser. In the meantime she is "cock of the walk" by being by herself so that builds up her self-confidence. She is no bother when she is away from the other children. She gets along very well with Mary Moore and they have lots of fun

together . . . So I think everything is getting along OK . . .
Pray that everything stays quiet for me to get home.

"The calm [and] sameness of her life is just what she needs,"
Mother Isabel assured Rose in a letter just before Christmas. "I am
so glad Mr. Kennedy gave you good news of our dear Rosemary,
[and] that he is pleased, with her. We, too, are very satisfied with
the result of this term. Rosemary is very well, [and] obviously
happy, [and] she has made much progress in many ways." Rose
had sent Mother Isabel a "little book on writing" and suggested
that the sisters get Rosemary to use it by convincing her "to use it
in view of teaching others." Writing remained a constant problem
for Rosemary, and though she "welcomed" the book "with joy,"
Mother Isabel had a more practical request. She had asked Eddie
Moore to get Rosemary "a black double-lined page to put *under*
her note-paper. The lines can be seen through it [and] this should
make her writing straight, [and] more even in size . . . I told her
I always had to have one to keep *my* lines straight!"

Rosemary was now completing tasks she had been unable to
do before: "She has some supervision of the children in the garden, she has also a stated time for reading to them; she prepares
[and] gives them their lunch in the middle of the morning; [and]
has many other occupations of a domestic kind which she is able
to do *alone*—not the least of which is putting away the dining
room things (china [and] silver) in the cupboard."

Mother Isabel was well aware of Rosemary's anxiety over her
parents' praise. "She thinks of you very specially [and] loves you
heaps, [and] loves to hear from you, [and] to get your approval
[and] her father's too," she reminded Rose.

Rosemary still struggled with her anger and frustration.
"Rosemary is making great efforts on her character, too," Mother

Isabel reported. "She asked me one day to tell her what faults she had, as faults spoil people. This struck me, showing me how much she thinks things out. We have had more talks, [and] she has been trying hard to 'think of what pleases others *before* what pleases herself,' *and* 'to be *nice* to people even when *she* thinks they are not nice to her.' She comes to me whenever anything upsets her, [and] we 'have it out'—along these lines." The Kennedys had been blessed with the near "perfect healing" Dorothy Gibbs had been praying for.

Joe would not return to England for more than three months after the holidays. Confident that Rosemary was well cared for, he scheduled a few days with his latest lover, writer and journalist Clare Boothe Luce, in Italy before returning to his post in London in early March. The British had, by now, soured dramatically on the ambassador. They felt betrayed by the United States for its not entering the war or providing more substantial material support, and Joe was increasingly marginalized because of his pacifist views and accommodating attitude toward Hitler. Roosevelt was tiring of Kennedy as well, and when he sent Undersecretary of State Sumner Welles to Europe to discuss possible peace settlements, Kennedy understood it as a stinging sign of his disfavor.

When Joe returned to London, he started working with Mother Isabel to keep Rosemary at Belmont House for the foreseeable future. "Rose[mary] met me when I came home and I had dinner with her. She has got a little fatter but her disposition is still great and Mother Isabel tells me she shows improvement all the time," Joe wrote Rose at home in Bronxville on the fourteenth of March. "I'm riding out to see them both tomorrow. I'm thinking about her future plans. Of course a lot depends on what is going to happen in England in the war." Two days later, German bombers attacked Scapa Flow in Scotland, forcing the temporary relocation of the British naval fleet. Within three weeks, Germany was invading Norway and Denmark on a seemingly unstoppable course across western Europe. Joe's plans for Rosemary were now being threatened.

Joe's visit to Belmont House went well: "I had a talk with Mother Isabel about [Rosemary] staying here and Mother Isabel says she is already working on it and she is selling Rose[mary] the idea to stay." He had taken Rosemary to lunch when she went to London for a doctor's appointment, and he claimed that he did not "have any trouble with her when she is alone. She's not 100% of course, but no real difficulty." He sent Rosemary back to school, along with sugar, a rationed wartime luxury, and other supplies. He spent Easter not with her, as she had hoped, but rather with Clare Luce at his new residence, Saint Leonard's in Windsor, while the rest of his family gathered at Palm Beach.

Rosemary seemed to like the idea of staying in England. Her appeals reassured Joe. "Darling Daddy," she wrote in March 1940, "Mother [Isabel] says I am such a comfort to you, never to leave you. Daddy, I feel honour because you chose me to stay. And the others I suppose are wild . . . P.S. I am so fond of you. And love you very much." The following month, Joe wrote Rose to reassure her that Rosemary was still thriving: "Her disposition is great and there is no question she is getting along very well. She has gotten fat again and I am trying to get her to go on a diet. I am not hopeful, but at least I can try." Rosemary's father and mother's fixation on their children's weight remained a constant theme in correspondence. Rosemary knew her father disapproved of the few pounds she had put on over the winter months, after having done so well the year before with her Elizabeth Arden diet. "I am so fond of you," Rosemary wrote again to her father after a weekend visit in the spring, concluding in her awkward, misspelled

wording, "Sorry. to think that I am fat you. think." Joe wrote to
Dorothy Gibbs in a rather harsh tone, urging her to help Rosemary lose more weight: "I was more than pleased to see Rosemary
Sunday. She was looking very well and seemed to be in excellent
humor. I do feel that she is getting altogether too fat and I told
her in no uncertain words. So I wish, if you could, you would
try to build up the idea that she should lose weight. I told her
that her mother would be very disappointed and also that I could
not have her picture taken for America if she remains as stout as
she is." Gibbs responded immediately, assuring Joe that Rosemary had indeed understood perfectly what he meant. "You must
have made a big impression on Sunday," Gibbs told him. "She remarked, yes my figure does look fat doesn't it? . . . What do you
suggest I can do about it?" Later that month, Rosemary wrote
hurriedly to her father, "Everybody thinks I am thinner."

Kennedy was increasingly frustrated with his work and his
standing in Britain and wanted to head home. His political future seemed more uncertain as war was looming closer to British shores. Throughout the winter, German armed forces had advanced across Europe, preparing for invasion of western European
nations in the spring. During May, the German military marched
through the Netherlands, Belgium, and Luxembourg, and into
France. Joe and Rose knew they would be uprooting Rosemary
from the supportive and comfortable environment of Belmont
House, but it was too risky, they believed, to leave her there without the assurance that her father could be nearby. The decision
as to when, exactly, to send her home was left open, but she was
told it would be in the coming months. Rosemary did not want
to leave and pleaded with her father to let her stay another year
at the Montessori school. By the end of May 1940, the Germans
were rapidly advancing on Paris, so Joe wrote quickly to Rose, in-

forming her that the situation had gotten so bad that he had decided to "get Rose and the Moores out to either Ireland or Lisbon. We will be in for a terrific bombing pretty soon and I'll do better if I just have myself to look after."

Rosemary received her end-of-year diploma from the sisters and then, much to her disappointment, flew to America at the beginning of June with the Moores. The separation from her friends and the nuns at Belmont House was extremely difficult for her. "Everybody here is so sorry that I have to leave," Rosemary wrote to her father in April. "All of the nuns are especially nice to me . . . I always get such a great welcome here . . . I am dreadfully sorry about leaving. I will cry a lot."

The Germans marched into Paris on June 14; any lingering doubts about bringing Rosemary home were erased with German bombers' arrival in the skies above England. By September, Roehampton, the convent school that Eunice, Pat, and Jean had attended near London, had been bombed twice, and the embassy had become a prime target for the German Luftwaffe. Rosemary's haven in Britain was over.

6

War on the Kennedy Home Front

THE PLAN TO have Rosemary sail on the American liner USS *President Roosevelt* in late May was changed at the last minute. German U-boat attacks had made sailing, even on a passenger ship, too risky. On May 28, 1940, the day Belgium surrendered, as many French residents living near the Belgian border were trying to flee to England, Eddie and Mary Moore escorted Rosemary aboard a flight from London to Lisbon, where they waited, no doubt impatiently, for a scheduled Pan Am flight to New York. Though Joe Kennedy needed Moore at his side during this tumultuous time in Europe, getting Rosemary safely home was her father's priority.

The Moores' anxiety over the last-minute departure as western European nations were succumbing to Germany's advancing army was exacerbated by bad weather and heavy fog. Their flight out of Portugal to the United States was unexpectedly detoured to Bermuda because of the poor weather conditions, but the three landed safely in New York on Saturday, June 1, a day later than scheduled. When Rosemary wrote her father a few days later, she did not mention anything about their adventurous flight home, except that Eddie Moore told her that he wasn't "forgetting our trip back." By the middle of June, Paris would see German tanks and soldiers march down the Champs-Élysées, beginning a four-year occupation. Within weeks, the Luftwaffe bombing of Great Britain had started.

Joe wrote to Rose in New York expressing relief that Rosemary and the Moores were safe at home and assuring her that in spite of German threats he felt confident that he would be secure in London. Joe fully expected that the Germans would invade England, "but once this has happened I will expect F.D.R. to send for me . . . since there won't be much for me to do, my place is home, I've done my duty." Rosemary could return to the care of the Assumption Sisters, he believed, "when things settle down here under any regime, [and] they [the nuns] will be delighted to have her back and I'm sure she'll come back hopping. This state of the world can't keep on long at this [level of] tension." Joe's seemingly blasé comment that England could be conquered by the Nazis—and that he was "sure" his daughter could return to live in a totalitarian state under a fascist government intolerant of people with disabilities—reflects his increasing disconnect with the English people and with his own democratic government.

Rosemary's twelve-year-old sister Jean reported to her father at the end of May, from the family home in Bronxville, New York, that everyone was thrilled that "Rosie" was returning home. But Rosemary would find the adjustment to life back in the States after a year of living apart from her family difficult and destabilizing. She missed her British friends and the Assumption Sisters at Belmont House. Perhaps most important, she missed the humane and practical educational and vocational program that had effectively groomed her to be a primary-school teacher's aide. Arriving back in Bronxville—a home she had spent little time in since 1929, when the Kennedys had purchased it—Rosemary was now a twenty-two-year-old woman, one still needing a structured environment and close monitoring. Instead of the nuns, who had supplied expert, loving guidance under which Rosemary had felt secure and successful, she would be back under the watchful eye of her often demanding and impatient mother. She would no longer have a special teaching assistant assigned to guide her on a daily basis, take her for walks, and share life with her, as Dorothy Gibbs had done so devotedly at Belmont House. There, she did not have to compete for attention with eight siblings until someone had time for her.

A packed schedule of visiting old friends and extended family members occupied a good deal of Rosemary's time in the first two weeks. She attended the World's Fair in New York City, saw the dentist, and called on a podiatrist who fitted her with new arch supports to combat an ongoing problem with ill-fitting shoes. She chatted with everyone she met, including the "Saks man," about her adventures in Europe. She attended the wedding of her friend Frances O'Keefe—the sister of her friend Mary from Miss Newton's and the daughter of Rose's childhood friend Ruth Evans O'Keefe—in Boston, accompanied by Rose. Her participation in these events would have been well choreographed, just as it had been in England. In America, as in England, Rose and Joe agreed that no one outside the immediate family should know the true extent of her limitations. Rosemary's inability to engage in the well-known Kennedy banter—the quick intellectual and comedic jousting that characterized the family's verbal competitiveness—would be noted during this time, as it had been before, as shyness by most observers and even some close friends.

Although she had matured physically, Rosemary remained

as emotionally and intellectually immature as a barely adolescent girl. Her friends and acquaintances, by contrast, had grown into mature young men and women. Fitting back into their lives would be difficult at best.

A trip to the Kennedy home in Hyannis Port in early June began quietly. Eunice complained to her father that she feared that the Kennedys would be the only ones racing their boats that summer; no one else had shown up yet. Since Rosemary could not handle a boat well enough to race by herself, Eunice, and sometimes Bobby, took her along as crew. Her youngest sister, Jean, ten years her junior, would accompany her to the movies when the water was too cold to swim.

Jack's graduation from Harvard on June 20 marked the true beginning of the Hyannis Port summer for the Kennedys. Jack and his Harvard friends descended just as the area's summer residents began to arrive in droves, and family and friends, acquaintances, and others from near and far filled the Kennedy household. The structured life that had given Rosemary a sense of purpose and self-determination at Belmont House was now gone. Family life swirled around her. Even within the confines of the Kennedy compound, athletic games and competition dominated daily life, but those competitive activities were now played at an adult level and were beyond her capability. The heated dinner conversations about politics and current events, the war, and Roosevelt's policies could not have included Rosemary.

Her siblings' lives had become more complicated, full, and varied. Traveling to distant tennis tournaments in which she competed kept Eunice away for parts of the summer, leaving Rosemary the odd one out more often than not. The younger children could not be a substitute for true friendship or replace the bond she shared with Eunice. Jack was consumed with the success of his first book, *Why England Slept,* and was so busy with book-signing engagements, socializing, and planning for law school in the fall that he had no time to accompany Rosemary to parties or drive her to places in his own car. Joe Jr. was busy with politics, attending the Democratic National Convention in Chicago as a delegate from Massachusetts; and Kick was preoccupied with her own social life, volunteering for the Red Cross, and privately absorbed by any news about her friends and the war preparations in England as Germany bore ever closer to its shores.

Efforts were made to be as inclusive as possible with Rosemary. Luella Hennessey, the family's longtime private nurse, observed that the children were "especially kind" to her, and Jack and Joe Jr., in particular, made sure that there was "always a place for her in the family's activities." But she was forced to spend "a good deal of her time with her younger brothers and sisters, rather than with those who were closest to her age." Hennessey believed this was because Rosemary "found it easier to share their interests; their dependence on her gave her a feeling of security and usefulness." But this was not entirely satisfying for Rosemary, who wanted to mingle with her older siblings and people her own age.

Joe Jr. and Jack shared their social lives with Kick, not Rosemary. "From her childhood, Kick had been . . . our eldest daughter because of Rosemary's disability," Rose later acknowledged. Smart, engaging, competitive, and confident, Kick was much admired, not only by her many friends and the friends of her brothers who vied for her regard, but in the family, too. Much attention rained down on Kick, an "enchanting child, girl, and young woman," Rose would later remark. "Never was there a girl who had so many gifts lavished upon her . . . She was lovely to look at, full of *joie de vivre* and so tremendously popular." Returning from

England months earlier had allowed Kick, now twenty years old, the occasion to seize increasing personal independence and freedom. She could spend more time with her brothers going to parties and dating some of Jack's buddies.

Kick initially bore some of the responsibility for making sure Rosemary was not left out of social gatherings with people her own age. Kick's friendly and outgoing personality could deftly orchestrate an evening full of fun for Rosemary, and, with the help of Joe Jr. and Jack, Rosemary's dance card was filled. "Jack would . . . take her to a dance and he . . . with Lemoyne Billings [would] take turns dancing with her," Eunice recalled. "She'd come home at midnight and [Jack would] go back to the dance." But Rosemary noticed that she mostly danced with her brothers and a few of their close friends. "Why don't other boys ask me to dance?" she would ask. In spite of Kick's efforts, Rosemary may have felt like the proverbial stepsister. Miriam Finnegan, a close friend of Rose's, once remarked, "I think there's so much made of Kick . . . that Rosemary is a little conscious of that and feels a little bit in the background."

Kick and Eunice helped Rosemary dress and put on lipstick, a ritual any twenty-two-year-old woman should have been able to do on her own. This added to Rosemary's feelings of inadequacy. Her sisters had to secretly watch her all night to make sure she "didn't spill things on her clothes or try to put on fresh lipstick herself." One can imagine the anxiety the younger sisters felt, worrying that Rosemary might smear lipstick or create an embarrassing dilemma at a dance.

Kick, though used to accommodating Rosemary, probably began to chafe, too, at the relationship with her sister. One close friend of Jack's recalled that it "was embarrassing to be around Rosemary sometimes. She would behave in strange ways at the table, and I think they all were at great pains not to seem embarrassed . . . She would appear there standing in her nightgown when everyone else was moving ahead so rapidly. I don't think she really existed in the lives of Jack and Joe Jr., not any longer."

After Eunice became closer to Rosemary during their time in London, the responsibility of monitoring and supporting Rosemary now fell most heavily to her, three years younger and less socially mobile than Kick. But Rosemary may have resented this family transition; she was the oldest sister, and she knew it. Friends were few, and her daily companions were her youngest siblings. She was more of a babysitter than a young woman embarking on life in an adult world.

Rosemary also felt keenly the separation from her father, who remained in London as the American ambassador. During those months when Rosemary and Joe had been the only Kennedys remaining in England, Joe had made Rosemary feel special and feel that he needed her. No longer having his support nearby, and now lacking the close relationship to her mother she had experienced as a very young child, compounded Rosemary's feelings of anxiety and isolation. Her father had made clear in a letter to Rose from England that Rosemary was "much happier when she sees the children [her brothers and sisters] just casually. For everyone's peace of mind, particularly hers, she shouldn't go on vacation or anything else with them." But such a separation during the early summer of 1940 hadn't proved possible; Rosemary was home, and her integration into the family was necessary. Lem Billings, a close friend of Jack's from Choate who spent time with the Kennedy family that summer at Hyannis Port, remembered that Rosemary "seemed to realize that no matter how hard she tried she would never even come within sight of" her brothers' and sisters' accomplishments. Rosemary became "aggressively unhappy, irritable and frustrated at not being able to do the things her siblings could do." The pressure to perform was overwhelming; after all, the children understood that "only their best was good enough." Luella Hennessey remembered the "fiercely fought" Monopoly tournaments, "Twenty Questions and Geography, quizzes and word games" the Kennedys engaged in that kept their "wits sharp and razor edge." "In a large family . . . there is a great deal of competition," Rose told biographer Robert Coughlan. "[The children] learned to be winners, not losers, in sports . . . We would spur them on . . . [but] when they were defeated, the reasons for this were analyzed." On the one hand, such expectations and levels of achievement were impossible for Rosemary, and on the other, the restrictions placed on her were noticeably greater than those for her siblings. "In our family," Rose admitted, "if you're not doing anything you're left in the corner."

Luella Hennessey recalled that in advance of one Kennedy party that summer, Rose asked her to take Rosemary to Hennessey's sister's house in nearby North Falmouth for the day. Hennessey obliged, calling for the family chauffeur, Dave Deignan, to drive them the twenty miles to her sister's home on Buzzards Bay. Though Hennessey had been hired by the family several years before, when Rosemary was eighteen years old, the two of them had not developed the deep bond that Hennessey had with the younger children. In fact, Rosemary, who called her "Laura" because she found it too difficult to say the name Luella correctly, complained that Hennessey "bosses me so."

Once they arrived at the home of Hennessey's sister, Rosemary behaved like the aristocrat she had been raised to be, especially during her two years in England. Drinking tea with grace, tipping the cup smoothly, Rosemary conveyed sophistication, not, in the parlance of the day, feeble-mindedness. Hennessey's sister noticed how easily Rosemary then gathered the household's four children and took them to the beach, where they swam and frolicked for hours. When the children tired of that, Rosemary sat them down and announced it was "reading time." Carefully and slowly, she read them selections from *Winnie-the-Pooh,* both a children's favorite and also one of the few books she could read with confidence.

When Dave Deignan arrived to pick up Rosemary and Hennessey, Rosemary bid Hennessey's sister's family goodbye with poise, waving to them like "she was Mrs. Astor." Upon returning to Hyannis Port, Rosemary immediately sat down and, with great difficulty, wrote out a personal thank-you note to Hennessey's sister. When she returned to the house after mailing the card at the post office, Rosemary broke down, lashing out with anger, exhaustion, and frustration. Eunice rushed to soothe her, the only person, Hennessey remembered, who could calm Rosemary's rages. Lem Billings remembered that "somehow, Eunice seemed to develop very early a sense of special responsibility for Rosemary as if Rosemary were her child instead of her sister. There was an odd maturity about Eunice which was sometimes forbidding but which clearly set her off from all the rest."

The family began to notice that Rosemary's earlier gains from her time in England, both intellectual and emotional stability, were receding rapidly. She was increasingly tense, irritable, and irrational. Rosemary clearly could not manage within the freewheeling but highly demanding style of her family. But even Eunice understood that Rosemary was struggling more than in the past. "She started to deteriorate," Eunice later recalled. "She didn't make such a good adjustment at home."

Rose confirmed Lem Billings's impressions of Rosemary's state of mind that summer, recalling that she became agitated quickly and unexpectedly. "Some of these upsets became tantrums, or rages, during which she broke things or hit at people. Since she was quite strong, the blows were hard." In Billings's recollection, "Every day there would be one terrifying incident after another: physical fights where Rosemary would use her fists and hit and bruise people." She also experienced convulsions. These attacks may have been epileptic seizures or a type of psychogenic non-epileptic seizure, which usually develop in young women in their late teens and early twenties. Some sufferers also have additional problems, including learning disabilities. These nonepileptic seizures are often brought on by increasing psychological and emotional stress, with depression and anxiety a common contributing factor. Though there is no way to tell what type of seizures Rosemary suffered from, any kind would have been frightening, exhausting, and debilitating. Treatment at the time would have included some form of sedative, like Luminal, the addictive barbiturate in red-pill form that Rosemary may have already been taking for years, to calm her after the worst of a seizure was over. In those days, however, treatment for epilepsy and nonepileptic seizures was limited and mostly ineffectual.

Rosemary's striking beauty—lovely features, a broad, perfect smile, and a buxom figure—continued to attract men's attention. Rosemary had proudly told her father earlier that summer that even that "Saks man" told her "he things [*sic*] I am the best looking of the Kennedys." In a household both highly sexualized on the male side and notably repressed on the female side, Rosemary's beauty was a special threat.

Lem Billings suggested an additional diagnosis to journalist Burton Hersh: Rosemary was "sexually frustrated," a view surely more telling about Billings's own sexual outlook than Rosemary's, but his belief was rooted in common views about intellectually disabled and mentally ill women—attitudes shared and feared by Rosemary's parents. Twenty years after women had finally gained the right to vote, society's lingering nineteenth-century ideas played heavily on social, religious, and scientific attempts to control women's more public and expressive sexuality. This had devastating consequences for the country's most vulnerable and weakest women, mentally ill and disabled women who faced victimization through forced sterilization and institutionalization at alarming rates.

Interestingly, in spite of being effervescent, outgoing, and flirtatious, the slim-figured Kick was viewed as less sexually suggestive than Rosemary. Though open and frank about sex in conversation, Kick had no experience with intimate sexual contact, and her male friends knew that her religious background would preclude her from engaging in any sort of premarital sexual activity. In fact, Kick wished privately to her best friend, Charlotte McDonnell, as many of her friends were "pairing up" and getting married, that she could remain single forever and go to parties, instead, every night. Yet no male contemporary of Kick's ever described this party girl as "sexually frustrated," and it was Rosemary's potential and physically obvious sexuality that her parents found dangerous.

WITH SUMMER ACTIVITIES at Hyannis Port in full swing, Rose found a way to insulate herself from the frenetic pace and the constant racket of so many people, radios, and dogs. She had built a small getaway cottage for herself on the family compound where she now retreated to read quietly, write letters, and relax while the hired help managed the chaos in and around the main house.

Rose already had made another arrangement to assure that Rosemary's special needs—and her own need for tranquility—

were met for the balance of the summer. Rose had become used to not having Rosemary around every day, and she had agreed with Joe that Rosemary would have difficulty around her active, competitive siblings. In anticipation of Rosemary's return, Rose investigated several summer camps, looking for options that would satisfy Rosemary's need for structure, attention, and usefulness. At nearly twenty-two, Rosemary would be too old to be a camper, however. Through family acquaintances, Rose found what she believed to be a positive placement, Camp Fernwood, in western Massachusetts. She approached its owners and directors, Grace and Caroline Sullivan, to discuss Rosemary. The two women were the daughters of Michael Henry Sullivan, an attorney and former chairman of the Boston School Committee. In 1909, he had become the youngest judge ever appointed to the bench in Massachusetts. Located along the shores of Plunkett Lake, in Hinsdale, Camp Fernwood was a Catholic summer sleepaway camp for girls ages six to sixteen. Rosemary seemed excited about attending the camp and about what she might be doing there during the summer. She believed, and no doubt was told, that she would be a "junior counselor," teaching youngsters as she had done in England. "But isn't it interesting," she wrote her father in London on the Fourth of July after arriving at the camp, "but [*sic*] me being a junior counsellor the first year. They thought I had experienced [*sic*] in <u>Arts</u>, and <u>Crafts</u> in Europe. So, I am teaching it now. I have <u>the</u> younger girls. And another girl Alice Hill, has the bigger girl in <u>Arts</u>, and <u>Crafts</u>. So, the two of us run it."

Rose should have given the Sullivan sisters some indication that Rosemary, an adult woman, was intellectually disabled, but it seems she did not share much with them—certainly not that the staff would need to monitor Rosemary every day to be sure she rested, ate properly, completed her tasks, and remained composed with the children; or that they would be called to calm her rages, to constantly reassure and compliment her, and to monitor her every move.

Whereas Kennedy family lore long perpetuated the myth that Rosemary was hired to be a counselor at the camp, Sullivan family records reveal a different story. In the spring of 1940, while Rosemary was still living in England and the Sullivan sisters met Rose in New York to discuss Rosemary's placement, they were completely unaware of the extent of her disabilities. All they knew was that Rose was hoping her twenty-two-year-old daughter—who had received Montessori training in England to become a teacher's assistant—could find a spot for the summer at the camp. She would require, Rose told them, a special counselor to accompany her at all times. Rose did not explain fully why this was so necessary. Terry Marotta, Caroline Sullivan's daughter, wrote that her mother later recalled that "she should have known the minute Mrs. Kennedy arrived [in New York] without her daughter that the girl was not as 'able' as Rose was leading them to believe." To Rose's relief, the Sullivans accepted Rosemary into the camp program—not officially as a paid junior counselor, but rather as a camper who needed guidance herself.

In a July 1 letter from Rose's secretary and the younger children's governess, Elizabeth Dunn, to the Sullivan sisters, Dunn conveyed Rose's requirement that the camp staff be "sure her [Rosemary's] arch supporters are in her shoes correctly" and that Rosemary sit at the "diet table if you can encourage her to." Additionally, Rosemary should "use Arts and Crafts Shop as much as possible. Have tennis lessons as often as practical," and "do exercises for her arches." These "very important" instructions were the ones Rose chose to convey—not suggestions on how to handle an adult woman prone to anger, or likely to be "fierce" with the children, or anxious about changes in her daily routine and environment. Clearly, in spite of her instructions concerning Rosemary, Rose gave little thought to the campers or to the abilities of Fernwood's staff to cope with Rosemary.

There were problems from the start. One family friend later recalled that the Fernwood staff did not realize that Rosemary's shoes were ill fitting until they noticed her feet bleeding. Frustrated, the Sullivan sisters took Rosemary to their own podiatrist in nearby Pittsfield, Massachusetts, to help relieve her intense discomfort. Rosemary may have consciously followed her mother's instructions about putting on a positive public face and not complaining, but in this case she was clearly carrying the mandate to the extreme. The sisters were shocked when they discovered that Rosemary did not properly dispose of her stained sanitary napkins but rather stored them in her camp trunk. They were deeply worried by Rosemary's habit of wandering off. Caroline Sullivan, whom Rosemary called "Cow" because she could not pronounce Caroline's nickname, "Cal," eventually had Rosemary sleep in her private quarters, with a bed placed up against the door to prevent her from wandering off in the middle of the night.

After three weeks, the Sullivans had had enough, and they requested that Rose come and take Rosemary home. Rose told them she could not come to the camp and that it was up to them to get Rosemary to New York, where Eddie Moore and Elizabeth Dunn would meet them on July 22. Before the Sullivans' decision to send Rosemary home, Rose had inquired about visiting her on July 27, on a trip that would coincide with the annual summer concerts held in the Berkshires, allowing Rose to enjoy some cultural entertainment while there. Now, however, it was important that she remain at the Maine Chance Beauty Spa, established by cosmetic pioneer Elizabeth Arden at her expansive estate on

Long Pond, in Belgrade, Maine. The news that Rosemary was once again going to be under her care, without Joe there to handle their daughter, as he had been doing to a greater degree while she was in school in England, sent Rose fleeing the turmoil.

On a "hot as hops" July day, Caroline Sullivan accompanied Rosemary to New York, requiring her to be away from the camp and her responsibilities there for two days. Posting a note from the Barbizon-Plaza Hotel, on Central Park South, after leaving Rosemary with Eddie Moore, Caroline wrote to her sister, Grace, that she "left the final ordeal at 7:10 [p.m.] with no mishaps."

Incredibly, it would be nine months before Rose would pay the bill for Rosemary's time at Camp Fernwood. After finally receiving a check from Rose, in mid-April 1941, which lacked her signature, the Sullivan sisters were stunned to read in the check's accompanying letter that Rose was challenging them regarding the amount of the invoice. "I see there is a $200 charge for tuition, and I suppose it is a fair charge, although Rosemary was only there three weeks. I did not discuss all the financial arrangements with you at all, of course, and I shall pay whatever is customary. I am merely bringing it to your attention in case you had not considered all the circumstances." The sisters returned the unsigned check for its required signature and expressed their frustration with the way they were being treated, outlining the "circumstances" that they had indeed "considered":

> Our charge is based on a half season, that is, 4 weeks. Since we don't accept anyone for a shorter period it is customary to receive tuition for the full period . . . We have charged you double the regular tuition of $100 per half season. This seems only fair since you requested that a counselor be particularly assigned to Rosemary and constantly be in charge

of her at all times. This was carried out and, as it so happened, she was so difficult of adjustment in our group of normal young children that, for the well-being of everyone I found it necessary to give my own attention to her, in addition to the special counselor assigned to her, in spite of my many other duties and heavy responsibilities. The situation turned out to be so impossible that after giving it every effort and a thoroughly fair trial, it seemed necessary to request from you the end of her stay at camp. There was such a very definite nervous effect upon the counselors that I did not feel it fair or safe to let any one of them accompany Rosemary to New York, and so it was my duty to do so although ordinarily my sister and I never leave the camp during the season.

The Sullivans assured Rose that Rosemary was "lovable and well meaning." Her effect on the staff and campers was so adverse, however, that they felt they "should not have kept her at camp as long as we did." Years later, Caroline Sullivan still bore lingering anger and disbelief over the way Rose had treated her, in addition to shock over Rose's disregard for the health and safety of her disabled daughter.

Eddie Moore barely had time to make arrangements for Rosemary; he had received a telegram from Joe in London on June 21 that Rosemary was leaving the camp immediately and that Elizabeth Dunn was heading to New York from Hyannis Port to help him take care of her. The two of them were expected to meet Rosemary and Caroline Sullivan on the evening of the twenty-second in New York. Fortunately, Moore had started investigating Rosemary's placement for the fall as soon as they had returned from London. He had made inquiries of the sisters at Belmont

House about American Catholic schools with Montessori programs similar to theirs. Moore visited Ravenhill Academy of the Assumption near Philadelphia, where he found a "better layout" than at the Convent of the Sacred Heart at Noroton, where Kathleen and Eunice had gone. The head of the convent school was the Reverend Mother Ann Elizabeth, who was intimately familiar with the Assumption school in England "and all the Nuns there," Moore reported. One of Ravenhill's nuns was an Englishwoman whose sister was an Assumption nun at Belmont House. Both she and Reverend Mother Ann Elizabeth had heard about Rosemary and were open to having her enroll at the school. The campus was set in the beautiful Germantown neighborhood of Philadelphia, and, Moore reported, "the Nuns are lovely." The Montessori program "will interest Rosemary because she can continue her studies," he assured Rose. Moore wrote to Joe in London and asked whether Mother Isabel could be encouraged to write a letter to the Assumption nuns in Philadelphia, as a sort of introduction and assurance of Rosemary's capabilities and potential. Though Moore had met the Reverend Mother in June with the idea that Rosemary would enroll in the fall, her failure at the camp forced a quick adjustment to those plans. He quickly secured arrangements to take Rosemary to Ravenhill, where the nuns could take charge of her immediately.

Rose remained secluded in Maine until August 5, more than a week beyond her scheduled departure, while Rosemary suffered emotionally from the sudden removal from Fernwood and the transition to a new school. Rosemary had been proud to be working as a "counselor" at the camp, where her self-esteem was buoyed by the perception of responsibility. She had left Fernwood and been whisked off to Ravenhill so quickly that she barely had time to pack; two duffel bags of clothes, books, pillows, and a tennis racket were left behind. On July 25, Rosemary sent two postcards and a four-page letter to the Sullivan sisters and the campers, expressing her deep sadness over and disappointment with her abrupt departure from the camp. "I tried to get up to see you [all], before I went, but Mr. Moore said there wasn't time," she wrote. Compounding her distress, Rosemary feared her father was displeased by her departure from camp; she so desperately wanted him to approve of her. "I am going to work so hard for my Daddy," she told her camp friends, "and he deserves it." "I knew nothing about" the plan to leave the camp, she wrote, "until my father wired from Abroad . . . It's not my fault, darlings . . . I have been crying over it. I know you all loved me so." Rosemary desperately wanted the campers and staff to write her and possibly arrange to see her in New York or Philadelphia during the upcoming school year. In his telegram, Joe had told her she was going to resume her Montessori training. "I am going to be a bit tired from all the studying, this summer and the fall," she told her friends. *Pray for me. God Bless You.* She poured out her feelings of love and gratitude to all the staff and begged the Sullivan sisters, "Write to me soon. I am lonesome for you."

Ravenhill Academy had been established in 1919 in a large Victorian mansion donated to the Archdiocese of Philadelphia. Providing education for girls in first grade through high school, the school attracted the daughters of some of the most elite business, political, and social leaders of the day. Grace Kelly, the famous actress who later became one of Hollywood's most illustrious stars before marrying the prince of Monaco, was a ten-year-old student there when Rosemary started classes that fall. The nuns spent their summers at Ravenhill Cottage, a Catholic retreat in Wildwood, not far from Atlantic City and Cape May, New Jersey. Since some of the boarding students at Ravenhill could not travel home for the summer break, they moved to Wildwood with the sisters. Rosemary spent the last part of the summer at this retreat, where she joined other students spending their days swimming, walking, and studying.

Classes at Ravenhill Academy in Philadelphia started on September 17, and the nuns had agreed to enroll Rosemary in the fall if she had a companion or tutor, like Dorothy Gibbs at Belmont House, accompany her. As she had done in the past, Rose sent inquiries to potential candidates for private tutor for Rosemary, and was still corresponding with some of them in late August. It is unclear whether a tutor was actually hired; within two months, at any rate, Rosemary was transferred out of the school. Ravenhill did not have a Montessori program similar to the one at Belmont House, nor a Mother Isabel. Still, the circumstances surrounding the failure of the sisters at Ravenhill to satisfactorily replicate the environment that had worked so well for Rosemary at Belmont House can only be imagined.

Rose anticipated the failure. By mid-September, when Rosemary was meant to be transitioning into classes at Ravenhill, Rose was making inquiries about committing her to a psychiatric hospital. Roseneath Farms Sanitarium was a private, fifty-bed psychiatric facility established in the 1920s on property abutting Ravenhill, a fact suggesting that staff at the Assumption school might have been involved in the recommendation to place Rosemary there. James J. Waygood, a highly respected psychiatrist, had been director of the hospital for nearly ten years. Rose clearly required letters of reference. The Reverend Thomas J. Love, a Jesuit priest and president of Saint Joseph's College in Philadelphia, told Rose at Dr. Waygood's request that "during the past ten or twelve years we have had some of our men there . . . The physical facilities afforded, combined with the excellence of the medical staff, leave little to be desired. I feel quite sure that should you place your daughter there, you will be eminently satisfied." Edward Day, a lawyer from Hartford, Connecticut, assured Rose in a reference letter written on September 20 that "Dr. Waygood has had an abundance of experience and is very understanding and wise in his treatment." Day had spent a year at Roseneath recovering from "a very severe illness . . . and as a result of it, I recovered my health completely and am as well if not better than I ever was." Rosemary would "have to be prepared for a period of adjustment," Day wrote cautiously, but she would find "genuine kindness and real understanding" from the staff. "If your daughter cooperates with Dr. Waygood and exercises patience . . . she will get well."

Whatever transpired in those few months with the Ravenhill nuns, the decision to send Rosemary to a psychiatric hospital indicates a possible serious decline in her state of mind. Eunice recalled that Rosemary "had begun to get sort of emotional . . . She was high strung and had quite a lot of temper tantrums all the time." It seems the hospital was ready to admit her; Rose and Joe may have been the ones to change their minds—she did not in fact go to Roseneath Farms.

By the third week in October, Rosemary was instead enrolled at Saint Gertrude's School of Arts and Crafts, an innovative Benedictine convent school in Washington, D.C. Other historians have assumed that Rosemary was engaged as a teacher's aide at the school, but in fact Rose and Joe paid tuition for Rosemary to take classes there, just as they had paid tuition for her to attend Camp Fernwood as a "junior counselor." Rose noted in her diary on October 29 that she and Joe, who had just been recalled from London by Roosevelt, "went to see the President in Washington." Roosevelt and many of his staff had become increasingly frustrated by Kennedy's isolationism in the face of heightened Nazi aggression, and the president had decided to force Kennedy's resignation. After having dinner with Roosevelt and spending the night at the White House, Joe went on to New York while Rose remained in Washington to visit Rosemary at Saint Gertrude's.

Founded in 1926 by Paulist priest–turned–Benedictine monk Thomas Verner Moore, Saint Gertrude's School of Arts and Crafts was the fulfillment of a long-held dream on Moore's part to provide services and educational opportunities to intellectually and developmentally delayed and handicapped children. Saint Gertrude's was also a training ground where nuns and young Catholic laywomen could acquire clinical skills while training as nurses and social workers at the Catholic University of America, in Washington, D.C., and its sister institution for women, Trinity College.

Saint Gertrude's enrolled girls ages seven to twelve who scored between 65 and 90 on IQ tests. Moore wrote that he hoped to "enable the retarded child to become a happy and useful member of society by placing him [sic] in an environment where the soothing and uplifting influence of religion will be constantly affecting him; where guided by this influence, he may develop right habits; where he can adjust himself as easily and happily as possible to the situations that arise; and where he can learn, if necessary, to become self-supporting through the achievement of work that is both interesting to himself and useful to others."

The school offered small classes, with low student-teacher ratios, in the typical academic subjects, augmented by arts-and-crafts lessons, music, dance, theater, and homemaking skills. Moore, a "priest-psychiatrist" who had a PhD in psychology from the Catholic University and was a highly respected professor there, believed that focusing on the "mentally disadvantaged" through the delivery of new techniques in psychiatric and psychological therapies combined with deep spiritual guidance offered a more holistic treatment for patients suffering from mental illness and disabilities. However small and incremental progress might be, Moore argued, the new therapies were worthwhile and should be part of Catholic social justice and pastoral care. Moore stood at the center of a group of colleagues who hoped to "integrate a progressive world view with traditional faith" in service of humankind.

Moore considered girls to be the most at-risk population, based partially on the widely held view that mentally ill and intellectually disabled girls were more likely, left to their own devices, to drift into prostitution. By establishing Saint Gertrude's for girls, Moore believed he was providing care and service to the most vulnerable in society.

When Moore first began developing his vision, in 1917, the Catholic Church offered little help to families with children suffering from a range of intellectual and physical disabilities. Over the next decade, Moore cultivated a "clear vision of what the Catholic Church needed to do for its mentally disabled members," and was determined to make the Catholic University a pioneer in achieving that goal. He knew that at the intersection of science and faith stood the promise of new clinical and social-service methods that could provide effective treatment and support for the mentally ill and disabled and their exhausted families. The close proximity of Saint Gertrude's to the Catholic University and Trinity College perfectly suited Moore's vision for an incubator that would test innovations in special education and would serve as a training ground for Catholic nuns and laypersons, who would then take their education and work to Catholic schools and institutions around the country.

But the church hierarchy was cool to the idea. The archbishop of Baltimore, under whose leadership Moore and the Catholic University operated, was direct in his disapproval: "Get all the assistance you can for the work that you are doing at St. Gertrude's, but for the present be good enough to drop all proposals for linking the University and Sisters' College [Trinity] with the work." In spite of this resistance, Moore continued his work. He attracted student teachers willing to volunteer at Saint Gertrude's, and colleagues and nursing students from the university and Trinity encouraged him to establish a clinical care center through which additional health services could be provided for mentally ill and disabled children. A sizable grant from the Rockefeller Foundation in 1939 and support from wealthy Catholic donors helped firmly establish the Child Center at the university. The center became an effective training site for Catholic professionals conducting pioneering research, and for "the treatment of emotional and behavior disorders." Moore launched a working relationship with nearby Saint Elizabeths Hospital, and some of that institution's psychiatrists were tapped to teach the Catholic University's newly expanded course offerings in psychiatry. By 1940, when Rosemary enrolled at Saint Gertrude's, the school's integration with the Child Center was firmly established. For Rose and Joe, the school may have seemed ideally suited to Rosemary's and their needs: a lauded therapeutic setting that could allow Rosemary to function as a teacher's aide, both for her own self-esteem and for the sake of public appearances.

Rose later recalled that during this time, however, "disquieting symptoms began to develop." There was a "noticeable regression" in Rosemary's mental and physical stability, and her "customary good nature gave way increasingly to tension and irritability." Her outbursts of rage came on more frequently and unpredictably. Rose's niece Ann Gargan—the daughter of Rose's sister Agnes—later revealed that Rosemary had become incorrigible at Saint Gertrude's. She defied the nuns, the staff, and their rules. "Many nights," Gargan told historian Doris Kearns Goodwin, "the school would call to say she was missing, only to find her out walking around the streets at 2 a.m." The nuns would bring her back, clean her up, and put her to bed. Her explanations about where she had been or what she had been doing made no sense, or else they made frightening sense. "Can you imagine what it must have been like," Gargan recalled, "to know your daughter was walking the streets in the darkness of the night, the perfect prey for an unsuspecting male?" Joe Sr. expected his children to keep "out of the [newspaper] columns," granddaughter Amanda Smith recalled. His fears that Rosemary would end up as fodder for gossip columnists profoundly informed his and Rose's efforts to keep her sequestered. What happened to Rosemary during that time has remained a mysterious and complicated story, with a thin trail of evidence and mostly conjectured interpretation. Even family members remain mostly in the dark about what truly happened to Rosemary during her time at Saint Gertrude's.

Rosemary remained at Saint Gertrude's through 1941. Joe, no longer ambassador but living in Palm Beach playing golf and keeping up with news of the war in Europe, had looked into having Rosemary attend Wyonegonic Camp in Denmark, Maine, during the summer of 1941, but there is no record of Rosemary having attended. That July, Joe sought the advice of Monsignor Casey at Saint Patrick's Cathedral in New York City about finding a new convent for Rosemary, but as the family had come to understand all too well, Casey could offer nothing suitable for a twenty-two-year-old intellectually disabled and emotionally troubled young woman. Rosemary was reenrolled at Saint Gertrude's, though Dr. Moore, worried about "her welfare and the effect of her behavior on others" at the school, seems to have been reluctant to have her back. In October, Joe tried to persuade Rosemary to consider a new placement somewhere in Philadelphia. It seems likely the Kennedys were reconsidering Roseneath Farms, since both the Assumption and Sacred Heart schools in Philadelphia had already done what they could for her. "How is my old darling today?" he wrote Rosemary from Hyannis Port on the tenth. "Eddie and Mary are coming down and they were thinking perhaps that they might take you for a trip up to Philadelphia to look the situation over up there." Fully aware that Rosemary might be resistant to the idea of making another transition, he offered what seems like a bit of a bribe. "Do you think Dr. Moore and the Nuns would like to have a picture show sometime this fall and also do you think the children would like it? If they would, what kind of picture do you think they'd like?"

By the second week in November 1941, Dr. Moore was again expressing concerns about Rosemary's behavior and her influence and effect on the other children at the school. A young woman, Miss Slavin, was hired to work with Rosemary and be a companion. "I trust that she will be able to help a great deal," Dr. Moore assured Kennedy before boldly soliciting a $25,000 donation from him. But the new companion made little difference, and Joe did not send a contribution to the school.

Joe had planned on taking Rosemary, Jack, and Kick to a Notre Dame–Navy football game in Baltimore on November

8, but it's unclear whether Rosemary joined the others. As Rose noted in her memoir, *Times to Remember,* she and Joe were coming to the conclusion that Rosemary was suffering from something other than intellectual impairment; "a neurological disturbance," Rose would call it, that "had overtaken her, and it was becoming progressively worse."

7

November 1941

JOE SR., if not other members of the family, felt Rosemary's behavior had now become a menacing disgrace to the Kennedys' political, financial, and social aspirations. Her late-night escapes from Saint Gertrude's left her vulnerable to sexual exploitation and unsavory liaisons with unknown men. Joe, who had been mostly out of the political limelight since his return from London and his resignation as ambassador a year earlier, was focusing his energy on his businesses and investments and traveling frequently to New York and Washington, D.C. He was also beginning to chart his eldest sons' political futures, and he could not risk the publicity from an unwanted pregnancy, venereal disease, or some other compromising situation. Family nurse Luella Hennessey believed that Joe "was so afraid of [Rosemary's] getting into trouble or of [her] being kidnapped. It would be better for her not to be exposed to the general public in case she ran away." But keeping her out of the public eye was proving impossible. "It would be better to almost 'close the case,'" Hennessey recalled Joe Sr.'s attitude at the time. "Then there wouldn't be any

more trouble." The latest reports from Saint Gertrude's only further fanned Joe's increasing anxiety over the family's reputation
and his deeply felt concerns about the mental and physical well-
being of his daughter.

It has been suggested that Joe Sr. spoke with doctors about
a very experimental brain operation for the treatment of serious
mental-health conditions, leucotomy—popularly known as prefrontal lobotomy—while he was still in England. But in fact the
procedure was not performed there until after he had left his ambassadorship, so it is unlikely he met with anyone there who had
expertise. It is more likely that it was through his many connections in Washington—possibly Thomas Moore at Saint Gertrude's—that he learned about the pioneering psychosurgery then
being performed at George Washington University Hospital by
Dr. Walter Freeman and his associate Dr. James Watts, then the
leading researchers in the field in the United States. Freeman and
Watts were on the faculty of the George Washington University
Medical School and were well known to the psychiatric and neurosurgical community in Washington. Moore had been collaborating on innovative approaches to the treatment of mentally ill
children with psychiatrists from Saint Elizabeths Hospital, the
city's federal psychiatric facility and one of the leading mental-
health institutions in the country. Both Freeman and Watts conducted research and observed patients at Saint Elizabeths, so a
connection through Moore seems highly probable.

Joe approached Rose about the option as a potential "cure" for
Rosemary's disabilities and increasingly moody and unpredictable behavior. Rose and Joe may have read an article on lobotomies in the *Saturday Evening Post* in May 1941. Highlighting the
work of Freeman and Watts, among others, the article mostly
praised the potential of the surgery to make mentally ill patients

who were "problems to their families and nuisances to themselves . . . into useful members of society." But the article also noted that some specialists in neurological disorders responded with "outright denunciation" of the technique. In the twenty years that she had been seeking answers to Rosemary's troubles from physicians, psychiatrists, teachers, and specialists of all sorts, Rose had encountered numerous suggestions and recommendations, including permanent institutionalization, medications, and other physical and psychological interventions, but none had done what she had hoped — to make Rosemary able to function in society appropriately and independently. The process had made Rose weary, and extremely wary.

Rose, nevertheless, enlisted Kick's help to investigate the psychosurgical option. By the spring of 1941, Kick had completed her studies in New York and moved to Washington, D.C., where she started working as a society columnist at the *Washington Times-Herald* for editor Frank Waldrop. There Kick met a reporter named John White. White later recalled to historian Laurence Leamer Kick's intense interest in a series of stories he was researching during that summer and fall on mental illness and treatment at Saint Elizabeths Hospital.

Kick confided in White about her older sister's intellectual impairments and more troubling mental-health issues. She asked him about the experimental brain surgery. The lobotomy procedure had been in practice in the United States for less than three years, and fewer than one hundred patients had undergone the surgery. Nearly all of them had been treated by Drs. Freeman and Watts at nearby George Washington University Hospital. White may have told Kick that Saint Elizabeths did not allow the experimental surgery in its own facility, in spite of its supporting Freeman and Watts with their research. The surgery involved cutting the white fibrous connective tissue linking the frontal lobes to the rest of the brain, relieving the violent rages and psychological and physical pain some severely mentally ill patients suffered. White told Kick that the results were "just not good"; he had seen for himself that after the surgery patients "don't worry so much, but they're gone as a person, just gone."

Kick quickly reported her findings to her mother. "Oh, Mother, no, it's nothing we want done for Rosie," Kick apparently told her. "I'm glad to hear that," niece Kerry McCarthy recalled Rose replying.

If Rose told Joe her misgivings about the surgery, he did not listen. She later told Doris Kearns Goodwin that "Joe took matters into his own hands." In keeping with his instinct to seek out the opinions and ideas of the most prominent specialist in whatever field of expertise he needed, he moved ahead and met with Dr. Freeman during the fall to discuss the doctor's latest surgical results. It is not known whether Joe explored any other of the several therapy options available in 1941 for treatment of Rosemary's perceived psychological problems, at a time when electric shock, insulin-induced coma, and other treatments were embraced as new miracle therapies by a small but growing group of psychiatrists and neurosurgeons. Luella Hennessey recalled years later that Joe had always asked her opinion about the children's health issues, but this time he did not. "I think he knew what I would have said," she explained.

Local and national media coverage of lobotomy research was quite limited at this time, in spite of the feverish advocacy with which Freeman presented his research to colleagues. Notwithstanding the mostly positive report in the *Saturday Evening Post* that spring, in August 1941, the *Journal of the American Medical Association* warned against the use of lobotomy until further research could be done. Freeman had participated in a panel at the annual American Medical Association meeting, in Cleveland, earlier that year on the efficacy of the prefrontal lobotomy. In response to Freeman's presentation, the editorial board of the *Journal* argued that "in spite of these improvements in the mental condition of some patients this operation should not be considered [as] there is ample evidence of the serious defects produced." The *Richmond Dispatch*—one of the first newspapers to report on the AMA's warning—informed its readers in August 1941 that "scientific knowledge is admittedly meager regarding the exact function of the . . . frontal lobes," and that the operation "should be considered as in an experimental stage."

Though the prefrontal lobotomy was not recommended for curing or treating intellectual and developmental disabilities, Freeman assured Joe of the efficacy of his experimental brain operation. "The doctors told my father it was a good idea," Eunice later told biographer Robert Coughlan. It would, Freeman's associate Watts argued, calm Rosemary's "agitated depression." She would become docile, less moody.

It is instructive that at the time Drs. Freeman and Watts were teaching and performing their experimental psychosurgery at George Washington University Hospital, when nearby Saint Elizabeths Hospital, long a pioneer in the treatment of the mentally ill, refused the two men's requests to perform lobotomies there. Saint Elizabeths was founded in 1855 by the federal government. Named the Government Hospital for the Insane, it became known as Saint Elizabeths during the Civil War, when the facility was called into emergency service to treat wounded soldiers who flooded hospitals in Washington by the thousands. After the war, and throughout the nineteenth and early twentieth centuries, Saint Elizabeths treated Civil War veterans and others suffering from psychological and neurological trauma, becoming the largest and most prominent public institution of its kind. The hospital treated about seven thousand patients, and its research, psychiatric training, and chronic-care facilities had become models for clinical programs and institutions around the world. But the superintendent, Dr. William A. White, refused to allow Freeman and Watts to experiment on mentally ill patients at Saint Elizabeths. He believed that patients could not make an informed decision about the risky surgery, nor could their often-desperate families make the decision for them. Freeman and Watts's research was limited to performing autopsies on deceased patients and observing mentally ill patients in the hospital's wards.

Psychosurgery remained, at the time, a small field and was relegated to a few institutions in the United States. By the time Joe was meeting with Freeman, Massachusetts General and McLean hospitals, both in Massachusetts, and a few state psychiatric hospitals around the country, including those in Delaware, Pennsylvania, Minnesota, New York, Missouri, New Jersey, and Connecticut, were experimenting with a few patients. Only a handful of neurosurgeons in Europe and Asia were beginning to perform the surgery. Dr. Freeman, moreover, was a psychiatrist, not a surgeon. He believed that surgical intervention into the brain to treat psychological disorders did not require the extensive surgical training that neurosurgeons spent years acquiring. Though neurosurgeons disagreed with Freeman, no certification process for the procedure had been established, and neurosurgeons were, at the time, powerless to stop him even if they had wanted to. Freeman's partner, Watts, a trained surgeon, performed most of the surgeries under Freeman's direction, though by the mid-1940s, Freeman was performing lobotomies himself.

In the days before sophisticated scientific understanding of

mental development and the inner workings of the brain, Freeman and a handful of colleagues around the world were convinced
that lobotomies were the much-longed-for cure for deep depression, mental illness, and violent, erratic, and hyperactive behavior.
But the procedure was never meant to be used on intellectually
disabled individuals. The physiological and psychological side effects of the surgery varied widely, but for the most part patients
suffered tremendously. The positive outcomes and effectiveness of
these therapies in treating a broad range of mental illnesses and
intellectual disabilities were small, though claims by practitioners painted a far rosier picture than the collective results indi-
cated. Doctors like Walter Freeman and his colleagues publicized
the few success stories and downplayed the failures — failures that
ranged from tragic loss of cognition to fatalities — which occurred
with frightening frequency. Professionals claimed these failures
were the patients' fault, a function of the deep flaws rooted in
their compromised physical condition and damaged psychology.
Nevertheless, in the summer of 1941, when the AMA warned
against the use of lobotomy and called for more studies, Freeman
and Watts were scheduling more lobotomies. "It is inconceivable," the editors of the *Journal of the American Medical Association*
wrote, "that any procedure which effectively destroys the function
of this portion of the brain could possibly restore the person concerned to a wholly normal state." Given Joe's reputation for as-
siduously gathering information to make informed decisions, he
must have been aware of the risks involved, even if Freeman and
Watts did not disclose the full details of the side effects and negative outcomes of the surgery.

Informed consent for such a potentially fatal and certainly debilitating operation had not yet been considered by the American
medical or legal system. Under the laws of the day, a woman like

Rosemary could be forcibly hospitalized and treated without her consent. The legal requirement giving patients power and control over their own medical decisions would be decades more in the making. Women were most frequently institutionalized by the order of husbands and fathers, whose will and opinion superseded the women's. A doctor's legal and medical responsibility to fully inform a patient of the potential risks of treatment did not become a requirement until the 1960s and was still contested ground well into the 1970s and 1980s.

Freeman and Watts were using their patients as case studies; there were no protocols, safeguards, or protections, nor were standards required or instituted by or upon the physicians as they experimented on their patients. The first lobotomy had been performed in Europe in 1935 by a Portuguese neurologist, Egas Moniz. Greatly criticized, Moniz was nevertheless convinced of the efficacy of slicing and disconnecting the frontal lobes from the rest of the brain. His first patients suffered from paranoid schizophrenia and depression; the patients seemingly improved after the surgery, giving Moniz the sort of proof he wanted to continue his studies. In truth, the patients' relief was only temporary. In time, the side effects of the surgery would become more troubling and more disabling to the patient than the initial illness. Ironically and tragically, by 1949, when Moniz received the Nobel Prize in medicine, thousands of patients around the world had received the questionable treatment. Many were permanently disabled; some were dead.

Shared views among a relatively few psychiatrists across the country fed a system that lacked or disregarded formal protocols, systematic analysis of medical procedures, and standards to define acceptable and unacceptable risks. There was no consensus as to which underlying disease or illness would benefit the most from lobotomy. With few options, some psychiatrists and neurosurgeons looked to the lobotomy as a possible miracle cure for mentally ill, depressed, and disabled patients. One patient subgroup included habitual criminals and juvenile offenders, but most were individuals whose behavior simply defied conventional norms and conservative boundaries. Lobotomies and other psychosurgical procedures were performed on patients who suffered from not only crippling depression but also undefined violent behavior, schizophrenia, obsessive-compulsive disorder, chronic pain, and bipolar and other mood disorders. The procedure was also used to treat perceived defective personality traits that included homosexuality, nymphomania, criminal behavior, and marijuana and drug addiction. Freeman would later describe potential patients as society's "misfits." Women, in particular, made up the largest group of lobotomy patients. Women who were depressed, had bipolar illness, or were sexually active outside the range of socially and culturally acceptable limits of the day—including single women exhibiting typical sexual desire—were considered candidates.

At McLean Hospital in Belmont, Massachusetts, one of the premier psychiatric hospitals in the nation, women represented eighty-two percent of the total number of lobotomy patients from 1938 to 1954. In hospitals across the country, women constituted between sixty and eighty percent of all lobotomy recipients, in spite of the fact that men comprised the majority of institutionalized patients.

Without informing Rose or the other children, Joe ordered the procedure to be done on Rosemary as quickly as possible. Joined by Freeman's unbridled and unethical eagerness to perform the surgery, Joe's desperate need to control Rosemary drove him to make the decision on his own.

Sometime between November 10, 1941, when Thomas Moore at Saint Gertrude's wrote to Joe about continuing problems with Rosemary, and November 28, when Joe said in a letter to a friend that he was heading to Washington to "visit with my two young-sters who are there"—he actually had three children living in the city, Jack, Kick, and Rosemary—twenty-three-year-old Rose-mary was admitted to George Washington University Hospital. Rosemary would be one of twenty-eight patients Freeman and Watts would operate on during the last nine months of 1941, and one of fewer than eighty patients they had treated surgically up to that time.

Did Joe tell his daughter she was going to have a surgery? Did she ask him questions about it, and did he answer them truth-fully? Did he convince her that it was her decision but that he wanted her to do it? Joe knew Rosemary loved her "Daddy" and would not want to disappoint him. Did he tell her that her be-havior had disappointed him, and that her mother and sisters and brothers were concerned and frightened by her? What did she think? We can only imagine.

Soon after Rosemary arrived at the hospital—whether it was Joe, or Eddie and Mary Moore, or a Saint Gertrude's staff mem-ber who accompanied her has not been recorded—the doctors and nurses would have explained to her that she would need to have her hair shaved off. Rosemary, who loved to be told how pretty she was, who loved to look attractive, would have her head shaved. Did she say no, as one of Freeman's other patients did when she heard she would lose her beautiful hair? Patient Case 10, Freeman would later write, gave "exaggerated attention" to her curls, preventing her from submitting to the surgery. Only after repeated assurances that Dr. Watts would make "every ef-fort . . . to spare these curls" did the patient acquiesce. Freeman thought such concerns were frivolous, because the surgery would erase patients' "undue" attention to physical appearance and they would afterward "go about or talk with others quite oblivious to the fact" that their heads were shaved.

Rosemary would have been strapped to a table and given local anesthesia to numb the area of the skull near the temples where Watts would bore two holes. Sedation, according to Freeman and Watts, was used only when a patient was highly agitated and in a "panicky state," a reaction that would have only increased as the procedure continued. Lobotomies had to be performed with the patient wide awake, allowing the physician to monitor the effects of each surgical cut to the brain. Freeman and Watts noted that most patients were anxious and fearful about the surgery. Patients, they wrote, underwent "unnamed tortures when having their hands and feet strapped to the operating table, their heads shaved to the vertex [top of the skull], and the outside world masked from view by the towels and drapes." Next came the "rattling of the instruments, the noise of the suction apparatus, and the menacing spark of the electro-cautery." Some patients told them they wanted to die right then and there. Others called for help. These terrifying moments were useful, the doctors assured their colleagues, as the patients' distress was often so great that the "additional trouble caused by the operation passes almost unnoticed."

Watts followed Freeman's instructions, drilling holes on both sides of Rosemary's head, near the temples. She would have heard the whir of the surgical tool drilling the "burr holes" into her skull. "Apprehension becomes a little more marked when the holes are drilled," the two men wrote of patients, "probably because of the actual pressure on the skull and the grinding sound that is as distressing, or more so, than the drilling of a tooth." No doubt she felt the pain from the "leucotome," the small, modified surgical instrument Watts and Freeman developed specifically for lobotomies, "produced by contact with the Dura," the outermost membrane covering the brain. Watts later recalled that with Rosemary he followed the procedure he normally used with his other patients: "I made a surgical incision in the brain through the skull. It was near the front. It was on both sides. We just made a small incision, no more than an inch." Through the openings on the sides of Rosemary's head, Watts inserted a specially made quarter-inch-wide flexible spatula into her cranium near the frontal lobes, turning and scraping as he moved deeper into her brain. Freeman asked Rosemary to sing a song, recite common verses, tell him stories about herself, count, and repeat the months of the year. At this point in the surgery, patients generally felt little pain, but their fear was palpable, their breathing rapid. Some tried to wrest their hands from the restraints or grab the nurse's hand with "painful intensity." Watts claimed Rosemary complied with their requests to recite simple songs and stories. Encouraged, Watts boldly cut more of the nerve endings from her frontal lobes to the rest of her brain. With the fourth and final cut, however, she became incoherent. She slowly stopped talking.

It would not take long—a few hours at the most—before the surgeons recognized that the surgery had gone horribly awry. Rosemary would emerge from the lobotomy almost completely disabled. Freeman claimed the procedure would produce a more docile, less moody Rosemary. The operation did far more than that. She could no longer walk or talk. It would take months of physical therapy and constant care before she would be able to move around, and then only with limitations. She would never recover the full use of her limbs. She walked with one leg and foot turned awkwardly in, creating a labored stride. She would have only partial use of one of her arms. She could speak only a handful of words. The operation destroyed a crucial part of Rosemary's brain and erased years of emotional, physical, and intellectual development, leaving her completely incapable of taking care of herself. The nurse who attended the operation was so horrified by what happened to Rosemary that she left nursing altogether, haunted for the rest of her life by the outcome.

In the hours, days, and weeks following lobotomy, patients like Rosemary experienced a wide array of postoperative reactions and symptoms. They vomited uncontrollably. Incontinence plagued some for weeks or months or longer. They were alternately restless and inert, many with expressionless faces, their eyes transfixed or drowsy-looking. Many picked at the surgical dressing on their head. Confused and frightened, many became extremely agitated and cried or laughed uncontrollably. Some would require help feeding, cleaning, and dressing themselves, as Rosemary would. Kennedy niece Ann Gargan, who lived with the family during the 1960s and later came to know Rosemary, recalled, "They knew right away that it wasn't successful. You could see by looking at her that something was wrong, for her head was tilted and her capacity to speak was almost entirely gone."

Rosemary's was one of several dozen case studies the doctors used in their volume on their research on prefrontal lobotomies published a year later, in 1942. Her case number remains unknown—none of the patients' names are revealed in the study—and her outcome, like the other failures, is relegated to footnotes and vague references. Freeman, Watts, and their university research colleague Dr. Thelma Hunt showed statistically few positive results—improved mood and less depression, less compulsive or destructive personal behavior, and fewer fears and anxieties—and, more important, they did not highlight the majority of long-term debilitating side effects of the lobotomies. According to their own records and published papers, many of their patients became more belligerent, more caustic, and less able to engage in positive social interactions. Many became more forgetful and self-absorbed, and often lacked emotion, even to the point of being uncaring toward loved ones around them. Some experienced heightened sexuality, even nymphomania. Binge eating, childlike behavior, insomnia, weepiness, and compulsive disorders emerged in some patients for the first time. Some began having epileptic-type seizures. Incontinence, catatonia, and the inability to walk, to use their hands and arms, or to take care of themselves plagued another subset of patients. Yet the research report concluded that "63% of the cases have resulted satisfactorily," while "in only 14% of the survivors can the results be considered bad." The authors obliquely reported that nine percent of their patients had died as a result of the surgery, and they did not mention which "bad" results affected the remaining fourteen percent. Two patients were still so "problematical" as of the research project's completion, in December 1941 — just a month after Rosemary's lobotomy — that they could not be categorized. Such disastrous results did not sway Freeman and Watts. Incredibly, they and Hunt claimed,

> Most of the patients are able to live fairly active, constructive lives, free from the harassing doubts and fears that characterized their illnesses, with their intelligence intact and their interests diverted outward. Many of them are better adjusted than they have ever been in their adult period of existence. Some of them are taking on new responsibilities and are equipped with sufficient energy and imagination to drive forward unhampered by the restraining influences that reduced them previously to vacillating insecurity. Al-

most all of them find existence more pleasurable, and they can adjust better in their environment.

Tens of thousands of patients would be forced to undergo lobotomies in the United States over the next two decades, and not until antipsychotic and antidepressant medications appeared in the 1950s was the surgery slowly replaced. Watts eventually abandoned his work with Freeman, but Freeman continued at a more feverish pace. A showman who craved attention and had an almost messianic belief that he could change people's lives with the procedure, he kept experimenting even while other physicians and medical specialists argued for more restraint and oversight. Determining that he could perform the surgery as well as a neurosurgeon, Freeman developed altered surgical instruments to reduce the time it took to complete a lobotomy. Over the next twenty years, he performed lobotomies on thousands of individuals—sometimes twenty or more a day—using a modified ordinary household ice pick that he would insert through the eye socket into the patients' frontal lobes.

Baby Rosemary and her brothers Joe Jr. (left) and Jack, with their mother, Rose, early 1919. *Courtesy John F. Kennedy Presidential Library and Museum*

Eunice, Kathleen, and Rosemary in Brookline, 1925, with Rosemary displaying the family's most exuberant smile.

Jack, Rosemary, Kathleen, and Joe, with Eunice on his shoulder. Joe worked long hours and was away from home often, but he valued his time with his children. On the beach in Cohasset, circa 1924.

Joe Jr. and Jack were the leaders among the Kennedy children, and the girls looked up to them. Cohasset, 1924. Left to right: Eunice, Jack, Joe Jr., Rosemary, and Kathleen.

Riding a bicycle, rowing a boat, playing tennis, and doing other athletic activities proved challenging for Rosemary. On her tricycle, 1924.

Rosemary's godfather, Eddie Moore, teaches her how to steer a sled, circa 1925. Over the years, the Moores' bond with Rosemary remained deep as they took on more responsibilities related to her education and care.

On the beach in Hyannis Port, 1930. Reading and writing remained a struggle for Rosemary, but she attained a fourth-grade level of proficiency.

Joe and Rose with eight of their nine children at Hyannis Port, 1931. The Kennedy parents encouraged close bonds among the children, which became a hallmark of the family dynamic in the years to come. Left to right: Bobby, Jack, Eunice, Jean, Pat, Kathleen, Joe Jr., and Rosemary. *Courtesy John F. Kennedy Presidential Library and Museum*

In her teens, Rosemary's smile belied difficult times as she slipped further and further behind her peers and siblings. *Courtesy John F. Kennedy Presidential Library and Museum*

Eunice (left) and Rosemary wave from aboard the USS *Manhattan* as they embark for England in 1938 to join their family.
© *Bettmann/Corbis*

Rosemary and her father at the 1938 opening of the London Children's Zoo. Joe, now the U.S. ambassador to Great Britain, and his family attracted near-constant media attention. This required vigilant control over Rosemary; note her father's firm grip on her arm.
© *Bettmann/Corbis*

Reporters greeted Kathleen, Rose, and Rosemary in the embassy garden as the women were leaving in May 1938 for their presentation at court to Britain's king and queen. Rosemary's gown was a favorite of the British press. *Daily Herald Archive/National Media Museum/Science & Society Picture Library*

Rosemary was delighted with all the attention. With only two weeks to prepare, she mastered the special curtsy and other social protocols required of young debutantes who gathered at the event. *Courtesy John F. Kennedy Presidential Library and Museum*

Joe's appointment as ambassador was a brilliant political and social achievement. The large Kennedy family offered endless fascination for a British public still overtly prejudiced against Catholics. Here the family poses for the press in 1938. Left to right: Eunice, Jack, Rosemary, Jean, Joe Sr., Teddy, Rose, Joe Jr., Pat, Bobby, and Kathleen. *Photograph by Dorothy Wilding/© William Hustler and Georgina Hustler/National Portrait Gallery, London*

While in England, Rosemary flourished under the patient and gentle guidance of Mother Isabel of the Assumption school. Mother Isabel was an early adopter of the Montessori educational method. *The Religious of the Assumption, Sister Therese Duross*

Rosemary at twenty years old. Her beauty drew attention while on a tour of Ireland with her sisters in 1938.

Rosemary with her Kennedy spirit in evidence, Kilcroney, Ireland, 1938. *Unidentified press photograph*

Kathleen started spending more time with newfound friends in England, leaving to Eunice the role of next-oldest sister to Rosemary. The younger Kennedy siblings and Rosemary enjoy a tour of Italy in 1939. Left to right: Bobby, Eunice, Jean, Pat, Rosemary, and Teddy. *Courtesy John F. Kennedy Presidential Library and Museum*

Rosemary and her father at an embassy social event, 1939. Rosemary's intellectual disabilities and unpredictable social skills required careful choreographing by the family at such events. Here Joe once again maintains a tight grip on his daughter's arm. © *Peter Hunter/Nederlands Fotomuseum*

At Eunice's debut and court presentation in 1939, a year after her own, Rosemary attracted much attention from admiring young men. Eddie Moore watches carefully as a young man asks Rosemary for a dance and she places his name on her dance card. © *Peter Hunter/Nederlands Fotomuseum*

In spite of looming war, the Kennedys kept Rosemary at the Assumption school, which had moved out of London to the safer English countryside. With Rose and all the other children back in the United States, Eddie and Mary Moore saw Rosemary frequently (here in 1940) while her father traveled and attended to his job as ambassador.

Rosemary's transition home from England was a difficult one. She was happy, though, to be a "junior counselor" at Camp Fernwood, in western Massachusetts, in 1940. The situation lasted less than a month, however, as the camp owners could not cope with her disabilities.
Courtesy Terry Marotta

Deeply saddened by her sudden removal from Camp Fernwood, Rosemary pours her heart out in a handwritten letter to Caroline and Grace Sullivan, July 1940. *Courtesy Terry Marotta*

Especially all the counselors

write to me

My love to each one!

ACADEMY OF THE ASSUMPTION
"RAVENHILL"
WEST SCHOOLHOUSE LANE
GERMANTOWN,   PHILADELPHIA, PA.

P.S: My regards to the Judge, And Eleanor Farr.

I am sorry you all had to lose me. It's not my fault darlings.

Have everybody write me a short little note, I have been crying over it. I know you all loved me so.

I am going to be a bit tired from all the service this summer, all the sailing. Pray for me! and the sailing. God Bless you

P.S. My love to the camp

Drs. Walter Freeman and James Watts popularized the prefrontal lobotomy in the United States. This photo accompanied a May 1941 *Saturday Evening Post* article that claimed, "The psychosurgeon usually succeeds in turning an ingrowing and a harassed mind outward and in transforming a personality." This was six months before Rosemary's operation.

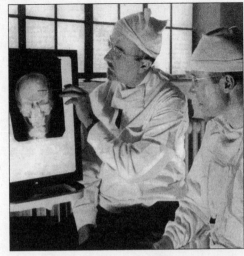

President John F. Kennedy presenting his pen to Eunice after signing the Maternal and Child Health and Mental Retardation bill in October 1963, less than a month before his assassination. *Courtesy John F. Kennedy Presidential Library and Museum*

In this August 21, 1964, photo, Eunice Kennedy Shriver is shown swimming with youngsters in a pool at a day camp for mentally challenged children in Fairmount Park, Philadelphia. *Associated Press*

Saint Coletta School, in Jefferson, Wisconsin, as it looked when Rosemary was moved there in the late 1940s. Her father would build a small cottage on the Saint Coletta campus for Rosemary and the several nuns who took care of her. *Hot Pepper Dave, Fort Atkinson, Wisconsin*

Rosemary, a caregiver from
Saint Coletta, and nephew
Anthony Shriver, who was
deeply inspired by Rosemary.
Courtesy Anthony Shriver

A rare press photograph of
Rosemary in her later years,
Hyannis Port, 1998. Still able
to walk with assistance from
two aides, Rosemary would
soon require a wheelchair.
© *Globe Photos/ZUMA Press/Corbis*

Rosemary
Courtesy Anthony Shriver

8

Rosemary Gone

JOE AND ROSE had decided earlier that fall to sell their Bronx-ville home and divide their time between Hyannis Port and Palm Beach. With Rosemary physically recovering at George Washington University Hospital; Eunice, Pat, Bobby, Jean, and Teddy in school; Joe Jr. in the service; and Jack and Kick in Washington, Rose was left to supervise the packing and moving of their furnishings over the Thanksgiving holiday. "The house was no longer a necessity," Rose wrote from the Plaza Hotel in New York City on December 5, in a letter sent to the children. Though they "all grew up there very happily, romping over the lawns in the spring and fall, and coasting down the sloping hill in the winter . . . I feel quite relieved and very free with nothing on my mind except the shades of blue for my Palm Beach trousseau." But Joe could not have kept the truth from her for very long. And it is clear that, even in those early days, Rose knew enough to decide on a stunning departure from her habit of writing a single letter, which included news about every family member and was copied and sent to each child. Rose in this letter did not include Rosemary's name. Rose's blithe tone would be remarkable for a mother who fully understood Rosemary's surgery or its outcome; perhaps she did not. Before, as Rose later reported, she "usually wrote to [the children] weekly [and] I conceived the idea of writing a letter with all the general family news on the first two pages. The general letter was typed by a secretary," and a "paragraph or two of news" about each child was included. A handwritten note specific to each child was then added by Rose, and the letters were mailed. For the next two decades, however, Rose never referred to Rosemary in her frequent, lengthy letters to all the other children and to family friends. Granddaughter Amanda Smith observed, while researching her book on Joe Kennedy, that during this time any mention of Rosemary ceased, "except obliquely in surviving family letters and papers."

The family was together at Palm Beach for Christmas, without Rosemary. It was a subdued holiday for the Kennedys—and for most Americans. The Japanese had bombed Pearl Harbor in a surprise attack on December 7. The United States declared war on Japan the next day, and by December 11, Congress had issued a declaration of war on Italy and Germany, Japan's allies. Much to Joe Kennedy's dismay, America had finally entered the war.

Kick and Pat left right after Christmas to spend New Year's with friends, and Eunice headed off to California to enroll at Stanford University. Joe Jr. returned to his air base in Jacksonville, Florida, where he had been training, and Jack left for Washington and his job at the naval intelligence office, leaving Rose in Palm Beach with Jean, Bobby, and Teddy. Joe Sr.—now firmly out of politics—was turning his attention to his sons' futures. He schemed to make Joe and Jack Massachusetts residents, even though their legal residence was now Florida, in the hopes that his eldest sons would soon enter politics. Rose's frequent family letters continued throughout the rest of the winter and spring of 1942, updating the siblings on what each of them was doing, in addition to supplying news and gossip about friends and acquaintances. Only one of the many letters written among the family members during the first year after Rosemary's surgery mentions her: Joe told Rose, who was living with Eunice in California, that he had "stopped off to see Rosemary and she is getting along very well nicely. She looks very well." To the family, Joe kept up a positive front about the whole matter. Joe's news about Rosemary was infrequent and vague and was directed specifically to Joe Jr., Jack, and Kick. Only six letters between the four of them with any reference to Rosemary survive from 1942 to 1944. No mention of the surgery or where she was living was reported in Joe's personal correspondence.

There is no record of Rose visiting her eldest daughter for more than twenty years. Certainly, there is no record of visits in the early postsurgery years. Ann Gargan later recalled that the lobotomy "was an absolute devastating thing, but once it was done [Joe] decided that he had to protect Rose from the heartbreak, believing it would shatter her to see her daughter that way while it would do Rosemary no good at all, since she no longer realized who she was." But Rosemary had not lost all cognitive ability, and the lack of contact with her siblings and parents on an ongoing basis probably made for a lonely and difficult recovery.

If Rose did not visit Rosemary, this does not mean Rosemary was cast out of her heart and mind. She chose to carry her pain privately. In her 1974 memoir, Rose wrote only that Rosemary had undergone an undisclosed type of neurosurgery. In a candid moment with Doris Kearns Goodwin years afterward, Rose bitterly explained that Joe "thought [the lobotomy] would help her, but it made her go all the way back. It erased all those years of effort I had put into her. All along I had continued to believe that she could have lived her life as a Kennedy girl, just a little slower. But then it was all gone in a matter of minutes." Rose's frankness is revealing: the lobotomy had injured her as much as it had Rosemary.

What Rosemary's siblings were told about the surgery and its outcome has not been fully recorded, but clearly it was little. Youngest sister Jean, then only thirteen years old, was told that Rosemary "had moved to the Midwest and had become a teacher—or maybe a teacher's assistant." Young Teddy was particularly troubled by Rosemary's sudden and unspoken disappearance from the family circle. At nine, Teddy feared that he "had better do what Dad wanted or the same thing could happen to me." There "will be no crying in the house," Joe told Teddy and his siblings, so whatever fears Teddy harbored, he kept to himself. The power of their father's commands carried tremendous weight with all the children. "Never violate people's privacy," he cautioned them in a powerful, unqualified directive.

Eunice's son Timothy noted in his memoir that for an untold number of years, "members of [Eunice's] family were in the midst of such a flurry of activity at that time that they apparently never questioned one sister's absence until much later." Jean concurred: "That was the way things were going then. We all just kept moving."

Remembering the struggles and tension the family endured when Rosemary was home on vacations, her siblings may have accepted that she was better off not seeing them. Or, perhaps, Joe told them some version of the truth. Certainly, Kick knew what her father had done, and Joe Jr. and Jack must have had a sense, if not outright knowledge.

Kick's surviving letters and diary reveal little. In one letter, however, she comes close to crossing a line. "Dear Daddy," she wrote sometime in the spring, four or five months after Rosemary's lobotomy, "the latest joke I meant to tell you last night about Washington is: A man is having terrible headaches so he went to a doctor who had a cure. The cure consisted of taking out the patient's brain, dusting it off every day for a week and then returning it. A week passed and the patient didn't come back for his brain. About two weeks later the doctor met him on the street and said, 'What about your brain. I've dusted it off consistently every day this week and you shouldn't be bothered with headaches any longer.' The man answered, 'oh that's alright, I won't need a brain any more, I have just gotten a job in Washington.'"

Eunice seems to have suffered particularly from Rosemary's suddenly vanishing, suggesting that perhaps Kathleen had confided what she knew their father had been thinking in the months before Rosemary's surgery and disappearance. Two months before the lobotomy, Eunice had enrolled at Sacred Heart in Manhattanville, now offering a full-fledged college program for women. Classmates observed that over the 1941 fall semester, Eunice became sick, depressed, and distant. They were stunned to discover when they returned from Christmas break that Eunice's room was empty and that she would not be returning for the spring semester. Rose, according to Eunice, had wanted her to go to Stanford instead, so Eunice obliged, but, she later said, she "did not have a good time [at Stanford] . . . I just didn't click." Rose claimed she preferred the location for Eunice's health. Perhaps Rose felt Eunice needed to be at a physical distance in order to accommodate the loss of Rosemary. Yet at Stanford, classmates remembered how very thin and unkempt Eunice was. Rose was so concerned about Eunice's health that she moved to Stanford during the spring of 1942 to stay with her daughter and even to attend classes with her. Photographs of Eunice from 1942 and 1943 show a terribly thin, frail young woman. Eunice later claimed she did not know where Rosemary was for at least a decade. Though Eunice would later be diagnosed with Addison's disease, it is probable that the stress of losing her sister only compounded her ill health.

ROSEMARY REMAINED FOR a short time at George Washington University Hospital, but was soon transferred to a private psychiatric facility called Craig House, located on the Hudson River fifty miles north of New York City, where the wealthy hid away their disabled, addicted, and seriously mentally ill family members. Its close proximity to New York made the facility the preferred hospital for the city's and the nation's business, entertainment, political, and artistic elite. Zelda Fitzgerald, the deeply troubled and depressed wife of American literary giant F. Scott Fitzgerald, spent months at Craig House in 1934, and actor Henry Fonda's second wife, Frances Seymour Brokaw, would spend several months there in early 1950, before committing suicide in her room.

Craig House offered the mentally ill or disabled loved ones of wealthy families a discreet rehabilitative environment that provided what psychiatrists of the day believed to be the best treatments available, including intensive, daily talk therapy, recreational activities, healthy food, and a serene atmosphere. Craig House boasted a high ratio of nurses and trained staff to patients—there were about thirty other patients when Rosemary arrived—and all the amenities associated with upper-class social and recreational pursuits, such as swimming, tennis, golf, and an assortment of indoor activities. Yet, in spite of its 350 acres of gardens, lawns, woods, and walking paths, its well-trained staff and comfortable surroundings, there would be no curative treatment for Rosemary. Her physical disabilities were as profound as her now-diminished intellectual abilities.

For Rosemary, learning to regain movement and control of her body—to eat, drink, communicate, walk, and interact with other people again—would take physical therapy and treatment beyond the capabilities or treatment options available at Craig House. It seems likely that Craig House was chosen for Rosemary as a temporary measure—yet she was to remain there for the next seven years.

There is evidence that Joe—but not Rose or any of the Kennedy children—visited Rosemary during her early years at Craig House, but he did so only a handful of times over a seven-year period. Rosemary's reaction to Joe during this time has not been recorded. Mary Moore saw her more frequently, and she probably played the role of Joe's confidante and informant about Rosemary's needs and the care she was receiving. Rosemary's personal and medical care continued to be extensive. Joe provided Rosemary with extra nurses and personal attendants—"private duty nurses, laundry, hairdresser, druggist, stationer, tailor"—to care exclusively for her at Craig House. These extra private benefits and resources, costing nearly $2,400 per month, were in addition to the nearly $50,000-per-year cost for treatment at Craig House, an exorbitant amount only the rich could afford at a time when medical-insurance coverage was in its infancy.

Joe communicated with the doctors and staff at Craig House, mostly through his secretaries, who took care of the monthly expenses and directed Craig House staff according to Joe's wishes. In a couple of letters written to Jack in 1942 and 1943, Joe briefly reported that Rosemary was swimming in the pool every day—a lifelong practice, as it was with her mother—and that she was "getting along quite happily," "looks very good," and "is feeling better." In letters to Joe Jr. and Kick written on February 21, 1944, Joe noted that "Rosemary is feeling quite well," a fact, he remarked, that rounded out the family news that "everyone is getting along quite happily." By the summer of 1944, Rosemary is no longer mentioned in letters to family members, a pattern that persisted for more than two decades.

MANY YEARS LATER, Rose was to call Rosemary's fate the first Kennedy tragedy. But the 1940s, the years Rosemary spent hidden at Craig House, brought yet more danger, death, and sorrow to the Kennedy household. During the fall of 1941, Jack joined the U.S. Navy. Earning the rank of lieutenant, he later became commander of a patrol torpedo boat, the *PT-109*. During the dark early hours of August 2, 1943, Kennedy and his crew were conducting patrols around the Solomon Islands when a Japanese destroyer rammed their relatively small wooden boat. The strike killed two crew members, but Kennedy and a number of other wounded men survived. They swam for hours to get to the closest island, with Kennedy pulling one of his wounded men along with him. With the help of local islanders, Kennedy and the men were rescued. Joe Kennedy kept his family in the dark about Jack's missing-in-action status; he decided to wait until he could confirm one way or another what had happened before telling Rose and the rest of the family. Before they could be told, however, the *Boston Globe* broke the news that Jack had been rescued, stunning Rose and the rest of the children and robbing Joe of his secret. After a short recovery, Jack returned to the South Pacific.

The war would soon take a deeper toll on the family. In August 1944, Joe Jr., a naval aviation officer stationed in England, knowing the extreme danger he faced, accepted a secret assignment to fly over the English Channel to northern France. The covert mission, Operation Aphrodite, entailed flying a BQ-8, a stripped-down B-24 bomber heavily laden with more than ten tons of explosives. The plan required Kennedy and another pilot, Lieutenant Wilford Thomas Willey, to eject as they approached their target—a Nazi military complex near Mimoyecques, in northern France—at which time their fellow airmen in two B-17s flying with them would remotely trigger the explosives over the target. But the remote trigger activated ten minutes too early, killing Kennedy and Willey instantly and nearly destroying the B-17s escorting them.

Kathleen was living in London when Joe Jr. was killed. It is difficult not to read Kick's war as shadowed by what she knew and felt about Rosemary's tragedy. Kick had remained in Washington, still writing society notes for the *Times-Herald,* but she missed her friends, nearly all of whom were vitally engaged in the war effort in England. Kick felt desperate to join them, but her parents objected. To get around their opposition, she signed on with the Red Cross. Her parents finally understood that they could not stand in the way of Kick's serving the war effort, like her brothers, and allowed her to set sail for England in June 1943.

Soon, Kick reunited with a former beau, William "Billy" Hartington, the son of the Duke and Duchess of Devonshire. Hartington had joined the British Army and was stationed near London, allowing the two to see each other frequently. The issue of marriage surfaced rather quickly, but Billy would not give up his Protestant faith, nor would Kathleen abandon her Catholic upbringing. The rift hurt them both. Over the months, however, their love deepened and, after much discussion with friends and a local Jesuit priest whom Kick had befriended in London, she agreed to marry Hartington and to raise their children as Protestants. The negative effect on her parents and family, however, would be more than she expected. Rose and Joe refused to give their approval. Just days before the wedding, Joe acquiesced, sending Kick a telegram: "With your faith in God you can't make a mistake. Remember you are still and always will be tops with me."

Even a noble title — Kick would become Lady Hartington, the future Duchess of Devonshire, on her marriage to Billy — could not sway Rose. On the advice of family friend Joseph Patterson, publisher of the *New York Daily News,* Rose checked into the New England Baptist Hospital in Boston, where, it was reported, she was "too ill to discuss the marriage." To Rose, Catholic doctrine was clear: marrying a non-Catholic was a mortal sin, and the church would neither recognize nor sanctify Kick's marriage. Kick's sisters, especially Eunice, rallied behind their mother, and nineteen-year-old Bobby lashed out at Kick, too. He felt personally challenged by her rejection; he imagined that her flagrant behavior was an unforgivable breach of their Catholic faith.

Joe Jr., stationed at Dunkeswell airfield, in East Devon, 220 miles southeast of London on the Plymouth coast, received a pass to travel to London to give Kick away at the May 6 ceremony in the Chelsea Town Hall. He was the only Kennedy family member in attendance; he would be dead in three months. Joe Jr. was willing to risk the wrath of his mother in order to support his younger sister; he liked Billy, and he had become particularly close to Kick during the preceding year. Rose was inconsolable over the marriage, "horrified [and] heartbroken." She checked herself out of the hospital the day of the wedding, flying to New York and then to Hot Springs, Virginia, where she would experience "much needed rest." "What a blow to the family prestige . . . We should think of a way to extricate her," Rose wrote privately in her diary in Hot Springs. Joe Jr., who probably understood what his family's fear of exposure had cost his oldest sister, responded to his parents: "As far as what people will say, the hell with them." But Rose refused to answer Kick's and Joe Jr.'s letters and cables. "The Power of Silence is Great," Joe Jr. cabled his father in desperation.

By the time of the wedding, Hartington had earned the rank of major, and not long after the marriage, he left with his unit for the front lines in Europe. On September 9, less than five weeks after his brother-in-law's fatal mission, Hartington was also dead, shot while liberating the town of Heppen in Belgium, then under Nazi control. Still in mourning for her brother, and living temporarily with her family in New York City, Kick experienced profound pain and isolation. The church offered no comfort. Because she had married a non-Catholic, the sacrament of Communion was now denied her.

Kathleen returned to England by the end of September to be with Billy's family and to attend his memorial service. While there, she found the love and comfort with his family that she had been denied by her own. Billy's sister Elizabeth recalled that she had "never met anyone so desperately unhappy. [Kick's] mother had tried to convince her that she had committed a sin in this marriage, so in addition to losing her husband, she was worried about having lost her soul."

Kick remained in England, serving with the Red Cross until the Japanese surrendered and the war was officially over, in 1945. Her years in England greatly changed her, and the estrangement from her family further shaped her decision to buy a small home in Smith Square in London and to build a life there.

Back in the States, Jack was laying the groundwork for a run for Congress—a plan that had originally been devised for Joe Jr. The Catholic vote for Jack was important, and Kick's marriage to a Protestant was problematic. The family believed that her presence on the campaign trail, and in church on Sundays with them, would be proof of her renewed commitment to her Catholic upbringing. After months of pleading by her father, Kick finally returned to New York that fall of 1945. The family assured the press she was returning home for good, though Kick in fact was vague about her plans.

Living apart from her family in her own hotel suite in New York, Kick tried to carry on an independent life. But she could not escape the stifling family responsibilities expected of her. Her father remained controlling, interfering in her private life and scolding her for her choice of friends and boyfriends. Her mother remained distant and cold.

Soon, her participation in the campaign and other Kennedy family events stopped. The press took notice, but by the winter of 1946, Kick probably did not care. The family had begun featuring the heroism of Jack and Joe during the war as part of the campaign rhetoric, ignoring Billy Hartington's sacrifice. Kick felt the snub deeply. Rejecting the pleas of her parents, who had seemingly done everything to isolate her, Kick moved back to London. She had seen enough of what happened to Kennedy daughters when they acted outside accepted social boundaries. For the next two years she renewed old friendships and spent time with her in-laws, who welcomed her warmly. She regained her love of the theater and parties, and as a titled war widow she started to rebuild her life.

Kick became romantically involved with the earl Peter Fitzwilliam, an immensely wealthy, decorated war hero with family estates in both Ireland and England, including the largest private house in England, Wentworth Woodhouse. Fitzwilliam was married, with a twelve-year-old daughter. Over the years, his wife,

Olive, had become an alcoholic, while he became a notorious womanizer; his adulterous affairs with women across Europe were legendary. Nevertheless, Kick and Fitzwilliam fell in love, and he decided to divorce his wife and marry Kathleen. In spite of efforts to keep their relationship secret, rumors spread rapidly in postwar London.

During the spring of 1948, Kick traveled to America to spend the Easter holiday with her family. Stunned by Kick's news that she would marry Fitzwilliam once his divorce was final, Rose was inconsolable—and furious. She threatened to cast Kick out of the family forever. Fearing Joe would side with his daughter and continue to support her financially, Rose took the step of threatening to leave Joe in order to "embarrass" him. She believed this threat would force Kick to choose her father over Fitzwilliam.

Rose was wrong. Kick sailed for Europe, heartbroken but more determined than ever to marry the man she loved. Rose made one more attempt to convince Kick, now a twenty-eight-year-old war widow, to reconsider, following her to London and appearing at her home. Rose told Kick she would never see her mother or siblings again, if Rose had anything to say about it. She would have no money of her own, no family. Was Fitzwilliam worth it?

Kick held out hope that her father would support her decision. She and Peter Fitzwilliam made plans to spend a few secret days together at Cannes, in the south of France, in May. In fact, Joe, traveling to Paris on business, had agreed to meet the two of them there on their way back to London. On May 13, the pair took off from London for Cannes in Fitzwilliam's private plane. A short, scheduled half-hour stopover in Paris was prolonged when Peter and Kick decided to have lunch with friends in the city. Their leisurely lunch cost them two hours of good weather, weather that was quickly turning stormy near the Cavennes Mountains. The pilot, who had been uneasy about the weather reports, strenuously objected to a takeoff, but Fitzwilliam overruled him. They flew directly into the violent storm, crashing into the peak of Le Coran. Kick, Peter, the pilot, and the copilot were killed instantly.

Joe, then in Paris and anticipating his meeting with Kick in a few days, learned of the news the next day. The family back home in the States was stunned. Unable to bear the responsibility, Joe left the funeral plans to the Duke and Duchess of Devonshire. Kick was buried next to Billy in the Hartington family plot, near Devonshire's Chatsworth estate. Joe was the only Kennedy family member, among two hundred guests, to attend the funeral service. Back in Hyannis Port, the family held a small, quiet service.

BY THE END of the decade, Craig House's proximity to New York and its connections to the city's elite may have made Joe uncomfortable. Jack, the war hero, had been elected to the House of Representatives by Massachusetts voters in 1947, and he was hopeful for a future Senate seat. The risk of having anyone discover that Rosemary was institutionalized and in such a debilitated state was a public-relations problem for a family with political ambitions. Joe did not want to explain why Rosemary had had a lobotomy, when it was performed, and what had happened to her afterward. Ironically, Joe's decision concerning the lobotomy had rendered Rosemary more, rather than less, of a threat to the Kennedy family aspirations.

Settling Rosemary in Massachusetts or Florida would have been more convenient for visits by the family, if they had wanted to or could visit her. But there were hardly any private facilities in those two states that were suited to Rosemary's needs. Patient abuse was also rampant.

McLean Hospital, offering residential care and treatment for the mentally ill at its Frederick Law Olmsted–designed campus in Belmont, Massachusetts, was an option not available to Rosemary. An institution that provided private care with the leading psychiatrists and specialists of the day, it attracted members of the nation's wealthiest and most famous families, much like Craig House. It did not, however, care for the physically disabled. While Rosemary may have benefited from an examination at McLean when her erratic and violent behaviors increased before her surgery, it was not suitable for her after the lobotomy, given the physical and intellectual impairments it caused.

In 1948, Joe consulted with one of his close friends and spiritual advisers, Boston's Catholic archbishop Richard Cushing. The Catholic Church had been building residential treatment and therapeutic hospitals, sanitariums, and special schools for decades. Among them was Saint Coletta School in Jefferson, Wisconsin, staffed and run by the Sisters of Saint Francis of Assisi. Serving about two hundred children, the facility offered care for mentally disabled adults as well. Cushing in fact had sought the support of the Saint Francis of Assisi sisters of Milwaukee to build a Saint Coletta school in Massachusetts in 1947.

Cushing's school, Saint Coletta by the Sea in Hanover, Massachusetts, was originally designed for a small number of children who lived at, and were schooled in, two small buildings on a 176-acre campus. Joe, through a newly established nonprofit philanthropic family foundation created in the memory of Joe Jr., called the Joseph P. Kennedy Jr. Foundation, would donate more than $100,000 to the building of a chapel, a children's playroom, three classrooms, and a dormitory for forty children there in 1948. Within ten years, another large donation of funds from the Kennedy Foundation would help the school expand to include separate residential homes, additional classrooms, and more recreational facilities for children and a few adults. But, in the late 1940s, the Massachusetts facility was not suitable for Rosemary—not because she could not be properly cared for there but because, as Archbishop Cushing told Joe directly, "it would be impossible to avoid public attention." Joe understood and probably agreed. Cushing encouraged Joe to send Rosemary to the Jefferson, Wisconsin, program. "There," he assured Joe, "and not Hanover, will solve your personal problems."

Joe worked through a friend and longtime business associate, John Ford, to make all the necessary arrangements for a transition. "Word has come from Mother Mary Bartholomew that the school at Jefferson, Wisconsin will co-operate in every way concerning the placement of Rosemary," Sister Maureen wrote to Ford from Saint Coletta at Hanover. "I am sure that everything can be arranged to Mr. Kennedy's entire satisfaction." Joe dispatched Ford to investigate the facility in January. "If you have time, I wonder if, when you are in Chicago [on business], you will run up to the school at Jefferson, Wisconsin, and have a talk with Mother Mary Bartholomew . . . You know just what I have in mind and, after an examination of the place and a talk with the Nuns, I am sure you will be in a position to tell me what you think. I thought I would follow it up with a visit myself, possibly in March or April," Joe wrote to Ford on New Year's Eve in 1948. "That is the most important unfinished business that I have."

Sometime in the early summer of 1949, Rosemary moved to Jefferson. Leaving familiar surroundings at Craig House, she was taken by train in the company of two sisters to Milwaukee, and then to Saint Coletta, about an hour away. Over the next fifteen years, Ford would visit with Rosemary at Saint Coletta, checking on her care. He handled the financial details, paying Saint Coletta's monthly invoices, and acted as intermediary between Joe and the sisters caring for Rosemary. Joe never saw Rosemary again.

Saint Coletta had been established during the mid-nineteenth century as a Sisters of Saint Francis of Assisi convent, which was eventually expanded to a religious boarding school for girls. In 1904, under the auspices of the Diocese of Milwaukee and administered by the sisters, the school was transformed into the Saint Coletta Institute for Backward Youth. The name was changed in 1931 to the Saint Coletta School for Exceptional Children, not only reflecting a change in understanding of people with intellectual and physical disabilities but also, according to the school, "for the residents, one of whom remarked, 'We don't walk backward.'" Located on more than two hundred acres, the school also encompassed an additional five-hundred-acre farm, where the sisters raised hogs, chickens, cows, and geese; operated a dairy; and grew vegetables and other foodstuffs, mostly to feed themselves and the school's patients. The school offered appropriate academic programs for the youngest residents and, for older, adult patients, vocational training for jobs in the community.

Sister Margaret Ann, a nun who oversaw Rosemary's later care at Saint Coletta, revealed that the 1949 transition to the school was traumatic. Rosemary "was very uncontrollable when she first got here," she recalled hearing from the sisters who cared for Rosemary at Saint Coletta during those early years. Unhappy and feeling "inferior to her brothers and sisters," Rosemary, as one caretaker later reported, eventually came to understand that "in God's eyes she has worth and value. She is a wonderful remarkable woman." Joe paid for a special one-story brick ranch-style cottage to be built for Rosemary, which also housed two specially trained nuns who could live with her full-time. Informally named the Kennedy Cottage, the house was near Alverno House, about a mile from the main Saint Coletta campus. It would become Rosemary's home for nearly sixty years. Alverno House served adults at the school who, like Rosemary, would need dependent care for their entire lives.

Settling into a routine, Rosemary found comfort and security, even friendship, with the nuns, staff, and patients. She was happy, the nuns reported, and was adeptly cared for and nurtured by the sisters, who became her substitute family. She took walks with the nuns, who kept her from curiosity seekers. Inquisitive reporters tried to find her and uncover her story, but the nuns were vigilant, thwarting attempts by journalists and others to speak with or photograph her. "A Mr. Rudy S. Holstein . . . stopped in and wanted to see Rosemary," Sister Anastasia from Saint Coletta wrote to John Ford. "We told him that Rosemary does not wish to see anyone without the parents' consent. Mr. Holstein said he was in the army with Joe [Jr.]." Joe was furious. "I do not know who Mr. Rudy Holstein is and I do not care who the rest of them were or what their arguments were—your rules still stand," he wrote to Sister Anastasia.

Rosemary received individual therapy and participated in social functions and occasional meals with staff and residents at Saint Coletta. Speech therapy and improving her motor skills remained priorities. In 1958, Sister Anastasia, who appears to have been the contact for the family during Rosemary's early years at Saint Coletta, assured Ford that special therapists and doctors were coming to work with Rosemary. Joe Kennedy made clear that he would cover these costs, no matter what they were. "All you have to do is to do it and send me the bill," he told Sister Anastasia. The trust fund Joe had set up for Rosemary many years before, as he had done for all his children, paid Rosemary's bills at the school. But, even without it, Joe would have made sure she was well cared for. A car used by her caregivers to take her on short trips into town, furs, and beautiful clothes guaranteed that she was still a Kennedy girl. Consistent and significant yearly donations were made to the school, as well.

ROSE CLAIMED TO her niece Ann Gargan that she was kept in the dark about the lobotomy for twenty years, well into Rosemary's life at Saint Coletta. Gargan recalled that Rose "had to piece the story together chapter by chapter." Heartbroken, angry, and disillusioned, Rose begged her friends and family advisers to tell her what had happened. Why, she asked, hadn't she been told? Luella Hennessey Donovan's response was echoed by them all: "Because I did not know."

Rose's claims ring false, however, given the historical record. Rose later claimed, in her 1974 memoir, that she and Joe consulted with "eminent medical specialists" who advised them that there was no choice, but that Rosemary "should undergo a certain form of neurosurgery." Joe had discussed the surgery with her, and, it seems, Rose asked Kick to further research its viability. Joe may not have asked for Rose's final permission, but clearly she was not in the dark once the surgery had taken place. Though little correspondence exists that explicitly defines what Rose learned and when about what happened to Rosemary, it is not possible that she remained as uninformed as she alleged.

Rosemary now lived wholly apart from her family identity. Unable to speak clearly, and deeply intellectually impaired, she no longer needed to compete with her siblings and had become, as one nun described her, less "goal oriented." Her "whole life is wrapped up in doing things she likes, like taking trips into town." Still a relatively tall woman, at five feet eight inches, Rosemary presented an imposing figure. For some time she had tended to carry more weight, and now, with physical limitations, she was heavier than she had been. In spite of her crippled limbs, however, she was strong and healthy.

Over time, Rosemary would indeed consider Saint Coletta her permanent home, and would make friends among the patients. One woman, Gloria, had become intellectually impaired when she suffered severe brain damage in a car accident on the night of her high school senior prom. A talented pianist, Gloria suffered a form of amnesia that prevented her from remembering what she had done a few minutes before. She could no longer learn new music, but she could beautifully play pieces she knew from before her accident. The two developed a friendship. Gloria, younger by five years, believed it was simply because Rosemary loved music and liked to hear her play, just as she had liked it when Rose played the piano for the children when they were young.

In one letter to Sister Anastasia, Joe expressed deep gratitude for the kindness and loving care the nuns and staff were providing Rosemary. In a remarkable moment of honesty, Joe told Sister Anastasia that Saint Coletta had offered "the solution to Rosemary's problem . . . a major factor in the ability of all the Kennedys to go about their life's work and to try and do it as well as they can."

9

Rosemary Made the Difference

AS JACK'S POLITICAL career took form and the White House looked like more than merely a dream, the Kennedys' allure as newspaper fodder for both the society and news pages only grew. Family weddings, social and charitable events, and political campaigns kept the Kennedy name in the public eye. Jack was elected to the Senate in 1952, beating Massachusetts's longtime Republican senator, Henry Cabot Lodge. The following year he married Jacqueline Bouvier of Newport, Rhode Island, four months after Eunice's marriage to Sargent "Sarge" Shriver, a lawyer hired by Joe to manage one of the family's largest real estate investments, the Merchandise Mart in Chicago. Bobby, while still a law student at the University of Virginia, had married Ethel Skakel in 1950, and Patricia followed in 1954 when she wed actor Peter Lawford. As this wealthy, glamorous, and now politically powerful Kennedy generation's influence was growing, Rosemary's whereabouts and activities posed a special challenge, one that was met with the oft-repeated false claim that she was teaching at a school for handicapped children in the Midwest and preferred her privacy.

The fact of Rosemary's intellectual disabilities—but not the lobotomy—was known to the small circle of advocates, many of them parents and siblings of the disabled, who belonged to the Massachusetts chapter of the National Association for Retarded Children. In 1955, according to Elizabeth Boggs, the parent of an intellectually disabled child and the president of NARC, the Massachusetts chapter contacted Cardinal Cushing about the possibility of approaching the Kennedy family to ask for its support for NARC programs and advocacy efforts. "We have tried to reach the Kennedy family through our channels in Boston, and we haven't gotten any response," Boggs remembered being told by John Fettinger, the president of Massachusetts NARC. "The Senator was, after all, the Senator from Massachusetts," Boggs stressed, "so that would have been the natural approach." Boggs recalled being frustrated two years later as well, when Jack did not endorse the first "mental-retardation bill"—which provided for rehabilitation and education programs—and did not attend the Senate hearings where testimony, including Boggs's, was given in support of the legislation. "He didn't have to tell the world that he had a retarded sister in order to support that legislation, and yet he didn't [support] it."

While campaigning in 1958 for a second term as senator from Massachusetts—and, under the guidance and encouragement of his father, preparing for a presidential run in 1960—Jack made a secret side trip to Jefferson, Wisconsin, to visit Rosemary for the first time since her institutionalization. What he knew about Rosemary's lobotomy and its outcome is unknown—but what he found shocked him. Confronted with the firsthand knowledge of

Rosemary's condition, Jack experienced a transformed sense of responsibility toward disabilities legislation.

In 1958, during the frenetic excitement of Jack's fledgling presidential campaign, Eunice approached her father about channeling more of the Kennedy Foundation's resources into researching the causes of, and treatment for, intellectual disabilities. Up to that point, the foundation had devoted more than eighty percent of its charitable giving to alleviating the suffering of the poor and needy through mostly Catholic and some Protestant institutions and programs, with the remainder funding construction projects related to facilities for children with intellectual disabilities. Eunice had been appointed to the foundation's board of trustees when it was established in 1947. Though her name does not appear often in the annual reports, she did take an active role in the foundation's administration. But now she made it clear that she wanted the foundation to focus on intellectual disabilities, and particularly on funding research into the biological causes of developmental and intellectual disabilities.

Eunice had become interested in social work during college, and upon graduation began working in various social-service agencies. Securing a position in the Justice Department for the National Council on Preventing Juvenile Delinquency, she began working on the problem of troubled and at-risk youth. Preferring more direct social service, she moved on to the federal penitentiary in Alderson, West Virginia, to counsel incarcerated women. Eventually landing back in Chicago to work with young offenders through the juvenile-court system and to volunteer at the Catholic House of the Good Shepherd, she met her husband-to-be, Sargent Shriver. After marrying, in 1953, Eunice devoted her time to her growing family but remained active in Jack's campaigns.

Now, the Kennedy Foundation captivated Eunice's attention

and served as an outlet for her passion for social justice. With her father's support, Eunice, in 1958, began investigating the status of research into intellectual disabilities by visiting hospitals and institutions that offered custodial care, treatment, and educational programs for the disabled. In August 1958, after visiting the Saint Coletta Home in Hanover, Massachusetts, and the Joseph P. Kennedy Memorial Hospital, serving handicapped children in Brighton, Massachusetts — the latter of which had been an early and rare exception to the foundation's typical funding commitments — Eunice wrote excitedly to her parents that these facilities were fertile grounds for research into intellectual disabilities. The hospital, she wrote, "is doing so much and doing it so well that they can take my money and spend it." She had spoken with the doctors about introducing research studies, and she believed that, with the help of the "fabulous nuns," the facility was a "gold mine for research."

Eunice and Sarge, a committed partner to Eunice in her cause, worked fast. They established a medical and scientific advisory board at the foundation and appointed Dr. Robert Cooke, head of pediatrics at Johns Hopkins University, to chair that board and to advise on strategies for research funding. The father of two intellectually disabled children, Cooke viewed the crisis of the disabled child not as a problem to be placed out of sight but as an area of pediatrics that needed attention. Medicine, he believed, should be "as concerned with care as cure." The Shrivers proposed to Richard Masland, director of the National Institute of Neurological Diseases and Blindness, that he establish a research center and clinical programs on child health at Johns Hopkins. Other doctors and scientists were consulted, and a new vision and mission for the Kennedy Foundation emerged.

Eunice felt the family could make a sizable impact in the field.

Social stigma, misunderstanding, and lack of knowledge about disabilities had contributed to a critical shortage of research and facilities. Eunice redirected the distribution of the foundation's funds to research into the causes of intellectual disabilities, pre- and postnatal care, education, and medical services. Educational outreach and support services, the construction of homes for the disabled, funding for research, and construction of research centers could now engage a significant portion of the foundation's financial resources. In 1957, a decade after its founding, the foundation had committed only seventeen percent of its gifts to research and programs devoted to developmental and intellectual disabilities. By 1960, this percentage had tripled.

Joe, never one to waste an opportunity to promote the family, understood that any foundation gift was sure to be covered in the press and would keep the Kennedy name in the news. His giving was also genuine, however, and many donations were gifted anonymously or with little fanfare or recognition. With a new vision in place—Eunice's vision—Joe quietly transferred control of the foundation's giving to her and Sarge.

Jack's eventual commitment to legislation in support of research and education coincided with the foundation's newfound mission. In 1958 he was one of eleven senators sponsoring modified legislation directing additional federal assistance to states to expand research and education for mentally disabled children. The legislation passed both houses of Congress and became Public Law No. 85-924–926, which became the foundation for Title III, a federal program supporting certain specialized education programs under the Higher Education Act of 1965.

THE FACT OF Rosemary's condition was not directly addressed by Jack's presidential campaign. In July 1960, *Time* magazine revealed in a feature article on Jack's campaign that "Rosemary, the eldest of the Kennedy daughters, was a childhood victim of spinal meningitis, [and] is now a patient in a nursing home in Wisconsin." The article did not directly state that she lived with intellectual disabilities, nor was it revealed that it was the lobotomy that had further disabled her. Joe Kennedy was quoted claiming, "I used to think it was something to hide, but then I learned that almost everyone I know has a relative or good friend who has the problem. I think it best to bring these things out in the open." It was only in a footnote at the end of the article that a diagnosis was implied:

> Rosemary's misfortune has resulted in the major Kennedy philanthropy, which is the good fortune of the mentally retarded, and typically, an all-absorbing project of the entire clan: the Joseph P. Kennedy Jr. Foundation. Since its inception in 1948, the foundation has spent $13.5 million on a dozen homes and hospitals for the mentally retarded in Massachusetts, New York, Illinois and California. This year $10 million is being spent recruiting eminent doctors, psychologists and psychiatrists to work on a dramatic new research program.

The *New York Times* reported in an article on Kennedy's campaign that same week that "Rosemary is in a nursing home in Wisconsin," but did not mention the reason.

John Seigenthaler, a reporter who was covering the presidential campaign for the *Nashville Tennessean,* was granted a rare interview with Joe Kennedy that July. "The story had just come out in *Time* that Rosemary had been 'mentally retarded,'" Seigenthaler recalled. "[Joe] said, 'I don't know what it is that makes eight children shine like a dollar and another one dull. I guess it's the hand of God. But we just do the best we can and try to help wherever we can.'" Eunice, Joe bragged to Seigenthaler, "knows more about helping the mentally retarded than any other individual in America."

In November 1960, Jack Kennedy was elected president, defeating Richard Nixon of California in a hotly contested race. Winning by the narrowest of margins—a mere two-tenths of one percent of the popular vote—Kennedy became the youngest man and the first Catholic ever elected to the presidency. Less than a month later, the publication of the National Association for Retarded Children, *Children Limited,* revealed in a photo caption that "the President elect has a mentally retarded sister who is in an institution in Wisconsin." A photograph of Jack Kennedy with the Pennsylvania branch president of the National Association for Retarded Children accompanied the statement on Rosemary. While there was no mention of Rosemary's lobotomy, this was the first time a clear statement was made about Rosemary's disability. The Kennedys, however, were still not ready to speak more openly about Rosemary's condition, forcing NARC to issue a bulletin immediately to all its affiliates cautioning them to not repeat the information. "No capital should be made of this," Elizabeth Boggs said was the message from NARC. The word was "that the family preferred not to have this, in fact, mentioned and we would respect their wishes in this matter as we would any other family's wishes."

EUNICE SEIZED HER opportunity once Jack was elected president. She persuaded her brother to establish the Committee on Mental Retardation and the National Institute of Child Health and Human Development (NICHD). Though the National Insti-

tutes of Health opposed a new institute on child health and development, on the grounds that it was unnecessary, heavy lobby-
ing by the Shrivers, Dr. Cooke, and many others helped get the
NICHD established by executive order within months of Kennedy's taking office. At the behest of Joe, and through Eunice's
powerful insistence, the institute was soon followed by a commission to study intellectual and developmental disabilities of children. President Kennedy established the President's Task Force
on Health and Social Security and funneled resources into the
moribund and obscure Department of Mental Retardation, then a
small office within the Department of Education. Dr. Cooke was
appointed to the commission, ensuring that the interests of children, in particular, would be well represented.

In the spring of 1961, an award-winning documentary film,
The Dark Corner, about the treatment of mentally disabled people
in Maryland, was shown at the White House. Written and nar-
rated by journalist Rolf Hertsgaard and produced by WBAL-TV
in Baltimore, the film had an enormous impact. By that summer,
the twenty-seven-member President's Panel on Mental Retardation got to work, and set a goal of delivering a report to the president within a year—a remarkably short amount of time, considering the enormity of the task.

The Shrivers had moved from Chicago to Maryland once Jack
was elected president and after Sarge was appointed head of the
newly created Peace Corps, one of President Kennedy's first efforts, to call on the nation's youth to volunteer two years of service offering technical, economic, and social resources to struggling communities around the globe. Focusing on the physical
well-being of disabled children, Eunice remembered all those
years that her mother and siblings had worked with Rosemary—
playing tennis, swimming, sailing, running, and more—and how

important those activities were to Rosemary's physical and emotional well-being. Eunice researched available programs offering such activities and found there were few, most of them sponsored by NARC, serving a small number of children across the country. Few children with intellectual disabilities were receiving any type of sports or fitness training, whether they were institutionalized, in school, or at home. Without wasting time, Eunice established Camp Shriver in the summer of 1961, a small day program for mentally handicapped and disadvantaged children on the Shriver estate, Timberlawn, in Maryland, where she hosted outdoor games and swimming. The camp was in full swing during the summer of 1962, pulling in volunteers from local colleges and universities to work as counselors for dozens of disabled children. Running, jumping, swimming, rope climbing, horseback riding, dancing, ball games, and more drew squeals of laughter from the children who attended the program.

LESS THAN A year after Jack's inauguration, on December 19, 1961, Joe Sr. had a stroke, paralyzing him and leaving him unable to communicate intelligibly. Wheelchair-bound and needing physical care until his death, eight years later, and unable to orchestrate and manipulate the careers, social aspirations, and political futures of his children, he suffered mutely as the world moved on. "He is still very vital and vigorous," Rose noted in her diary in the spring of 1963, "about expressing his wishes and gets cross and impatient if we cannot understand him and if he is not handled properly. He uses his arm and his leg to push or whack the nurses." Joe, in his debilitated body, had now lost the ability to walk and speak, just as his powerless daughter once had.

During the fall of 1962, just before the highly anticipated President's Panel on Mental Retardation report was due, the *Sat-*

urday Evening Post published an article written by Eunice entitled "Hope for Retarded Children." In it, Eunice revealed in detail the struggles her family faced trying to find ways to accommodate Rosemary's many physical, intellectual, and emotional needs throughout childhood and young adulthood. "She was a beautiful child," Eunice wrote, "but in early life Rosemary was different. She was slower to crawl . . . walk and speak." Her parents, Eunice revealed, tried to keep her at home rather than institutionalize her. "Keeping a retarded child at home is difficult. Mother always said the greatest problem was to get other children to play with Rose and to find time to give her all the attention she needed and deserved." The whole family worried about Rosemary—would some accident befall her, or would she get lost if she wandered away? When she was twenty-two, Eunice admitted, Rosemary's behavior became more "irritable and difficult." An institution where she could live "with others of her own capacity . . . where there was no need for 'keeping up,' or brooding over why she can't join in activities as others do," was the solution. Blending statistics on intellectual and developmental disabilities and acknowledging the lack of resources to help create "chances for useful lives" for the disabled, Eunice spelled out a vision for funding research, education, and vocational-training programs. The article delivered hope that with training, appropriate medical care, community support, and federal and private resources, people with disabilities could lead productive, happy, independent lives. Eunice, however, did not reveal that Rosemary had been subjected to a debilitating lobotomy.

On October 17, 1962, three days after the CIA discovered that the Soviets were building missile sites in Cuba, President Kennedy signed Public Law No. 87-838, authorizing the establishment of the National Institute of Child Health and Human Development under the auspices of the National Institutes of Health. The institute would focus exclusively on the "complex process of human development from conception to old age," and would fund research into the causes of birth defects and intellectual and physical disabilities. Five days later, just as the Cuban missile crisis was unfolding and a month after Eunice's *Saturday Evening Post* article was published, the President's Panel on Mental Retardation released its first report. In spite of being distracted by the "great gravity" of potential nuclear war, the president paid close attention to the pioneering document. Topping the list of recommendations were new laws to protect and provide for people with disabilities, a reorganization of federal agencies and offices to accommodate a new emphasis on the disabled, and funding for the new federal programs and initiatives.

Elizabeth Boggs later credited Eunice's *Saturday Evening Post* article with helping to pave the way for public acceptance of the many recommendations made in the report. The Kennedys followed the release of the panel's report with a gala dinner, hosted by the Kennedy Foundation, in Washington, D.C., in December 1962. Seven hundred and fifty guests filled the ballroom of the Statler Hotel, including members of Congress, the Supreme Court, the cabinet, and leaders in the realm of science and medicine. The president presented the Kennedy Foundation's first International Awards in Mental Retardation, recognizing outstanding achievements in the scientific and medical field of intellectual disabilities, advocacy, and outreach. Five doctors, chosen from a worldwide list of more than four hundred scientists and practicing physicians, and NARC were the inaugural recipients, and they received cash prizes and grants to support their individual research projects and programs. The event also set the stage for the president to deliver his "Special Message on Mental Illness and Mental Retardation" to Congress on February 5, 1963.

In the fall of 1963, President Kennedy signed two important pieces of legislation. The Maternal and Child Health and Mental Retardation Planning Amendments of 1963 encouraged states to update and improve programs for the intellectually disabled, and authorized funding for pre- and postnatal care linking families to resources and services to help prevent disabilities. Also, in October, Kennedy signed the Mental Retardation Facilities and Community Mental Health Centers Construction Act, which provided funding for research centers—several of which were connected to large university-hospital networks—as well as community inpatient centers.

The legislation marked a turning point in the government's commitment to providing resources for the disabled. President Kennedy was assassinated, however, within weeks of signing the bills, and, with his loss, the power of the Kennedys on Capitol Hill diminished quickly and considerably.

The loss of access to the White House forced Eunice to refocus the energy she had spent marshaling the resources of enormously influential contacts in Washington and across the country. By 1968, her Camp Shriver had matured into a professional charitable organization dedicated to addressing the needs of intellectually and physically disabled youth through similar camps in a few cities across the nation. But Eunice yearned for more national acceptance of the program. In a joint venture with Chicago's Park District and the Kennedy Foundation, the first Special Olympics, originally conceived by Anne Burke, a phys-ed instructor and a Chicago parks employee with experience working with the intellectually disabled, took place in the eighty-thousand-seat Soldier Field stadium in Chicago that July. The event featured Olympic-style summer games for one thousand disabled young people from across the country and Canada. Though fewer than one hundred spectators showed up to watch the first games, Eunice—still mourning the death of her brother Bobby, assassinated during a presidential-campaign event in Los Angeles in early June—welcomed the athletes and announced both the Kennedy Foundation's commitment to funding Special Olympics training programs and a promise to host another international event every two years. The games, Eunice had quickly come to realize, showed not only how important athletics were in the lives of disabled children but also that the Special Olympics was the way to promote the foundation's vision. The Special Olympics today reaches more than four million disabled athletes in year-round programs in nearly two hundred nations around the globe.

DURING THIS TUMULTUOUS decade for her family and the nation, and reflecting her ongoing public commitment to the disabled, Eunice, more privately, after her father's stroke, took over responsibility for Rosemary's care. She monitored Saint Coletta's educational, physical, and mental-health services. She conferred with Rosemary's doctors, companions, and nurses, making sure Rosemary received the best and most advanced care. This was during the period when Joe's stroke required round-the-clock nursing care at home, and Rose was preoccupied with managing his care. Rita Dallas, one of Joe's nurses, recalled that Rose "was nervous and uncomfortable around illness of any kind and she had gone through severe shock in trying to cope with her husband's condition." Though Eunice started visiting Rosemary when she took over the management of Rosemary's care at Saint Coletta once Joe became an invalid, it is not known when the rest of the family began visiting her.

With the partial truth about Rosemary having been revealed, especially by Eunice's *Saturday Evening Post* article, in 1962, and with Joe still a burden but no longer a controlling force, Rose was liberated enough to travel across the country giving speeches about "mental retardation." Her effectiveness at bringing attention to the issue of intellectual disabilities and her personal relationship to the cause made her a powerfully effective spokesperson. Yet even while dismantling the shroud of shame and secrecy surrounding intellectual disabilities, she kept a very important detail of Rosemary's life—the lobotomy—a secret. A *National Enquirer* article in the late fall of 1967, titled "The Tragic Story of . . . THE DAUGHTER JFK'S MOTHER HAD TO GIVE UP," revealed some of the family's trials caring for Rosemary within the fabric of such a high-energy, competitive family. Quoting liberally from Eunice's *Saturday Evening Post* article and from some of the speeches Rose had been making on behalf of the intellectually handicapped since 1963, the story recounted how Rosemary's limitations slowly emerged, and how, after years of effort and searching for a medical cure, Rose and Joe realized that Rosemary was permanently disabled. When the family returned from England, the article reported, "Rosemary showed disturbing signs of going backward." The family had no choice but to "accept the unanimous verdict." Rosemary "would be better off in an institution, away from the pressures and complexities of the world."

Rose received hundreds of letters from parents across the nation, thanking her for being a beacon of hope. Grieving, burdened parents expressed tremendous relief and feelings of fellowship with the mother of a president and a family of high achievers. They felt encouraged as they struggled at home to care and provide for their disabled children. Most did not have the financial resources the Kennedys had to provide for their loved ones. Rose knew this, and it moved her.

Rose's faith was one thing she could honestly share with others. Her letters to other parents of disabled children, following a common format using a few variations to suit particular cases, held up her faith as a source of strength, while highlighting her own exceptional loss. Noticeable, too, was Rose's belief—which she shared widely in these letters—that Rosemary's life could mean little.

> Thank you very much for your letter . . . None of us can understand the ways of Almighty God—the crosses which he sends us, the sacrifices which he demands of us. But he loves us and He has a particular plan in this life for each of us.
>
> He has sent you a retarded [son or daughter], He took away my three stalwart sons—young men, well equipped and eager to devote their time and talents to His work on earth. And He left me my handicapped daughter, mentally and physically unable to help herself or anyone else.
>
> Life is not easy for any of us, but it is a challenge and it is up to us to pray, to resolve to be strong and not be a burden to our family and our friends. If we keep busy mentally and physically, we do not have time to dwell on what might have been but we are filled with a desire to accomplish something worthwhile for the future.
>
> My prayers and best wishes are with you.

After Bobby's assassination, in June 1968, Joe's health deteriorated rapidly. He died, from complications of his stroke, in November 1969.

According to Barbara Gibson, who joined the Kennedy household staff as a secretary in 1968, Rose first visited Rosemary at Saint Coletta at some point in the early 1960s, after Joe had suffered his stroke. There is no indication from Rose's personal papers that she made any trips to visit Rosemary before then, even though she campaigned for Jack in Milwaukee, a few miles from Saint Coletta, during his presidential run in 1960. Once Joe had become disabled, and Eunice's article in the *Saturday Evening Post* had appeared and received a warm reception by readers, Rose may have felt the time had come to see her daughter.

Whenever it was, Rose's visit upset Rosemary; Sister Margaret Ann recalled being told by the sisters who cared for her at that time that Rosemary recoiled from her mother. Though she was unable to speak many words, Rosemary's anger toward Rose was apparent to everyone around her. The nun felt, "in the back of my mind," that Rosemary remembered having the surgery and that "her mother didn't show up." Sister Margaret Ann learned from other caregivers that Rosemary "was taking it out on her mother" during Rose's initial visits. "The way I understand it," the sister revealed, "Mrs. Kennedy would come out [to Saint Coletta] and would go back [home] very upset. I wasn't here when Mrs. Kennedy was here, but they said that Rosemary never accepted her."

Perhaps such a reaction kept Rose from visiting frequently. Rose's surviving correspondence reveals no contact with Saint Coletta until 1969. "Sometime I should like St. Coletta to have a swimming pool as a gift from Rosemary," Rose wrote to Father Thomas J. Walsh at the school in February, nearly nine months before Joe died. "I know she has enough money to finance one, but . . . if it is possible . . . I prefer to have a large swimming pool which all the children could use, not a small one like they have now, and which is used only during the summer." Clearly, Rose had been to Saint Coletta and was aware of its facilities. "I know swimming is important to Rosemary and these children. At home she swam well and enjoyed it a good deal, and it is of course of untold advantage to her health." The swimming pool would be built and funded by the trust fund Joe had established for Rosemary nearly four decades earlier.

In March 1970, four months after Joe died, Rose was still in mourning, but she ordered games from a Hyannis toy store to be sent to Rosemary for Easter. She visited Saint Coletta early the following December, flying to Milwaukee to spend a couple of hours with Rosemary before returning to New York in a short, fifteen-hour round trip. On December 17, Rose directed her secretary, Diane Winter, to write Sister Charitas—one of the nuns then caring for Rosemary—and ask her to buy "some little gifts for Rosemary for Christmas from her mother." Rose, Winter wrote to the nun, "really did not know Rosemary's sizes," nor what Rosemary needed. "I wish," Rose wrote in a round-robin letter to the rest of her children on the same day, "you would send [Rosemary] a little gift for Christmas. Any little novelty would probably do, or a cute painting for her room."

Rosemary's longtime physician at Saint Coletta, Dr. Harry A. Waisman, died in March 1971. Waisman, a specialist in pediatric developmental disabilities, had been the director of a research center established at the University of Wisconsin during President Kennedy's administration and funded by the Kennedy Foundation. "I am sure we are all very grateful to him for the advice and treatment he recommended for Rosemary, as her health during the past years has been excellent," Rose wrote to Sister Sheila, the administrator at Saint Coletta. This news, however, left a void in Rosemary's care that Rose was unprepared to accommodate. So she abdicated the responsibility: "I am forwarding your letter to Mrs. Shriver, since I believe she talked over the idea of a physician with her Father when Rosemary first went to St. Coletta. I am sure she will be able to advise you." Eunice had only recently returned to the States after her husband, Sarge, had completed a two-year appointment as ambassador to France. She told Sister Sheila to choose a new doctor for Rosemary, "as you know the best doctors in the area." Dr. Raymond W. M. Chun, a pediatric neurologist and researcher at the University of Wisconsin and a colleague of Waisman's, was recruited by Saint Coletta to take Rosemary as a patient.

The assignment of a new doctor to Rosemary brought changes to her care. New speech, occupational, and physical therapists began working with her. Sister Charitas wrote to report that their efforts seemed to be helping Rosemary, but, she pondered, "if [only] this could have been done twenty some years ago right after the operation . . . of course at that time not much was known of scientific therapy." The elimination of some medication also brought out a talkative Rosemary. "It seems the longer she is off medication the more vocal and expressive she becomes," Sister Mary Charles wrote to Rose. "She at times amazes us with a complete and correct sentence."

More changes were on the horizon. Sister Charitas, who had been caring for Rosemary almost exclusively since 1963, was nearing retirement. Finding her replacement would be easier than transitioning Rosemary to a new caregiver. "Because we feel that Rosemary needs a younger person, one with greater physical vigor and vitality to pursue the program recommended by the professional personnel on our staff, we have accepted Sr. Charitas' retirement," Sister Sheila wrote tactfully. "Sr. Paulus, who has also been with Rosemary for the past several years will assume the major responsibility for her . . . We are pleased with the progress that she made within the year and are hopeful that it will continue." Sister Charitas was not quite ready to retire, however. "My doctor . . . said that organically I am fine for my age," Sister Charitas wrote to Rose. "He thinks if I just took care of Rosemary and nothing else this would be ideal." She told Rose also that "Rosemary responds to me better than to [the other nuns]. So . . . I am happy to do all I can for her." It would be several more months before Sister Paulus and several other nuns would transition to caring for Rosemary full-time and Sister Charitas would move on to a retirement home.

The construction of the new swimming pool at Saint Coletta began in earnest that spring of 1971. Eunice visited in mid-June and approved of the progress, and Rose followed with a visit later that month, after vacationing in Europe for several weeks. Perhaps flustered by the hurried nature of the less-than-twenty-four-hour trip, Rose forgot to give Rosemary a photograph of Joe — in "a rather expensive frame" — which she inadvertently left in her suitcase. Rose's secretary mailed it to the school; there is no record of what Rosemary's reaction was to the photograph, if indeed she had one.

Rosemary spent her fifty-third birthday that fall surrounded by the nuns and fellow residents. She received a canary — she named it Skippy — as a gift. He "sings his little heart out for her," Sister Charitas reported to Rose. "She loves it and calls it by name." Rosemary also had a poodle named Lollie. "Woe be to us if we dare raise our voice to Lollie," the sister confided. "[Rosemary] takes it as a personal offense." Lollie liked to take Rosemary's exercise ball and jump on a chair. Rosemary would scold

Lollie "with all the indignation she can command [by shouting,] 'Lollie, Lollie, get off of there.'"

Sister Charitas transitioned to retirement by November, and three nuns were now responsible for Rosemary's round-the-clock care. Rosemary was finding it "difficult to adjust to three different persons after being used to one person to take care of her," Sister Mary Charles wrote to Rose. "But we feel she is doing well at that. I believe it is an injustice to her to have only one person look after her, and when this person is no longer with her, she seems lost and frustrated." The nuns were struggling with finding a routine that worked for Rosemary, while encouraging her to share in the responsibility of mundane daily activities. "Many times the three of us march with her to the bed room and each one does something for her, or even suggest that she help us with the ceremony," Sister Mary Charles wrote. "I tell her she is the Princess and we are her three attendants. She loves this. After all the main thing Rosemary wants is love and attention." Sister Paulus reported that when she took a rare night out to go to a concert in Madison, Rosemary complained to the other sisters, "I don't like the maid going out!" The sisters were confident, however, that Rosemary could adjust to new ways of doing things.

After failing to make a promised visit in October — she made a month-long trip to Europe instead — Rose flew out to Wisconsin in early December 1971. Something displeased Rose during her visit, because in early January, Eunice fired off a letter complaining that Rosemary was not getting enough exercise. "I would like to emphasize again my mother's and my concern that Rosemary be kept on a good strong physical education program. This should include, I would hope, at least an hour's walk every day, plus a swim once a day when the new pool is built. Even in bad

weather or when it is cold." Madeline Sulad, another of Rose's secretaries, followed up a few days later. "Mrs. Kennedy wanted you
to know," she wrote to Sister Paulus, "that she hopes Rosemary
is swimming now and that she is not having to wait for the new
pool to be built." Rose seems to have forgotten that the old pool
was not accessible in the wintertime. "She feels that, if Rosemary
wears a warm fur coat to and from the pool you now have, she
should be able to enjoy a swim every day."

Rose directed her secretary to write to Saint Coletta to ask that
all of Rosemary's medical reports be sent to her. "Mrs. Kennedy is
very involved at this time in writing her memoirs . . . [but] Mrs.
Kennedy would like to be sure that any progress report on Rosemary be sent to her at the same time one is sent to Mrs. Shriver."
Though she wanted to be more actively involved with Rosemary's
care, Rose did not want sole responsibility. Her dependence on
Eunice in this regard was strong. Days before Christmas 1971,
Rosemary tripped and fell on the flagstone walk in front of her
cottage, landing her in the hospital to receive stitches and an
overnight stay for observation. Though the sisters and health-care
professionals reported the accident to Rose on the twenty-ninth,
Rose may have felt they had not included her as readily as she expected. In March 1972, Rose wrote again to Saint Coletta, reiter-
ating her interest in being informed of Rosemary's status. "Mrs.
Shriver has followed Rosemary's regime very closely during Mr.
Kennedy's prolonged illness, as I was confined at home during
that period, but now I have no obligations and I am free to devote
time and effort to her difficulties." Rose had not been involved
in Rosemary's care since her institutionalization, thirty years earlier. The sudden interest no doubt created some adjustment on
the part of Saint Coletta. "We understand Mrs. Shriver takes most

direct responsibility for Rosemary, but we will make sure that you get copies of all our communications," an administrator from Saint Coletta assured Rose.

Rose's new relationship with Saint Coletta developed at the same time that she was collaborating with ghostwriter Robert Coughlan on her autobiography, *Times to Remember.* Over several months' working with Rose in 1972 and during several interviews, Coughlan pressed the issue of Rosemary's condition and her whereabouts. Though Coughlan knew Rosemary was at Saint Coletta in Wisconsin, Rose took only an incomplete step forward to the truth. "Her mind is gone completely," she assured him. "But that was due to an accident which I don't really discuss. But I am going to say in here [*Times to Remember*] that there was an accident and she became worse. So people won't become discouraged and think that children do become worse but it was due to an accident."

When Coughlan asked Rose to explain the "accident," she refused. But she felt compelled to explain the situation to him again, repeating herself in a way suggestive of someone meaning to create and stick to a narrative "which is true":

> Rose had an accident, and so her condition deteriorated. Because I didn't want to discourage people because she was getting on quite well and she did have this accident. I wasn't going to go into [it,] [but] her condition did deteriorate otherwise they'd think that the child was well until she was 20, 23 or 24 . . . well enough to travel, it would be discouraging for other people to think then she suddenly retrogressed so I said, which is true, that there was an accident and in which her brain was further damaged and so [it] was found expedient and necessary really better for

her to go to this home in Wisconsin where she is very well taken care of with the nuns of St. [Coletta].

Within a month of one of Coughlan's interviews with Rose about Rosemary, in January 1972, Eunice did tell Coughlan what had happened to Rosemary. The "accident" was in fact surgery that removed "a small section of the brain . . . but it didn't work." She told Coughlan that she couldn't understand "why they permitted [it], but that was 30 years ago and it was acceptable then . . . but of course you wouldn't do that today." It seems unlikely that Eunice would not have conferred with her mother on this point before mentioning it to Coughlan. Nevertheless, the fact of the lobotomy was not revealed in *Times to Remember,* and it would remain secret for a decade more.

Rose was forthcoming with Coughlan concerning her feelings that, as the mother of eight other children who also needed her, she had shortchanged them by spending so much time with Rosemary as a child. "And then I think sometimes, of course, children don't always understand the circumstances — when they are little, they don't know why certain things are done, and they feel resentful." Her daughter-in-law Jackie assured her that Jack had never felt slighted, in spite of Rose's belief that he, in particular, did. Rose told Coughlan that the survival of Rosemary and the loss of three of her sons "is a puzzle — is a question, too — why God took three sons who were equipped and wanted to work for the government and for humanity, and left my daughter who is incapacitated. But, as I said, that is one of those things about life we cannot understand — God's ways we can't always understand, as I have said before."

When the children got together to review Coughlan's manuscript of *Times to Remember,* each carried his or her own perspectives and anxieties to the editing of the book, and each made some significant changes. Eunice was particularly troubled by Rose's quoting of Rosemary's childhood letters. "She was sure," historian Laurence Leamer noted, "that the nuns had helped write [the letters], and they made Rosemary seem too normal."

Rose would continue to monitor Rosemary's care from afar. In August 1972, Rose complained to the sisters at Saint Coletta that one of Rosemary's physical-therapy appointments had been canceled because it conflicted with a regularly scheduled hairdressing appointment. "I cannot understand why it happened when Rosemary has so much free time," Rose wrote to Sister Sheila. "Her hair is easily shampooed by one of the Sisters, if necessary, and afterwards rolled on Carmen (electric) curlers, which can be bought at any department store." Two weeks later, Rose wrote again, instructing Sister Paulus to "buy presents for Rosemary and sign the cards from her brother and sisters." She was also interested in sending some artificial flowers for Rosemary's birthday—Rose could not visit herself because she would be leaving for Europe on an extended vacation—but she could not recall the color scheme in Rosemary's cottage. Sister Paulus agreed that the sisters would purchase presents for Rosemary and sign the cards "as you suggested," adding that Rosemary's "walls, drapes, and davenports are green, and the floor is multicolored: red, rust, yellow, brown, so almost any colors would fit in nicely."

Rose's demands from afar may have been particularly trying given that the sisters were already doing so much. In a post-Christmas letter that December, Rose singled out the flaws in Rosemary's appearance in a photograph the nuns had just sent her. Noting, first, her pleasure at receiving a "very good photograph of Rosemary from Sister Prudenz," she proceeded to criticize the clothing the sisters had been asked to purchase for Rosemary. "I think her clothes are usually very pretty, but a dress with a circular design . . . gives her a more rounded silhouette than a dress with a straight pattern." In this regard, Rose did not single Rosemary out for particular criticism. Just a couple of weeks later, Rose wrote to Jean, criticizing her for a fashion faux pas. "I happened to notice that your long evening gloves were rather loose at the top," she noted.

In June 1973, apparently not satisfied with the way the sisters at Saint Coletta managed their time, Rose requested a full accounting of what each nun did for Rosemary. Sister Mary Charles responded by outlining in detail what each sister was responsible for. Sisters Juliane, Paulus, and Mary Charles participated in Rosemary's therapy — walking, swimming, and playing ball — in addition to carrying out daily grooming, laundry, meal preparation, chauffeuring, shopping, and housecleaning. They played games, sang songs, read, and played cards with Rosemary, "do[ing] the little things for her I know she likes," Sister Mary Charles wrote. "We are a family and Rosemary is the object of our love and concern."

Rose told Coughlan in 1972 that she had considered bringing Rosemary home for a visit, "but I don't think that I will. Because she is used to it out there. She has her own home and her own car and people that she is used to being near." Two years later, however, in 1974, Rose decided to bring Rosemary to Hyannis Port for a summer visit, the first trip Rosemary had made to her former home in more than thirty years.

Sister Margaret Ann recalled telling Rosemary that she would be going home for a visit. Rosemary responded with two words: "Bronxville" and "European." Bronxville, of course, was the last home Rosemary knew. "European" represented some of Rosemary's most happy times, when she was living with the Assumption Sisters at Belmont House, and the great historic, cultural, religious, and recreational sites she had toured across Europe. Rose was very anxious about Rosemary's upcoming visit. "I was wondering if we should get a hospital bed for my daughter," Rose wrote to Sister Sheila. Assured that Rosemary would be fine in an ordinary bed, Rose made plans for a short, one-week visit at the end of July.

Saint Coletta preferred to have two sisters accompany Rosemary, but Rose insisted that one was all she would pay for. In the commotion of gathering Rosemary's luggage at the airport, Rosemary wandered off. A frantic search ensued, and she was discovered wandering in the parking lot. This first visit apparently went well enough, though, for Rose to make plans to take Rosemary to Palm Beach for an Easter visit in 1975. But Rose couldn't cope with Rosemary alone. "Of course, I would like you to be here, since she relates to you so well," Rose wrote to Eunice in January, in anticipation of Rosemary's visit, adding that "Pat might be able to do the job also." Rose had become increasingly close to Eunice in the years since Kick's death, and even more so after the deaths of her sons Joe, Jack, and Bobby. When asked which child was her favorite, Rose would later remark, "I don't have a favorite. I love all my children and I have never shown any favoritism . . . never. I've tried to do all I could for all of them. The children tease me about this . . . they all think Eunice is my favorite. Maybe she is . . . just a bit. If she is it is because she's the hardest worker. She has helped me so much in my work with the retarded."

On April 17, 1975, a week or so after the Easter visit, Rose sent a letter to Pat, "to remind you not to forget to visit Rosemary [at Saint Coletta]." Two months later, Rose, who had made only brief and infrequent visits to Saint Coletta, wrote another letter, this time to both Pat and Jean, requesting that they make a trip to see Rosemary. Apparently, they did not fulfill the obligation as Eunice readily did. It seems that the issue of visiting their disabled sister caused tension between siblings. "With reference to Eunice," Rose wrote in response to a complaint from Jean, "she has been a source of great joy and consolation through the years because she keeps in constant touch with Rosemary. You remember I asked you to go see her when Eunice was in Paris [in the late 1960s], but you said you could not make the effort—a great disappointment to me." Jean's response remains unrecorded. But Rose was intolerant of any excuse. The next letter promptly informed Jean that Rose would not accommodate Jean's family at Palm Beach for the Easter holidays. Mother–daughter tension ran deep; as Laurence Leamer observed, Jean remained angry with her mother for many years.

The pace of Rosemary's visits increased; her Easter 1975 visit was followed by another at the end of the year. Jim Connor, the family's driver and sometime bodyguard, later recalled Rosemary's arriving for a visit to Palm Beach accompanied by two nuns over the Christmas holiday. Once at the house, Rosemary "came bouncing up the steps there and she said, 'Mommy. You momma, me baby.'" Whether Rosemary bounced up the stairs is questionable. Another family staff member recalled Rosemary occasionally saying "Kathleen." The photographer who had come to take the annual holiday photos remembered Rosemary being very "fidgety," so much so that the family questioned whether she should be made to sit for the portrait.

By the late 1970s, Rosemary was making twice-yearly trips to her family's two residences. The regular visits put a great strain on Rose, especially as she aged. Rose Kennedy's secretary Barbara Gibson, whom Rosemary called "Arbarb," recalled Rose becoming increasingly agitated and nervous as the day of Rosemary's arrival approached. With Rosemary present, sadness and anxiety would envelop Rose. Gibson, who later erroneously claimed that Rosemary was never mentally disabled but merely dyslexic, witnessed the estrangement between Rose and Rosemary. One day, while Rose was swimming with Gibson in the pool at Hyannis Port, Rosemary's aides from Saint Coletta took her out for a swim as well. The nuns encouraged Rosemary to get in the pool while Rose was there, but she refused. Gibson watched as Rosemary, seated in a chair instead, looked "straight ahead, like a dutiful child who has been punished for misbehavior." Rose whispered, "Oh, Rosie, what did we do to you?" Rosemary's nurses and companions found the trips to Palm Beach and Hyannis Port stressful, too, recognizing the frustration and alienation that Rosemary felt in her mother's presence.

Kerry McCarthy, Rose's great-niece and the granddaughter of Joe's sister Loretta, also recalled the emotional toll Rosemary's visits took on Rose. On one occasion, Rose tried to find a connection with Rosemary, asking her if she remembered Kerry's grandmother Loretta. Stroking Rosemary's black hair, kissing her gently, and hugging her while she watched television, Rose became wistful. "Rosie . . . Rosie . . . Rosie . . . Remember when you learned to write and you wrote Aunt Loretta from England? Remember that, Rosie, remember?" Rosemary just ignored her, rocking back and forth in her chair. Rose began to sob uncontrollably. Kerry helped her aging aunt back upstairs.

Rose could not find new common ground—she relied on the old habits and former ways, creating stress for Rosemary and disappointment for herself. Barbara Gibson often noted Rose's distant attitude. She recalled Rose's instructions to throw away Rosemary's diaries that had been uncovered during a search through family papers in the early 1970s, when Rose was working on her memoir. Troubled by the request to dispose of the diaries, Gibson — who insisted Rosemary had been a normal but psychologically troubled young woman — says she retrieved them from the trash. Gibson believed that Rose was trying to erase any documentation of Rosemary's true mental capacity. She claimed that the Kennedy Presidential Library in Boston refused to accept the diaries into its collection when she offered them. Interestingly, in writing two books about the Kennedys, Gibson quoted only from letters already in the possession of the library, though she attributed those quotes to the supposed diaries.

What did Rosemary understand about the many joys and losses the rest of the family had endured together over the prior thirty years? Some reports claimed that Rosemary had secretly attended her brother's presidential inauguration, but that is not true. She remained in Wisconsin, watching the swearing-in on television with staff and friends. The television would also reveal President Kennedy's assassination to her. According to the *Milwaukee Sentinel,* "President Kennedy's sister, Rosemary, learned of his assassination while watching a television broadcast from Dallas, Tex., where he was shot." Confirmation from a spokesperson at the school was chilling: "She knows he is dead . . . She was watching on television." Jack had been her escort to so many dances and social events when they were young. Both Joe and Jack had lovingly teased her and treated her like the little sister she was. Bobby had grown up and become a man, but he, too, was assassinated, in 1968. Her brothers had loved her, she had felt their love, and now they were gone.

The Moores were gone, as well — Eddie had died in 1952 and Mary in 1964. They had been like parents to Rosemary. Mary had visited Rosemary at Craig House, and continued visiting once Rosemary was settled in Wisconsin, maintaining the close bond she and Eddie had shared with Rosemary since her birth.

Thrown back into the family homes with her now-mature siblings, who had spouses and numerous children she did not know, Rosemary showed confusion and frustration. Encounters between Rose and Rosemary were often short and scarring. Rosemary, Sister Margaret Ann believed, blamed Rose for not protecting her, as a child expects a mother to do.

Eunice, Teddy, and Rosemary's numerous nieces and nephews helped make her visits more pleasant. As Rose herself became feeble, senile, and uncommunicative during the last decade of her life, the rest of the family ensured that Rosemary's visits were more enjoyable, and perhaps less stressful. They had parties for her with her favorite cakes and sweets, music, and more. Rosemary beamed with delight.

Eunice visited with Rosemary far more than any of the siblings. As she had done when they were teenagers and young adults, Eunice accompanied Rosemary to church, to restaurants and shopping, on long walks, on sailing excursions, and to the beach. They had gone dancing together, seen the sights of Europe together, and witnessed the ordination of a pope together. Now, as Rosemary's caregiver, Eunice vowed to do many of the things they had done as youngsters, and more. She took Rosemary to Special Olympics events, for instance, determined that Rosemary remain active and engaged. If Rosemary was reluctant, Eunice would be firm with her. As a child and young woman, Eunice had been able to soothe Rosemary's rages and to elicit cooperation from her when no one else in the family could. Now, Eunice had seemingly less patience, though more purpose.

Barbara Gibson recalled watching Eunice force Rosemary into

swimming or sailing when she did not want to do those things. Though Eunice was acting as the siblings had once done when they were young—cajoling and criticizing one another for failure to comply with an activity—one of Rosemary's companions, Sister Juliane, disliked such forced treatment for Rosemary. "Eunice has no compassion for human weakness," the nun remarked. Eunice's son Anthony Shriver recalls one afternoon's sail to a local Cape Cod restaurant with his mother, Rosemary, and a friend. While they were at the restaurant, the weather turned foul. Eunice insisted they sail home in spite of the storm. Anthony, reluctant but not one to challenge his mother, tried to help the unwilling Rosemary back into the boat, a difficult endeavor. Frustrated, Rosemary burst out, "Damn Anthony, get away from me." In spite of the fact that her words were generally limited and that she often used phrases repetitively, Rosemary had no trouble expressing herself in this instance.

Life with Rosemary could be unpredictable. During one outing, Eunice took her sister to Saint Peter's in Chicago for Sunday Mass. Afterward, Eunice and the two nuns from Saint Coletta who were accompanying Rosemary stopped to look at religious books displayed in the vestibule of the church. Bored or distracted, Rosemary wandered away. Eunice and the sisters prayed and searched while dozens of Chicago police officers looked for Rosemary along the city's busy sidewalks. "If you know Rosemary," Sister Sheila later told a reporter, "you could understand how that could happen. She likes to walk. The rest of the Kennedys are browsers." Five hours later, she was spotted several blocks from the church, looking in store windows, by a local television reporter. "Are you looking for Eunice?" the reporter asked. Rosemary replied yes, but the reporter wasn't so sure Rosemary knew where she was or what she was doing.

Eunice's children became extremely close to Rosemary, too. As their disabled aunt, Rosemary would deeply move them as children and adults. Anthony Shriver became founder and chairman of Best Buddies International, a global volunteer organization that facilitates employment opportunities and leadership development for people with intellectual and developmental disabilities through one-on-one friendship and mentoring programs. Once settled with a family of his own, Anthony built an additional room to accommodate Rosemary's visits to his Miami home. "A Kennedy through and through," he believes his aunt to have been, someone whose personality shone through even with limited language and physical abilities. "She was very strong and determined," sometimes frightening Anthony's young children with her forcefulness. But her love of swimming brought them all together in the pool.

Anthony's brother Timothy, who replaced their mother as chairman and CEO of Special Olympics in 2003, remembers Rosemary being a frequent visitor to his family home when he was a child. Though her language was terribly limited—often she repeated the words *babies, mother,* and *Eunice*—he remembers that she loved to take long walks, swim, and play card games. She loved to eat sweets, often demanding dessert before the main course at dinner. She loved to be "prettied up" and was easily brought to smiles by a simple compliment about her hair or outfit. As Rosemary aged, however, her mobility became hampered, slowly decreasing over time until finally, in her last years, she used a wheelchair.

Even though Eunice claimed her work with the disabled was not inspired by Rosemary, both Anthony and Tim believe otherwise. Perhaps Eunice, who so idolized her brother Jack, could not imagine that it was her sister Rosemary who had helped define the family's passion for the disabled. In fact, Tim believes that Rosemary belonged at the center of the Kennedy family story, because it was she, through her self-determination and the struggles that she faced, who had transformed them all. Certainly, both nephews feel that Rosemary inspired them—Tim to carry on his mother's work at Special Olympics, and Anthony through Best Buddies. "The interest [Rosemary] sparked in my family towards people with special needs," Anthony claims, "will one day go down as the greatest accomplishment that any Kennedy has made on a global basis."

Shriver brothers Robert and Mark have also found ways to support the family commitment to the disabled. With the musician Bono, Robert helped found DATA (Debt, AIDS, Trade in Africa), which advocates for the eradication of poverty through education, debt reduction, development assistance, and campaigning for access to treatment for AIDS and malaria in Africa; and Mark serves as senior vice president of U.S. programs for Save the Children. Eunice's only daughter, Maria Shriver, sits on the boards of Special Olympics and Best Buddies, and has earned two Emmy Awards for her documentary film work on Alzheimer's disease, a debilitating dementia that claimed her father Sarge's life and memories.

Their mother, however, would be the most powerful moving force behind the cause of the disabled, pushing public and private institutions and foundations to sponsor and provide services, to fund and conduct research, and to make accommodations for the intellectually and physically challenged. Once locked away or institutionalized, people with developmental, intellectual, psychological, and physical disabilities can now participate in life and integrate in communities in ways that seemed impossible when Rosemary was a child and young adult. They are able to go to school, live independently, and receive life-saving medical and psychological care and mobility accommodations—and more. Eunice's son Tim revealed in an interview that when he asked his mother what drove her so hard, she told him, "anger." He said, "After watching the struggles of her sister and visiting institutions and seeing this enormous amount of human suffering, and at the same time coming from a place where women didn't have equal opportunity in sports, she just couldn't take it anymore." *Sports Illustrated* called Eunice a "revolutionary," but Rosemary's life was the spark firing Eunice's sixty-year effort on behalf of the disabled. Rosemary, Eunice believed, "sensitized . . . us all to the gifts of the vulnerable and the weak."

ROSEMARY AND EUNICE'S brother Ted, a senator from Massachusetts for more than forty-seven years, would take over as legislative champion for the cause of the disabled by initiating, sponsoring, and supporting hundreds of pieces of legislation. He believed that Rosemary "taught us the worth of every human being." Working tirelessly and often across the partisan aisle with Senate and House colleagues, like Orrin Hatch, a Republican senator from Utah, Ted helped pass major social and civil rights legislation. His efforts include the Education for All Handicapped Children Act (1975), the Americans with Disabilities Act (ADA) and the Child Care Act (both passed in 1990), and the Ryan White AIDS Care Act of 1990; he increased funding for the National Institutes of Health and many more educational, housing, medical, and support-services programs. The ADA specifically prohibited discrimination on the basis of disability, forcing the inclusion of millions of people with disabilities in education, housing, employment, sports, and more. Hatch said that even though he and Kennedy differed much on policy and philosophy, he "never doubted for a minute [Ted's] commitment to help the elderly, the ill, and those Americans who have been on the outside looking in for far too long."

The Kennedys did not do this work alone. They were often guided by dozens of organizations, agencies, and institutions serving and representing the disabled. Parents' groups and specialized organizations representing the blind, deaf, physically disabled, mentally ill, and others demanded awareness, support, accommodations, research, and funding. And the Kennedys heard them. When Ted achieved passage of the ADA, he said, "Many of us have been touched by others with disabilities. My sister Rosemary is retarded; my son lost his leg to cancer. And others who support the legislation believe in it for similar special reasons. I cannot be unmindful of the extraordinary contributions of those who have been lucky enough to have members of their families or children who are facing the same challenges and know what this legislation means."

AS ROSEMARY AGED, her angry flashes of temper diminished dramatically. As she learned to soothe herself and communicate her needs more effectively, Rosemary settled into a comfortable routine, fostering a sense of happiness and peacefulness that had often eluded her as a younger woman. Every transition continued to be difficult, but the sensitivity of the nuns and the awareness on the part of the Kennedys to this consideration, honed over decades, helped smooth anxious moments. At one point Rosemary needed surgery for an injured knee. Aware that a hospital setting could generate tremendous fear and apprehension, the family arranged for her to spend several days in the hospital beforehand, to become acclimated. With a Saint Coletta aide at her side at all times, the surgery and recovery proceeded with minimal trauma.

The Kennedy wealth and Rosemary's personal trust fund could pay for such attentive care.

Sister Margaret Ann became Rosemary's consistent companion at Saint Coletta for the last two decades of her life. Rosemary's daily routine varied little—she liked it that way—with the exception of intermittent doctors' appointments or trips into Jefferson to go shopping or to have dinner. At six thirty every morning, Sister Margaret Ann would turn on the lights in Rosemary's bedroom. "Rosemary's very cooperative. She helps you turn her out of bed. Usually I put her shoes on right away," Sister Margaret Ann told historian Laurence Leamer, "and she will push her foot into the shoe . . . She's been putting her foot out for shoes all these years." After taking her to the bathroom to wash up, Sister Margaret Ann helped Rosemary get dressed. "Her arms go out and her feet go out, and she will button her buttons. I will take out a couple things and make sure they match, and I'll let her choose. I know that when I buy something new she will choose the new thing."

Daily activities included a simple volleyball game with a balloon or some other manual play to challenge Rosemary physically and mentally. A swim therapist would work with her in the pool, funded with $300,000 from Rosemary's trust fund, and often Rosemary did not want to leave the water. She generally ate lunch in her own cottage, though sometimes she shared a meal with other residents and staff in the communal cafeteria. There were certain people with whom Rosemary preferred to spend time. They would hold hands, play games, and look at pictures together. Sister Margaret Ann noted that people were drawn to Rosemary even with her limited speech and mobility. She had "a magnetic personality. I go to the mother house and everybody asks 'Where's Rosemary?'" Evenings were spent quietly in her cottage, sometimes watching television.

Rosemary loved music and dance, though sometimes it was a challenge to get her to participate, and gentle persuasion was employed. She attended daily Mass. "She knows her prayers by heart, like 'Hail Mary' and the meal prayer," Sister Margaret Ann told Leamer. "I think mass means a lot to her. The word 'Jesus' means a lot to her." The sister believed these were indelible memories etched into her mind from the years before her surgery. Her presurgery life remained a mystery to her, however, Sister Margaret Ann believed. "There's a picture on the wall of Rosemary in a long dress with her mother waiting to be presented to the king. I think she remembers, but it's hard to tell because she can't tell you. But if you have a program like the Academy Awards with long dresses, she loves it, and she sits there watching so happy." That picture, from the debutante ball in London in 1938, also included Kathleen in her beautiful gown.

Rosemary Kennedy died at the age of eighty-six on January 7, 2005, at Fort Atkinson Memorial Hospital in Wisconsin, near Saint Coletta. She had outlived her mother by ten years. News of Rosemary's death noted that her sisters Eunice, Jean, and Pat and her brother Ted were at her side.

IN A SPEECH Rose gave around the time of her memoir's publication, for the first time she credited Rosemary with making a contribution of value: "I cannot attempt to judge that which has been given to me nor that which has been taken away. I could not begin to measure the pride, the pain, the enduring love, but I do sense and I do believe that Rosemary's gift to me is equal to the gifts of my other children. By her presence I feel that she, too, has asked something terribly important of us. With her life itself she too has shown us direction, given us purpose and a way to serve. That has been her gift." By the time Rose died, in January 1995, at the age of 104, she may actually have come to believe those words.

Eunice did. In a speech she gave in 2007, Eunice revealed that

> my life [has been] lucky in the adversity I encountered. I am lucky that I experienced the sting of rejection as a woman who was told that the real power was not for me. I am lucky that I saw my mother and my sister, Rosemary, treated with the most unbearable rejection. I am lucky that I have had to confront political and social injustice all over the world throughout my career.

> You might say, "Why are you lucky to have had such difficult experiences?" The answer is quite simple: the combination of the love of my family and the awful sting of rejection helped me develop the confidence I needed to believe that I could make a difference in a positive direction. It's really that simple: love gave me confidence and adversity gave me purpose.

> You will not be surprised to know that I believe that those were also the experiences that shaped President Kennedy. Truthfully, I believe Rosemary's rejection had far more to do with the brilliance of his Presidency than anyone understands. Yes, he was our country's greatest champion of what we used to call "mental retardation." To this day, his legacy of innovation in creating NICHD, The University Affiliated programs, and the President's Council remain unmatched in American History. But beyond the specific work he did for people with intellectual disabilities, I

believe it was Rosemary's influence that sensitized him . . .
Remarkably, I think I can say that not one author among
the thousands who have written about him has understood
what it was really like to be a brother of a person with
intellectual disability. And tonight, I want to say what I
have never said before: more than any one single individual, Rosemary made the difference.

Through the loving, indomitable spirit of Rosemary, the Kennedy family found one of its greatest missions, and in doing so
changed millions of lives.

Author's Note

I VIVIDLY REMEMBER reading Rosemary's obituary in the *Boston Globe* in early January 2005. I knew who she was, but I was quite surprised that she had lived so long and in such obscurity. I was struck by the barely essential facts presented in the obituary and sensed that there was much more to her story. What had happened to Rosemary, and why didn't we know more? Surely, in the twenty-first century, the fact of intellectual disability and mental illness in families was no longer something to hide. I would soon discover otherwise.

I would not have the opportunity to begin researching Rosemary's life until 2008, after I had finished another book project. Fortunately, I live near Boston, with easy access to the John F. Kennedy Presidential Library and Museum, where Rose and Joe Kennedy's personal papers had been deposited. Only recently had Rose Kennedy's diaries and scrapbooks been opened to the public, so I was among the first people to see many of these intimate records for the first time.

Within a year, however, my work would be suddenly derailed.

My then nineteen-year-old son was diagnosed with schizophrenia. Suddenly, our family was faced with how to provide a safe, therapeutic environment where we hoped he could be "cured." Options were few and extraordinarily expensive. We sent him far away to highly recommended residential treatment programs, and we were convinced he would get better. We missed him terribly, and he missed us. Compounding our pain was the realization that the stigma of mental illness is still alive and well. Many people we knew — some family members, friends, associates — stumbled in conversations with us about his diagnosis. Some blamed us for his condition. We felt inadequate and, at times, hopeless.

Once my son stabilized — with the aid of good clinicians and thoughtful caregivers — I was able to return to Rosemary. It was with a new, more personal understanding that I now viewed Rosemary's experience and her family's reactions.

Scores of biographies have been published about the Kennedy family and its individual members during the past sixty years; many of these have been invaluable sources for my writing on the Kennedys and are found in the notes for this book. In these accounts, though, Rosemary is treated as a peripheral member of the family, an outlier whose contributions mattered little to the larger story of her famous parents and siblings. Early biographers relied on what the Kennedy family told them about Rosemary or on what they could uncover through press coverage; both of these sources were tightly controlled versions of the truth. During the 1980s, Doris Kearns Goodwin was given unprecedented access to Joseph P. Kennedy's personal papers, held by the family foundation in New York City, for her biography *The Fitzgeralds and the Kennedys*. Goodwin interviewed dozens of family members, business associates, and friends of the family, who supplied her with new information about the Kennedy lives. Goodwin delivered the clearest understanding up until then of Rosemary's disabilities. Most important, she was the first to reveal that Rosemary had undergone a lobotomy. But Rosemary was one of scores of characters in Goodwin's book. I knew there was more to be found in the newly opened Rose Kennedy collection at the John F. Kennedy Library.

IN THE YEARS since Goodwin's work, numerous biographers have retold the same snippets of stories about Rosemary, positioning her as a minor figure in the lives of the Kennedys and revealing little more than what Goodwin had already uncovered. I believed that if I could put Rosemary at the center of this dynamic family story, where she belongs, it would open a new chapter on the roles of the Kennedy women and the powerful impact one sibling had on her entire extended family.

During the 1990s, the Kennedy family foundation gifted the Joseph P. Kennedy Papers to the John F. Kennedy Library in Boston, at the same time placing severe restrictions on access to them by researchers. Over the past two decades, the deed of gift has allowed for the periodic release of previously closed material, offering fresh resources for biographers. Rose's collection of papers complemented the larger and less accessible Joseph P. Kennedy Papers, and the two collections together revealed more deeply the personal thoughts and deeds of not only Rose and Joe but their children as well. While Rosemary's personal paper trail had been quite thin—a few letters were scattered through both collections—the most recent and broadest unveiling of both collections offered a whole new chapter in the quest to understand Rosemary's life. Unlike other Kennedy biographers, I have had access to all of Rosemary's known letters, and some of them are seen here for the first time.

Letters from some of Rosemary's teachers and caregivers illuminate for the first time the array of educational and therapeutic settings Rosemary experienced. I was intrigued by Mother Eugenie Isabel's success with Rosemary at the Assumption School in England. That led me to research Dr. Maria Montessori and to meet with the Assumption Sisters in Worcester, Massachusetts. They shared recollections and their personal file on Mother Isabel, who had been taught personally by Montessori. Mother Isabel possessed remarkable gifts as a teacher and spiritual guide, and her influence is still felt today in Montessori classrooms across this country and abroad.

I viewed these newly available sources within the context of their times. I was able to paint a disturbing portrait of the societal attitudes toward the intellectually disabled—attitudes that informed Rose and Joe's flawed decisions in their desperate search to find medical and psychiatric "cures" for Rosemary's disabilities. They faced a fragmented and indifferent medical, social, and cultural environment—an environment hauntingly revealed in many letters from psychiatrists, educators, pediatricians, and other physicians that spanned decades of Kennedy frustration, desperation, and profound denial. However, dozens and dozens of letters that Rose and Joe wrote to and received from Rosemary's governesses, doctors, guardians, and teachers, as well as business associates, lawyers, and Catholic priests and nuns, among others, reveal near-constant attention to Rosemary's needs. This correspondence allowed me to piece together an accurate progression of the events that led to Rosemary's tragedy.

In addition to the letters from so many of those employed by Rose and Joe to care for Rosemary, the Kennedy bills and receipts and other items related to Rosemary's education, housing, health, and social life were revealing. Much of this material remains inaccessible to the public and researchers; pink sheets marked "Withdrawal" are sprinkled throughout the collections. In subject files labeled as correspondence related to Rosemary Kennedy, withdrawal sheets indicate the removal of hundreds of documents dating between 1923 and the 1970s. This leaves significant gaps in the historical record. A large amount of the withdrawn material is associated with Rosemary's treatment and care after her lobotomy. Because of the Health Insurance Portability and Accountability Act (HIPAA), sponsored by Rosemary's brother Senator Edward M. Kennedy and passed by Congress in 1996, the medical records related to Rosemary's surgery, performed in the fall of 1941 by Drs. Freeman and Watts, are permanently inaccessible. That act, combined with the fact that Rosemary could not tell anyone what happened that November 1941 day at George Washington University Hospital, ensures that her medical information will remain inaccessible in perpetuity.

Nevertheless, contemporary medical journals, scientific research, and popular articles of the day informed my understanding of the thinking and methods of health-care professionals who were deeply misguided by their own prejudices. My research into the state of treatment for people with disabilities and mental illness in prewar America reveals a profoundly ignorant medical establishment and educational community. And my discovery that Freeman and Watts's lobotomy research, including detailed case studies, appeared within months of Rosemary's lobotomy brings us chillingly close to her tragic experience.

Additionally, I was fortunate to be given access to the private personal papers of one of the Massachusetts camp directors who spent a month with Rosemary in the summer of 1940 and to interview her daughter, Terry Marotta. I interviewed Anthony and Timothy Shriver, two of Eunice Kennedy Shriver's sons, who recalled memories of Rosemary and her frequent visits to their home. They, like most of their generation of Kennedys, are as unclear about Rosemary's early life as a Kennedy, her disabilities, and the reason for her tragic lobotomy as are most historians.

As the mother of a disabled child, I am grateful to Rosemary and to her siblings, particularly her sister Eunice, whose advocacy continues to give us the language to forge ahead with more conversations and action on behalf of the mentally ill and the disabled.

Acknowledgments

I OWE A TREMENDOUS debt of gratitude to the John F. Kennedy Library Foundation and the archivists at the John F. Kennedy Presidential Library and Museum. Their patience and dedication to providing an exemplary research environment, their extraordinary knowledge of the library collections, and their familiarity with resources beyond the library made my work possible. Stephen Plotkin, Michael Desmond, Stacey Chandler, Abigail Malangone, Karen Abramson, and the various interns whom I met over the years in Textual Reference were always cheerful and supportive, and offered valuable suggestions and guidance when I hit many a brick wall. To Maryrose Grossman and Laurie Austin in the Audiovisual Archives, thank you for tracking down every photograph of Rosemary you could find, and for pointing out film clips that I would have overlooked. These images gave me a glimpse of the vibrant young woman Rosemary was on the eve of her lobotomy, making the surgery all the more tragic to me.

I am grateful for early interviews with Anthony Shriver and

Timothy Shriver. Though they admittedly knew little about Rosemary's life before the surgery, their love for her was clear through their reminiscences and helped me see her as a much-loved woman whose life had a tremendous impact on their entire family. Charles Baker, one of Joseph P. Kennedy's nephews, remembered Joe Kennedy Sr. as a powerful force within the family whose decisions were never questioned. I deeply appreciate the Religious of the Assumption in Worcester, Massachusetts: Sisters Therese DuRoss, Nuala Cotter, and Coreena Garcia provided not only their personal recollections and biographical file on Mother Isabel Eugenie but also a warm afternoon with hot tea, cookies, and an introduction to their religious order and its mission.

I am very grateful to Terry Marotta—a beautiful writer and neighbor—who shared with me her personal family papers detailing her mother and aunt's experiences with Rosemary at the camp they ran in western Massachusetts, and Rose's callous treatment of them. Dr. Reese Cosgrove explained the current state of the practice of surgical lobotomy—an operation rarely performed today and highly regulated—and the important positive outcomes it can offer for certain severely mentally ill patients.

I am humbled by the extraordinary work of the many, many biographers who have researched and written about the Kennedy family over the past fifty years. I could not have written this biography if they had not conducted many of their interviews with Kennedy family members, friends, and acquaintances who are now gone. Some of them were privy to documents that are no longer available to historians because of legal issues and retractions by the Kennedy family. Fortunately, through their published works, I have been able to patch together many missing pages that have been pulled from the Kennedy family collections at the Kennedy Library. I hope that someday all the documents in those collections, with the exception of medical records protected by HIPAA laws, will be opened for all researchers to access.

This book could not have happened without the unwavering support of my agent, Doe Coover, who saw Rosemary's obituary at the same time that I did and knew that I should write about her. Thank you, Doe, for your excellent diplomacy, business sense, good humor, fabulous lunches, and deep friendship. And to my editor, Deanne Urmy, who is the best editor I have ever worked with, thank you for your patience. Your extraordinary eye for detail and skillful editing have made this a far better biography than I could ever have dreamed of writing.

And to my husband, Spencer, who, along with Doe and Deanne, endured years of stops and starts to this project, thank you for your loving patience and support, and for falling for Rosemary along with me. I could not have done this without you.

Notes

ABBREVIATIONS

DKG   Doris Kearns Goodwin, *The Fitzgeralds and the Kennedys* (New York: Simon & Schuster, 1987)

DN   David Nasaw, *The Patriarch: The Remarkable Life and Turbulent Times of Joseph P. Kennedy* (New York: Penguin, 2012)

EKS   Eunice Kennedy Shriver

EM   Edward Moore

EMK   Edward Moore Kennedy

JFK   John Fitzgerald Kennedy

JFKPL   John F. Kennedy Presidential Library and Museum, Boston, Massachusetts

JPK   Joseph P. Kennedy Sr.

JPKJR   Joseph P. Kennedy Jr.

JPKP   Joseph P. Kennedy Papers, John F. Kennedy Presidential Library and Museum, Boston, Massachusetts

KK   Kathleen "Kick" Kennedy Hartington

LL, *The Kennedy Men*

           Laurence Leamer, *The Kennedy Men, 1901–1963: The Laws of the Father* (New York: Morrow, 2001)

LL, *The Kennedy Women*
> Laurence Leamer, *The Kennedy Women: The Saga of an American Family* (New York: Villard, 1994)

RFK   Rose Fitzgerald Kennedy

RFKP   Rose Fitzgerald Kennedy Papers, John F. Kennedy Presidential Library and Museum, Boston, Massachusetts

RMK   Rosemary Kennedy

TTR   Rose Fitzgerald Kennedy, *Times to Remember* (1974; repr., New York: Doubleday, 1995)

1. A HOME BIRTH

page

2 *The closing of theaters:* "City Sends Even Nurses to Boston to Fight Spread," *Bridgeport (Conn.) Telegram,* September 20, 1918.

this viral infection: J. K. Taubenberger and D. M. Morens, "1918 Influenza: The Mother of All Pandemics," *Emerging Infectious Diseases* 12, no. 1 (January 2006): 15–22, http://wwwnc.cdc.gov/eid/article/12/1/pdfs/05-0979.pdf.

"All the city was dying": "Recollections of Miss East and Miss Franklin," n.d., School of Public Health, Department of Nursing, box 8, folder 1, Simmons College Archives, Boston.

Nearly seven thousand residents: Alfred J. Crosby, *America's Forgotten Pandemic: The Influenza of 1918* (Cambridge: Cambridge University Press, 1989), 60–61.

"If during the absence": Charles Sumner Bacon, *Obstetrical Nursing: A Manual for Nurses and Students and Practitioners of Medicine* (Philadelphia: Lea & Febiger, 1915), 151.

3 *She could not give Rose an anesthetic:* Barbara Gibson and Ted Schwartz, *Rose Kennedy and Her Family: The Best and Worst of Their Lives and Times* (New York: Birch Lane Press, 1995), 47.

The nurse demanded: Ibid., 54, based on interview with Barbara Gibson, Rose Kennedy's longtime secretary.

"I had such confidence": TTR, 66, 68.

Dr. Good and his colleagues: "Children Born at Home," diaries, August 23, 1971, RFKP, box 5; see also ibid., 68.

4 *When holding Rose's legs together:* LL, *The Kennedy Women,* 137, based on interviews with Luella Hennessey Donovan, a long-time Kennedy nursemaid and governess who did not help deliver Rosemary but spent many intimate years with the family; and an interview with Eunice Kennedy Shriver by Robert Coughlan, February 26, 1972, RFKP, box 10.

"A dainty girl": "Ex-Mayor Thrice a Grandfather," *Boston Sunday Globe,* September 15, 1918.

"sweet and peaceable": "Children Born at Home," RFKP, box 5; see also *TTR,* 131.

"The quiet and peace": "Children Born at Home," RFKP, box 10.

5 *This pace:* DN, 57.

6 *Classrooms were horribly overcrowded:* Martin Lazerson, *Origins of the Urban School: Public Education in Massachusetts, 1870–1915* (Cambridge, Mass.: Harvard University Press, 1971), 11–12.

7 *Between the late 1890s and 1920:* William DeMarco, *Ethnics and Enclaves: Boston's Italian North End* (Ann Arbor, Mich.: UMI Research Press, 1981), 21–24; see also Twelfth Census of the United States (1900), Thirteenth Census of the United States (1910), Fourteenth Census of the United States (1920), U.S. Bureau of the Census, Massachusetts, Suffolk County.

His decision to run: DKG, 105–6.

8 *He had run against Patrick Kennedy:* TTR, 23.

9 *Rose during this heady time:* Scrapbook, 1907–1929, RFKP, box 121. An undated news clipping indicates that Rose was voted the "most beautiful girl graduate" by the male graduates of Dorchester High School. Rose later revealed that it was her father who used a friendly journalist to write up the article—much to Rose's embarrassment, because she believed it was not true.

"his love for her": DKG, 91.

"To my mind": Ibid., 105.

10 *"My father":* TTR, 53–54.

her father was excessively conservative: Ibid., 23.

11 *Frustrated by the discrimination:* Thomas H. O'Connor, *The Boston Irish: A Political History* (Boston: Northeastern University Press, 1995), 150.

12 *"safety valve":* Lazerson, *Origins of the Urban School,* 19–23.

"public schools were training grounds": Interview with nephew Edward Fitzgerald in DKG, 104.

Under the leadership: Joseph W. Riordan, *The First Half Century of St. Ignatius Church and College* (San Francisco: Crocker, 1905), 199.

"the peril of the age": "People in Print," *Donahoe's Magazine* 56 (July–December 1906): 385–86.

13 *Fitzgerald enrolled his children:* DKG, 152–55.

Rose was eager: Ibid., 132.

Fifty-five percent: Boston, Massachusetts, School Committee, *Documents of the School Committee of the City of Boston for the Year 1910* (Boston: City of Boston Printing Department, 1910), 14–20; *only 12 percent of all students:* "School Document No. 16–1907," *Annual Report of the School Committee of the City of Boston, 1907* (Boston: Municipal Printing Office, 1907), 38.

From 1900 to 1920: Barbara Miller Solomon, *In the Company of Educated Women: A History of Women and Higher Education in America* (New Haven, Conn.: Yale University Press, 1985), 46–47, 63–64; see also Thomas D. Snyder, ed., *120 Years of American Education: A Statistical Self Portrait* (Washington, D.C.: National Center for Education Studies, 1993), 69.

14 *"There was screaming":* Interview with Kerry McCarthy in LL, *The Kennedy Women,* 61.

15 *"heeding the siren call":* DKG, 142–44.

"I was furious": LL, *The Kennedy Women,* 61.

16 *"My greatest regret":* Interview with RFK in DKG, 144.

"the propagation of the devotion": Remigius Lafort and Cardinal John Farley, *The Catholic Church in America, Undertaken to Celebrate the Golden Jubilee of His Holiness, Pope Pius X,* vol. 2, *The Religious Communities of Women* (New York: Catholic Editing Company, 1914), 68.

"I knew Latin": Interview with RFK in DKG, 146.

"ethics, metaphysics": Lafort and Farley, *Religious Communities of Women,* 445–46.

17 *Rose's course of study:* Tracy Schier and Cynthia Russett, eds., *Cath-*

olic Women's Colleges in America (Baltimore, Md.: Johns Hopkins University Press, 2003), 46–47, 264.

"Let religion be": Women of the Spirit: A History of Convent of the Sacred Heart, Greenwich, 1848–1998 (Greenwich, Conn.: Convent of the Sacred Heart, 1999), 11–12.

"Under such training": Lafort and Farley, *Religious Communities of Women,* 497.

"It took teamwork": TTR, 50.

Her father pushed other suitors: DKG, 219–20.

Even Fitzgerald's chauffeur: TTR, 50–57.

18 *The grandson of immigrants* and following: For a history of Irish Boston, see O'Connor, *Boston Irish,* 128–65.

19 *it was a privilege to travel: TTR,* 26.

"practical things of this world": Ibid., 27–28.

"foundation and the crowning point": Women of the Spirit, 8.

"pure like Mary": Daughters of the Charity of Saint Vincent De Paul, *Manual of the Children of Mary, for the Use of All the Establishments, Schools, and Orphan Asylums of the Sisters of Charity* (New York: P. J. Kennedy, 1878), 9–10.

"Purity, Humility": Ibid., 63.

20 *"It came to me":* Interview with RFK in DKG, 185.

"a model of perfection": Daughters of the Charity of Saint Vincent De Paul, *Manual of the Children of Mary,* 448.

Rose wrote home: TTR, 31, 34.

21 *"more and more in love":* Interview with RFK in DKG, 218.

His schemes and following: DKG, chaps. 10–16; and DN, 36–55.

22 *After a honeymoon:* "Daughter of Former Mayor to Wed Today," *Boston Globe,* October 7, 1914.

"We owe them": "Mary and Eddie Moore," 9; "Diary Notebook: A Married Life, 1 of 2," August 23, 1971; both in RFKP, box 5.

23 *"They derived vicarious pleasure":* "Mary and Eddie Moore," RFKP, box 5.

Mary Moore helped: "Children Born at Home," RFKP, box 5.

loved them like cherished: TTR, 59–60.

"shadow, his stand-in": Gloria Swanson, *Swanson on Swanson: An Autobiography* (New York: Pocket Books, 1980), 357.

2. THE MAKING OF A MOTHER

24 *"There were no signs"* and following: *TTR,* 131.

25 *"bear with submission":* Daughters of the Charity of Saint Vincent De Paul, *Manual of the Children of Mary, for the Use of All the Establishments, Schools, and Orphan Asylums of the Sisters of Charity* (New York: P. J. Kennedy, 1878), 68–69.

26 *"impression of the suffragettes":* LL, *The Kennedy Women,* 109; see also interview with Rose Fitzgerald, *Boston Post,* August 17, 1911.

   Her father ridiculed Boston suffragists: "House Votes for Suffrage," *Boston Daily Globe,* May 22, 1919. Fitzgerald eventually changed his views in time to vote in favor of ratifying the Nineteenth Amendment giving women the right to vote when he was a congressman from Massachusetts for a brief few months in 1919.

   her suffragist mother-in-law: John F. Kennedy National Historic Site, Brookline, Massachusetts, National Park Service, http://www.nps.gov/jofi/photosmultimedia/virtualtour.htm.

   participation in the Ace of Clubs: TTR, 40–41.

27 *"life was flowing past":* Interview with RFK in DKG, 301–2.

   Joe had always worked late: Gail Cameron, *Rose: A Biography of Rose Fitzgerald Kennedy* (New York: Putnam, 1971), 91.

   "reputation for being a ladies' man": Unidentified Fitzgerald relative, quoted by DKG, 303.

28 *"The old days are gone":* Interview with RFK in DKG, 307.

   she could be an asset to him: "Background Materials," 26–28, RFKP, box 12.

29 *"the most successful luncheons":* Ibid., 27–28.

   "Joe's time was his own": TTR, 63.

   "the great new experience" and following: Ibid., 64.

30 *"Why worry him?":* "My Mother and Birth of Baby," diaries, RFKP, box 5.

   if "you need more help": Interview with RFK in DKG, 307.

31 *"deliberate cultivation":* Resolution 68 of the Lambeth Confer-

ence, quoted in Lord Bertrand Dawson, "Sex and Marriage," *Birth Control Review* 5, no. 12 (December 1921): 7.

"This idea of yours" and following: Interview with Marie Green in DKG, 392.

32 *"a completely new and different environment"*: "Joe in Show Business and Movies," diaries, RFKP, box 5.

"I had heard": Ibid.

"trusted one another implicitly" and following: Ibid.

"formula for survival": Rita Dallas and Jeanira Ratcliffe, *The Kennedy Case* (New York: Putnam, 1973), 41.

"Gossip and slander and denunciation": TTR, 37.

33 *even more reason*: DKG, 304.

"challenge" and *"joy"*: Diaries, RFKP, box 5.

"On {a mother's} judgment": "Being a Mother," diaries, RFKP, box 4.

"an emaciated, worn out old hag": "Children Born at Home," diaries, RFKP, box 5.

34 *"responsibility of the family"*: "My Mother and Birth of Baby," diaries, RFKP, box 5.

song called "Bed Bugs and Cooties": "Mrs. K's 1923 Diary," diaries, February 25, 1923, RFKP, box 5.

"The children are fine": Telegram, JPK to RFK, April 8, 1923, JPKP, box 1.

35 *"Dear Rosa"*: Telegram, JPK to RFK, May 13, 1923, JPKP, box 1.

"Gee, you're a great mother": "Mrs. K's 1923 Diary," April 3, 1923, RFKP, box 5.

"Home Manager . . .": "The New Woman in the Home," in Ellen Carol DuBois and Lynn Dumenil, *Through Women's Eyes: An American History with Documents,* vol. 2, *Since 1865* (New York: Bedford/St. Martin's, 2009), 531–32.

36 *"The bottles for the babies"*: "Children Born at Home," RFKP, box 5.

"Kennedy desperation": "Card Catalogue," diaries, RFKP, box 5.

37 *"emaciated . . . fat"*: "Children Born at Home," RFKP, box 5.

"great leaders in their country": "Leadership," diaries, RFKP, box 5.
"They learned to be winners": Ibid.
"good old fashioned spanking" and following: "Physical Punishment," diaries, RFKP, box 5.

38 *The Moores:* See 1920 U.S. Census, Charlestown Precinct, Suffolk County, Massachusetts.

39 *"There I was with seven children"*: Rose Kennedy, interview by Robert Coughlan, January 7, 1972, RFKP, box 10.

40 *"read the papers"*: "Children Born at Home," RFKP, box 5.
when Rosemary was a year and a half old: TTR, 131.
"could not steer a sled": Rose Kennedy, interview by Coughlan, January 14, 1972, RFKP, box 10.
"I realized": "Diary Notes on Rosemary Kennedy," RFKP, box 13.

41 *"the best little talker"*: Diaries, February 14, 1923, RFKP, box 1.
Rosemary stuck her tongue out: Diaries, April 1, 1923, RFKP, box 1.
"I often wondered": "Married Life," diaries, August 23, 1971, RFKP, box 5.
"wasn't a bring-them-to-the-bosom kind of mother": Interview with Paul Morgan in LL, *The Kennedy Women,* 191.
"When we have a number of children": "Different Children," diaries, RFKP, box 5.

3. SLIPPING BEHIND

43 *"deficient"*: Arnold Gesell, *What Can the Teacher Do for the Deficient Child? A Manual for Teachers in Rural and Graded Schools* (Hartford, Conn.: State Board of Education, 1918).
"I had never heard": "Diary Notes on Rosemary Kennedy," RFKP, box 13.
"mental retardation was not": Ibid.

44 *"went away to school"*: Ibid.
"one {child} may be smart": "Different Children," diaries, RFKP, box 5.

"I did not know": Hank Searls, *The Lost Prince: Young Joe, the Forgotten Kennedy* (New York: Ballantine, 1969), 37. See also school register for Edward Devotion School, Edward Devotion School Manuscripts Collection no. 337, folder 1, JFKPL; and "Diary Notes on Rosemary Kennedy," RFKP, box 13.

"I talked to our family doctor" and following: "Diary Notes on Rosemary Kennedy," RFKP, box 13; and Searls, *The Lost Prince,* 37.

45   *"retardation"* and *"arrested growth"*: See, for instance, Elmer E. Liggett, "The Binet Tests and the Care of the Feebleminded," *Journal of the Missouri State Medical Association* 15, no. 5 (May 1918): 157–60; and Thomas G. MacLin, "Defective Mental Development with Special Reference to Cases Showing Delinquent Tendencies," *Institution Quarterly* 11, no. 4 (December 1920): 59.

an IQ test: "Diary Notes on Rosemary Kennedy," RFKP, box 13.

the Otis Intelligence Test: Stephen Colvin, "Principles Underlying the Construction and Use of Intelligence Tests," in *The Twenty-First Yearbook of the National Society for the Study of Education: Intelligence Tests and Their Use,* ed. Guy Montrose Whipple (Bloomington, Ill.: Public School Publishing Company, 1922), 21–23.

"I was told": "Diary Notes on Rosemary Kennedy," RFKP, box 13.

46   *Eunice finally succumbed:* "Former Mayor's Daughter Dies: Eunice J. Fitzgerald Martyr to War Work," *Boston Herald,* September 26, 1923.

Rose spent months: "Around Town," *Boston Post,* January 13, 1924.

47   *Traveling to Wall Street* and following: "Joe in Show Business and Movies," diaries, RFKP, box 5.

48   *The family:* Joe McCarthy, *The Remarkable Kennedys* (New York: Dial Press, 1960), 22, 53.

The large Riverdale estates: Fred Ferretti, "Uptight in Riverdale," *New York Magazine,* October 6, 1969, 31.

49   *"excellent boys school"*: "Joe in Show Business and Movies," diaries, RFKP, box 5.

50 *"were like fish out of water"*: LL, *The Kennedy Women,* 177–78.

52 *"Rosemary just plugged"*: Interview with Doris Hutchings in ibid., 177.
"Her lack of coordination": TTR, 132.
"heavy on her feet": "Diary Notebook B: Rosemary," 1972, RFKP, box 5; see also Eunice Kennedy Shriver, "Hope for Retarded Children," *Saturday Evening Post,* September 22, 1962.
She could not cut meat: Shriver, "Hope for Retarded Children."
"experts in mental deficiency": TTR, 132.

53 *"I think she was partly epileptic"*: EKS, interview by Robert Coughlan, February 26, 1972, RFKP, box 10.
"agitated": Gloria Swanson, *Swanson on Swanson: An Autobiography* (New York: Pocket Books, 1980), 392–94.

54 *"I had seen him {Joe} angry"*: Ibid., 393.
"a very sore subject": Ibid.
In spite of Rose and Joe's efforts: TTR, 134.

55 *"idiots"* . . . *"imbeciles"* . . . *"morons"*: Knight Dunlap, *The Elements of Scientific Psychology* (St. Louis, Mo.: Mosby, 1922), 357.
"purgatory": Burton Blatt and Fred Kaplan, *Christmas in Purgatory: A Photographic Essay on Mental Retardation* (Syracuse, N.Y.: Human Policy Press, 1974).

56 *Dark, dirty* and following: Jeffry L. Geller and Maxine Harris, *Women of the Asylum: Voices from Behind the Walls, 1840–1945* (New York: Doubleday, 1994), 320–21.
"terribly frustrated": "Diary Notes on Rosemary Kennedy," RFKP, box 13; see also TTR, 132.

57 *"two classes"*: Robert Whitaker, *Mad in America: Bad Science, Bad Medicine, and the Enduring Treatment of the Mentally Ill* (New York: Basic Books, 2002), 44.
fears of the "immigrant hordes": Ibid., 48–53, 172.
Some of the most prominent industrialists: Ibid., 46–49.

58 *"visiting the iniquity"*: Leila Zenderland, "The Parable of *The Kallikak Family,"* in *Mental Retardation in America: A Reader,* ed. Steven Noll and James W. Trent Jr. (New York: New York University Press, 2004), 168–69. See also Deuteronomy 5:9.

At that time: The Code of Canon Law 913 of the Roman Catholic Church; see Charles George Herbermann, ed., *The Catholic Encyclopedia* (New York: Encyclopedia Press, 1913). In 1995, the United States Conference of Catholic Bishops restated its guidelines to be inclusive of people with disabilities.

the Roman Catholic Church: See, for instance, Bernie Malone, "Catholic Church Denies Sacrament of Holy Communion to Down Syndrome Child," *IrishCentral.com,* January 19, 2012, http://www.irishcentral.com/news/catholic-church-denies -sacrament-of-holy-communion-to-down-syndrome- child-137710088-237427501.html#.

"My parents": Shriver, "Hope for Retarded Children."

59   *Rose would wait:* Diaries, August 23, 1971, RFKP, box 5.

4. FIVE SCHOOLS

60   *Founded in 1912 and following:* David Brind, *Researching the Mind, Touching the Spirit: The Helena T. Devereux Biography* (Philadelphia, n.d.), http://www.devereux.org/site/DocServer/HTD-Bio.pdf?docID=281, 3.

61   *"disabilities need not cause":* Ibid., 7.

"I am sure": Letter, JPK to RMK, November 13, 1929, JPKP, box 1.

"made the necessary social adjustments": "Report on Rosemary Kennedy," June 23, 1930, JPKP, box 26, as quoted in DN, 153.

developmentally appropriate work: Norma E. Cutts, "The Mentally Handicapped," *Review of Educational Research* 11, no. 3 (June 1941): 267; see also DN, 152.

"outbursts of impatience": DN, 153.

62   *Her parents had gone off:* Ibid.

busy settling the children: DKG, 417.

The basement featured: Edward M. Kennedy, *True Compass* (New York: Twelve, 2009), 39.

63   *"You were in charge":* TTR, 70.

"doctors, educators, and psychologists": Ibid., 133.

64 *"social adjustments":* "Report on Rosemary Kennedy," June 23, 1930, JPKP, box 26, as quoted in DN, 153.
   low self-esteem and low confidence: Ibid.

65 *"dislikes exerting the effort":* Report from Devereux School, November 21, 1930, JPKP, box 26, as quoted in DN, 153.
   "I am working": Letter, RMK to RFK, November 17, 1930, JPKP, box 1.

66 *"Did you ask":* Ibid.
   "Dear Eunice": Letter, RMK to EKS, April 13, 1931, JPKP, box 1.

67 *"She was tremendously popular":* Diaries, August 23, 1971, RFKP, box 5.
   "defectives": Elmer E. Liggett, "The Binet Tests and the Care of the Feebleminded," *Journal of the Missouri State Medical Association* 15, no. 5 (May 1918): 157–60; and Thomas G. MacLin, "Defective Mental Development with Special Reference to Cases Showing Delinquent Tendencies," *Institution Quarterly* 11, no. 4 (December 1920): 59.
   "would run away": "Diary Notes on Rosemary Kennedy," RFKP, box 13.

68 *A bus from the private boys' day school:* "Changes in Way of Life," diaries, RFKP, box 5. Eventually Rose would enroll her daughters in the Sacred Heart boarding school in Noroton, Connecticut.
   She resented having a companion: "Diary Notes on Rosemary Kennedy," RFKP, box 13.
   Neighbors in Bronxville: Interview with Paul Morgan in LL, *The Kennedy Women,* 192.

69 *her teachers at Devereux:* "Report on Rosemary Kennedy," June 23, 1930, JPKP, box 26, as reported in DN, 153.
   "Dear Mother and Daddy": Letter, RMK to RFK and JPK, June 2, 1934, RFKP, box 13.

70 *"Of course we are deeply interested":* Letter, Margaret McCusker of Sacred Heart at Elmhurst to RFK, October 17, 1934, RFKP, box 13.

71 *"raised Cain first week":* Telegram, JPK to RFK, October 6, 1934, RFKP, box 12.

"I had a very firm": Letter, JPK to Helen Newton, October 15, 1934, JPKP, box 26.

"retarded children": Letter, Helen Newton to RFK, spring 1936, JPKP, box 26.

Newton observed: Ibid.

72 *"October 1, 1934":* Letter, RMK to JPK, October 1, 1934, JPKP, box 26.

Ruth Evans O'Keefe: Dr. John O'Keefe, interview by Ron Doel and Joseph Tatarewicz, Goddard Space Center, Greenbelt, Md., February 2, 1993, http://www.aip.org/history/ohilist/32713.html. Ruth Evans graduated from Sacred Heart Convent in Marmoutiers, France, and was a classmate of Rose Fitzgerald's at Sacred Heart at Blumenthal. Ruth then attended Wellesley, graduating in 1911, and married Edward Scott O'Keefe in January 1916. She was very active in the Massachusetts League of Women Voters, child-labor reform, labor reform, and prison reform; see also "The Man Who Had to Be No. 1," *Boston Record American,* January 6, 1964.

73 *"I think it is fine":* Letter, JPK to JPKJR, October 2, 1934, JPKP, box 1.

"thought she was very nice": Letter, JPKJR to JPK, n.d. (ca. spring 1936), in *Hostage to Fortune: The Letters of Joseph P. Kennedy,* ed. Amanda Smith (New York: Penguin, 2001), 175.

74 *"condemnation of Hitler"* and following: Letter, JPKJR to JPK, April 23, 1934, in Smith, *Hostage to Fortune,* 130–31.

"Congenital mental deficiency": "Law for the Prevention of Offspring with Hereditary Diseases (July 14, 1933)," in *German History in Documents and Images,* vol. 7, *Nazi Germany, 1933–1945,* http://germanhistorydocs.ghi-dc.org/pdf/eng/English30.pdf. Source of English translation: U.S. Chief Counsel for the Prosecution of Axis Criminality, *Nazi Conspiracy and Aggression,* vol. 5 (Washington, D.C.: United States Government Printing Office, 1946), document 3067-PS, pp. 880–83.

"far beyond his necessary requirements": Letter, JPK to JPKJR, May 4, 1934, in Smith, *Hostage to Fortune,* 133.

75 *"October 15, 1934"*: Letter, RMK to JPK, October 15, 1934, RFKP, box 13.

76 *"Mother sent me"*: Letter, JPK to RMK, December 8, 1934, JPKP, box 1.

"It would do Rose{mary} good": Letter, JPK to JFK, October 10, 1934, JPKP, box 1.

"The reason I am making": Letter, RFK to Mr. Steel, Choate School, January 18, 1934, RFKP, box 12.

77 *They did other things:* Letter, RMK to JPK and RFK, March 1, 1936, RFKP, box 13.

"learning the names": Letter, RMK to RFK, January 19, 1936, JPKP, box 1.

"blue evening dress": Ibid.

"My dear Rosemary": DKG, 357.

78 *"Darling Mother and Daddy"*: Letter, RMK to JPK and RFK, March 1, 1936, RFKP, box 13.

79 *"Every time I would say"*: DKG, 360.

"If I said to her": "Rose Kennedy: 'Rosemary Brought Us Strength,'" *Catholic Digest,* March 1976, 36.

80 *"nervous impulses"*: Charles H. Lawrence, "Adolescent Disturbances of Endocrine Function: The Importance of Their Recognition and Treatment," *Annals of Internal Medicine* 9 (1936): 1503–12. See also A. P. Cawadias, "The History of Endocrinology," *Proceedings of the Royal Society of Medicine* 34 (1941): 303–8.

"I would do anything": Letter, RMK to JPK, October 15, 1934, RFKP, box 13.

"Some years ago": Letter, JPK to Frederick Good, October 15, 1934, JPKP, box 26.

81 *"spent {a} very pleasant visit"*: Telegram, Frederick Good to JPK, October 18, 1934, JPKP, box 26.

"in pretty good spirits" and following: Letter, Frederick Good to JPK, October 24, 1934, JPKP, box 26.

"considerable improvement": Letter, JPK to Charles Lawrence, November 21, 1934, in DN, 223.

82   *injections would not have helped:* The use of hormones to treat a variety of mental-health problems in teens and young adults was becoming more popular during the 1930s, though its success as a treatment was doubtful. One case study reported by a team of neurosurgeons and psychiatrists from Massachusetts General Hospital and McLean Hospital highlighted the story of one teen boy suffering from epileptic seizures, agitation, and depression. His initial treatment included injections of "pituitary extract," or hormones. The result was dismal, and the boy's seizures, depression, and uncooperativeness continued. He was then treated with phenobarbital, a barbiturate and anticonvulsant, also to no effect. Finally, at the age of seventeen, he was subjected to not one but two frontal lobotomies after the first one seemed to make him worse. Two years later the boy was clearly disabled, with a diminished IQ and slowed speech patterns, but he functioned enough to play a little tennis, exercise in a gym, and do a little work outside. Most importantly, his father reported to the doctors, the boy was now more compliant and cooperative, a significant change from the troublesome boy who had caused the family so much heartache and worry. "Reports of a Partial Frontal Lobectomy and Frontal Lobotomy Performed on Three Patients: One Chronic Epileptic, and Two Cases of Chronic Agitated Depression," *Psychosomatic Medicine* 3, no. 1 (January 1941).
      "she is 100% O.K.": Letter, Frederick Good to JPK, January 26, 1935, JPKP, box 26.
      Dearborn had conducted and following: See Herbert Langfeld, "Walter Fenno Dearborn: 1878–1955," *American Journal of Psychology* 68, no. 4 (December 1955): 679–81.
83   *"department store":* Letter, Walter F. Dearborn to RFK, June 28, 1937, in DN, 265.
      "Rosemary seems" and following: Letter, Walter F. Dearborn to RFK, October 11, 1935, JPKP, box 26.
84   *"Sorry to say":* Letter, RMK to JPK and RFK, January 12, 1936, RFKP, box 13.
      "Please show it to her father": Letter, Helen Newton to RFK, April 1936, JPKP, box 26.

85 *"I received this idea":* Ibid.
"There are days": Ibid.
"I wrote thanking you": Ibid.
86 *"She is not only attractive":* Letter, Mary Baker to RFK and JPK, March 27, 1936, JPKP, box 26.
"a period of intensive study": Ibid.
87 *"An occasional evening":* Ibid.
"definite instructions": Ibid.
88 *All the arrangements:* Letter, J. G. Vaughn to Edward Scott O'Keefe, April 3, 1936, JPKP, box 26.
"I have had from 15 to 20 years": Letter, Helen Newton to RFK, August 17, 1936, in DKG, 497.
"Music, French, Advanced English": P. Sargent, *Handbook of Private Schools,* 27th ed. (Boston: P. Sargent, 1943).
She was able to enroll: Invoices, Universal School of Handicrafts to Joseph Kennedy, 1936–1937, RFKP, box 128.
Rose hired: Letter, Amanda Rohde to RFK, July 21, 1937, RFKP, box 128.
89 *"A sister":* "Girlhood," diaries, RFKP, box 11.
"It appears to me": Letter, Amanda Rohde to RFK, October 18, 1936, in DKG, 496–98.
90 *"Rosemary has been allowed":* Letter, Amanda Rohde to RFK, October 18, 1936, JPKP, box 26, in DN, 264–65.
"intellectual blocking": Letter, Walter F. Dearborn to RFK, June 28, 1937, JPKP, box 26, in DN, 266.
"handicraft" classes: Letter, Amanda Rohde to RFK, (July) 1937, JPKP, box 26.
91 *She was accompanied:* Memorandum, M. E. Brown to Mrs. Waldron, September 28, 1937, JPKP, box 26.
"We took a boat": Postcard, RMK to JPK and RFK, n.d., RFKP, box 128.
"the boys over here": Letter, RMK to KK, July 15, 1936, JPKP, box 1.
92 *"When I last talked"* and following: Letter, Mollie Hourigan to RFK, July 9, 1937, JPKP, box 26.

"I read your letter": Letter, RFK to Mollie Hourigan, July 13, 1937, JPKP, box 26.

93   *"I shall always be"* and following: Letter, Mollie Hourigan to RFK, July 23, 1937, JPKP, box 26, in DN, 264–66.

5. BRIEF HAVEN IN ENGLAND

96   *A "grotesque appointment": New Republic,* July 1934, quoted in DN, 210.

Joe was responsible: DN, 204–11.

97   *Kennedy set about hiring* and following: Ibid., 254–79.

Kennedy and his staff and following: Ibid., 267–70, 278–79.

100   *"were used to seeing":* "Changes in Way of Life," diaries, RFKP, box 5.

The Dionne quintuplets: See Steven Mintz, *Huck's Raft: A History of American Childhood* (Cambridge, Mass.: Harvard University Press, 2004), 233–34.

101   *"dispense moral advice":* Ibid., 251.

One in five children: Ibid., 234.

Joe set sail: "Kennedy Departs, Attended by 'Foes,'" *New York Times,* February 24, 1938; see also DN, 284.

102   *Rose set sail:* "Married Life," diaries, RFKP, box 5.

Kathryn "Kiko" Conboy: Interview with Luella Hennessey Donovan in LL, *The Kennedy Women,* 151, 176.

"regular family fare": "Presentation at Court," diaries, RFKP, box 5.

New York School of Fine and Applied Art: The school is now Parsons The New School for Design in New York City.

103   *The* Boston Globe *reported:* "Rosemary Kennedy in Baptist Hospital," *Boston Globe,* April 6, 1938.

"Rosemary has been in Boston": Letter, EM to JPK, March 23, 1938, JPKP, box 144.

"very well and happy": Letter, EM to JPK, April 6, 1938, JPKP, box 144. The details of Rosemary's ailments have been specifi-

cally redacted from the letter by the Joseph P. Kennedy Foundation.

"a graduate of Sacred Heart Academy": "Rosemary Kennedy in Baptist Hospital."

104   *"they have been so sweet":* Letter, EM to JPK, April 6, 1938, JPKP, box 144.

USS Manhattan, *on April 20:* "Two Kennedy Girls Sail," *New York Times,* April 21, 1938.

playing "department store": Jerome Beatty, "The Nine Little Kennedys—and How They Grew," *Woman's Day,* April 1939, 16.

Aside from commenting: "Presentation at Court," diaries, RFKP, box 1.

106   *"very rich in pageantry":* "Presentation at Court," diaries, RFKP, box 5.

"lovely days": Ibid.

107   *"not to have one lady bobbing":* "Presentation at Court," diaries, RFKP, box 1.

"knew the type": Ibid.

108   *status-hungry citizens pressuring: TTR,* 196.

This year it would be: Ibid., 196–97.

"Cinderella . . . jewels were added": Diaries, "Presentation at Court, RFKP, Box 1.

"ran into my husband's room": TTR, 197–98.

109   *matching embroidered train:* "The First Court of the Season," *London Times,* May 12, 1938.

Eunice would later remember: EKS, "My Court Presentation," RFKP, box 129.

"Victorian posie": "First Court of the Season."

At 9:30 sharp: "300 Debutantes Bow at 1st Court, American List Is Reduced to 7," *New York Times,* European ed., May 12, 1938, diaries, RFKP, box 2.

The ballroom: EKS, "My Court Presentation," RFKP, box 129.

110   *"Prince Frederick of Prussia":* Beatty, "Nine Little Kennedys," 39.

Rose would later complain: TTR, 197.

"Court observers noticed": "300 Debutantes Bow at 1st Court";

"Seven Americans Presented to King," *New York Times,* May 12, 1938. See also Ibid., 196–99.

111   *"severe gowns of white":* Unidentified newspaper clipping, June 2, 1938, diaries, RFKP, box 1.

"about six midshipmen": KK, diary, 1938–1939, RFKP, box 128.

Though invitations for both: Invitation, Ambassador of the U.S.S.R. to Rosemary and Kathleen Kennedy, March 1, 1939, RFKP, box 128; and "Presentation at Court," diaries, RFKP, box 1.

112   *"Almost go mad":* "Diary Notes on Rosemary Kennedy," August 17, 1938, RFKP, box 1.

113   *"The Ambassador to the Court of St. James":* Maria Riva, *Marlene Dietrich* (New York: Knopf, 1992), 469.

Kick had "assumed the role" and following: Ibid., 469–70.

114   *During the latter part:* Assorted correspondence, August–September 1938, RFKP, box 13.

"plenty of attention": Letter, EKS to JPK and RFK, n.d. (August 1938), RFKP, box 13.

"When Joe phoned": Diary notes, September 13, 1938, RFKP, box 1.

"I had to settle": "Presentation at Court," diaries, RFKP, box 12.

115   *"on the verge": Convent of the Sacred Heart Finishing School for Girls,* school pamphlet, 1938, JPKP, box 26.

help "a bit with my duties": "Presentation at Court," diaries, RFKP, box 1. See also *TTR,* 185–86.

Courses in literature: Convent of the Sacred Heart Finishing School for Girls, school pamphlet.

116   *"remarkable progress":* Letter, Mother Isabel Eugenie to JPK, April 3, 1939, RFKP, box 13.

"American government apply": DN, 364.

117   *"collapse of the British Empire":* JPK, quoted in ibid., 368.

Rosemary and her siblings: "St. Moritz Data," JPKP, box 137.

"Everything is so beautiful": Letter, RMK to JPK, December 26, 1938, JPKP, box 2.

"Album for Dr. Montessori": Letter, RMK to JPK, February 27, 1939, JPKP, box 2.

118 *Mother Isabel had been trained:* "Sr. Isabel Eugenie, Educator, Writer," *Philadelphia Inquirer,* May 17, 1983.

119 *Through this method:* See American Montessori Society, http://www.amshq.org/; Montessori Foundation, http://www.montessori.org/; Maria Montessori, *The Montessori Method: Scientific Pedagogy as Applied to Child Education in "The Children's Houses,"* trans. Anne E. George (New York: Stokes, 1912); Sheila Radice, *The New Children: Talks with Maria Montessori* (New York: Stokes, 1920); and Josephine Tozier, "The Montessori Schools in Rome: The Revolutionary Educational Work of Maria Montessori as Carried Out in Her Own Schools," *McClure's* 38, no. 2 (December 1911): 123–37. Maria Montessori was nominated three times for the Nobel Peace Prize (in 1949, 1950, and 1951).

"The first idea": Tozier, "The Montessori Schools in Rome," 128.

"diploma for being a child of Mary": Letter, RMK to JPK, February 27, 1939, JPKP, box 2.

"This diet of Elizabeth Arden": Letter, RMK to JPK, February 27, 1939, JPKP, box 2.

121 *The Kennedys were seated* and following: LL, *The Kennedy Women,* 273. See also DN, 374–75.

Mother Isabel had personally seen: Interview by the author with the Assumption Sisters in Worcester, Mass., December 13, 2014.

122 *"leg show":* Letter, JPK to Arthur Houghton, August 29, 1939, quoted in DN, 397.

"little brassiere{s}": Diary, June 13, 1939, RFKP, box 2.

Belmont House: The estate is now a golf club.

"toasted Belmont": Letter, Dorothy Gibbs to JPK, September 13, 1939, RFKP, box 13.

123 *"marked improvement":* Letter, Dorothy Gibbs to EM, October 10, 1939, as quoted in DKG, 594.

"to fight incendiary bombs": Letter, Mother Isabel Eugenie to JPK, September 23, 1939, JPKP, box 26.

124 *"she was going to be the one":* Letter, JPK to RFK, September 18, 1939, in *Hostage to Fortune: The Letters of Joseph P. Kennedy,* ed. Amanda Smith (New York: Penguin, 2001), 379–80.

Joe also arranged: Letter, JPK to RFK, September 18, 1939, in Smith, *Hostage to Fortune,* 379.

"No one could watch": EKS, quoted in "The Tragic Story of . . . the Daughter JFK's Mother Had to Give Up," *National Enquirer,* November 5, 1967.

"empty head": Edward Shorter, *The Kennedy Family and the Story of Mental Retardation* (Philadelphia: Temple University Press, 1984), 31–33. This quote was found in a draft of an article, ghostwritten for Eunice Kennedy Shriver for the *Saturday Evening Post* in 1962, called "Out of the Shadows." Some of these more personal reminiscences were deleted from the final published article.

"looked out for her": Edward M. Kennedy, *True Compass* (New York: Twelve, 2009), 26.

Joe wrote that Mary Moore: Letter, JPK to RFK, October 11, 1939, in Smith, *Hostage to Fortune,* 515.

125 *"Please God":* Letter, Dorothy Gibbs to JPK, September 13, 1939, RFKP, box 13.

"a magical key": Eileen Foley, "Montessori Revival: A Magical Key to Learning — or Not?," *Philadelphia Sunday Bulletin,* February 21, 1965.

Noted for her selfless devotion: Essay on Mother Isabel, written for inclusion in the Spring 1983 issue of the *Ottawa Montessori School Newsletter,* Sister Isabel Eugenie File, courtesy the Religious of the Assumption, Worcester, Mass.

"She {Rosemary} is contented": Letter, JPK to RFK, October 11, 1939, in Smith, *Hostage to Fortune,* 394.

"She loves being the boss here": Ibid.

126 *"I don't see any point":* Letter, JPK to RFK, October 23, 1939, in DN, 422, from Nasaw's personal collection.

"Now as to Rosie": Letter, JPK to RFK, November 13, 1939, in DN, 426, from Nasaw's personal collection.

127 *"welcomed . . . with joy":* Letter, Mother Isabel Eugenie to RFK, December 20, 1939, JPKP, box 26.

"She has some supervision": Ibid.

"She thinks of you" and following: Ibid.

128   *he scheduled a few days:* DN, 432.
      Roosevelt was tiring of Kennedy: Ibid., 433.
      "Rose{mary} met me": Letter, JPK to RFK, March 14, 1940, RFKP, box 13.

129   *"I had a talk":* Letter, JPK to RFK, March 20, 1940, RFKP, box 13.
      "Darling Daddy": Letter, RMK to JPK, (March–April, 1940), JPKP, box 26, in Smith, *Hostage to Fortune,* 412.
      "Her disposition is great": Letter, JPK to RFK, April 26, 1940, RFKP, box 13.
      "I am so fond of you": Letter, RMK to JPK, April 4, 1940, RFKP, box 13.

130   *"I was more than pleased":* Letter, JPK to Dorothy Gibbs, April 23, 1940, RFKP, box 13.
      "You must have made": Letter, Dorothy Gibbs to JPK, April 24, 1940, RFKP, box 13.
      "Everybody thinks": Letter, RMK to JPK, April 25, 1940, RFKP, box 2.

131   *"get Rose and the Moores out":* Letter, JPK to RFK, May 20, 1940, in Smith, *Hostage to Fortune,* 432.
      "Everybody here is so sorry": Letter, RMK to JPK, April 13, 1940, RFKP, box 13.

6. WAR ON THE KENNEDY HOME FRONT

132   *German U-boat attacks:* "G-Men Search Ship Sailing to Save Americans," *Chicago Daily Tribune,* May 25, 1940.
      Their flight out of Portugal: "Clipper's Mail Removed Again," *Palm Beach Post,* June 1, 1940; "Envoy's Daughter Home on Clipper," *New York Times,* June 2, 1940; "Clipper, 21 on Board, Puts In at Bermuda," *New York Times,* June 1, 1940.

133   *"forgetting our trip back":* Letter, RMK to JPK, June 4, 1940, RFKP, box 13.
      "but once this has happened": Letter, JPK to RFK, June 7, 1940, JPKP, box 2.

"Rosie" was returning home: Letter, Jean Kennedy Smith to JPK, May 28, 1940, quoted in *TTR,* 226.

She missed her British friends: See letters, RMK to JPK, June 4, 1940; Dorothy Gibbs to JPK, June 8, 1940; Mother Teresa to JPK, June [?], 1940; JPK to Mother Teresa, June 18, 1940; JPK to Reverend Mother Isabel, July 10, 1940; JPK to RMK, August 8, 1940; JPK to Patsy Cunningham, August 31, 1940; and JPK to RMK, September 10, 1940, all in RFKP, box 13.

134 the *"Saks man":* Letter, RMK to JPK, June 4, 1940, RFKP, box 13.

135 *Eunice complained:* Letter, EKS to JPK, June 1940, in *TTR,* 227.

Since Rosemary could not handle: EKS, interview by Robert Coughlan, February 26, 1972, RFKP, box 10.

Her youngest sister, Jean: Letters, Jean Kennedy to JPK, June 24, 1940, in *TTR,* 228; and RFK to JPK, June 24, 1940, in *Hostage to Fortune: The Letters of Joseph P. Kennedy,* ed. Amanda Smith (New York: Penguin, 2001), 446–47.

athletic games and competition: TTR, 226–32.

136 *Kick was preoccupied:* Lynne McTaggart, *Kathleen Kennedy, Her Life and Times* (New York: Dial Press, 1983), 82–83.

the children were "especially kind": Luella Hennessey Donovan, "My Happy Life with the Kennedy Babies," *Good Housekeeping,* August 1961.

"From her childhood": TTR, 246.

an "enchanting child": DKG, 362; and ibid.

"Never was there a girl": "Kathleen Kennedy," diary notebooks, RFKP, box 13.

137 *"Jack would . . . take her":* EKS, interview by Robert Coughlan, February 26, 1972, RFKP, box 10.

"Why don't other boys": Rose Kennedy, "Rosemary Brought Us Strength," *Catholic Digest,* March 1976, 36–37.

In spite of Kick's efforts: McTaggart, *Kathleen Kennedy,* 70–87.

"I think there's so much made": TTR, 134.

"didn't spill things": Interview with EKS in DKG, 360.

it "was embarrassing to be around Rosemary": Interview with a close friend of Jack Kennedy's in LL, *The Kennedy Women,* 303.

138 *"much happier when she sees the children"*: Letter, JPK to RFK, October 11, 1939, JPKP, box 2.

Rosemary "seemed to realize": Interview with Lem Billings in DKG, 640.

"aggressively unhappy": Ibid.

139 *"only their best"*: Donovan, "My Happy Life."

"fiercely fought" Monopoly tournaments: Ibid.

"In a large family": "Leadership," diary notebooks, RFKP, box 5.

"In our family": "The Tragic Story of . . . the Daughter JFK's Mother Had to Give Up," *National Enquirer,* November 5, 1967.

calling for the family chauffeur: David Deignan expenses, 1939–1940, JPKP, box 8.

"bosses me so": Interview with Luella Hennessey Donovan in LL, *The Kennedy Women,* 304.

Drinking tea and following: Ibid.

140 *"she was Mrs. Astor"* and following: Ibid.

"somehow, Eunice seemed to develop": Interview with Lem Billings in DKG, 363.

"She started to deteriorate": EKS, interview by Robert Coughlan, February 26, 1972, RFKP, box 10.

141 *"Some of these upsets became tantrums"*: *TTR,* 245.

"Every day there would be": Interview with Lem Billings in DKG, 640.

a type of psychogenic nonepileptic seizure: See literature on nonepileptic seizures from the Epilepsy Foundation, at http://www.epilepsyfoundation.org/answerplace/Medical/seizures/types/nonepileptic/weinonepilepsy.cfm.

after the worst of a seizure was over: Letter, RMK to JPK and RFK, March 1, 1936, RFKP, box 13. See also EKS, interview by Robert Coughlan, February 26, 1972, RFKP, box 10.

In those days: See discussion of anticonvulsant medications, including Luminal and Dilantin and other Phenytoin-based sedatives, at Pub Med Health, U.S. National Library of Medicine, National Institutes of Health, http://www.ncbi.nlm.nih.gov/pubmedhealth/PMH0000549; "Triumph in Epilepsy," *New*

York Times, June 3, 1940; and Waldemar Kaempffert, "Science in the News," *New York Times,* June 2, 1940.

Rosemary had proudly told: Letter, RMK to JPK, June 4, 1940, RFKP, box 13. Rosemary's nephews Timothy and Anthony Shriver both recalled that Rosemary loved to be told she was beautiful. Author interviews with Anthony Shriver and Timothy Shriver, October 8, 2008, and November 2, 2010, respectively.

"sexually frustrated": Interview with Lem Billings in Burton Hersh, *Edward Kennedy: An Intimate Biography* (New York: Counterpoint, 2010), 522. See also LL, *The Kennedy Men,* 156.

142   *This had devastating consequences:* See Jeffrey L. Geller and Maxine Harris, *Women of the Asylum: Voices from Behind the Walls, 1840–1945* (New York: Anchor, 1994), 247–325 in particular.

Though open and frank: McTaggart, *Kathleen Kennedy,* 103–4.

many of her friends were "pairing up": Ibid., 91.

She had built a small getaway cottage: TTR, 239–42.

143   *"But isn't it interesting":* Letter, RMK to JPK, July 4, 1940, RFKP, box 13. Rosemary was also excited about the upcoming wedding of her friend Elaine, the daughter of Dr. Walter Dearborn, who had treated Rosemary during the mid- to late 1930s. According to Rosemary, Elaine had asked her to be her maid of honor.

144   *She would require:* Interview by author with Terry Marotta, daughter of camp director Caroline Sullivan, April 2, 2013.

"she should have known": Terry Marotta, "Eunice and the 'Other Sister,'" *Exit Only* (blog), August 12, 2009, http://terrymarotta. wordpress.com/; interview by author, April 2, 2013; and e-mails to author, April 1 and 8, 2013.

Dunn conveyed Rose's requirement: Letter, Elizabeth Dunn to Caroline T. Sullivan, July 1, 1940, private collection of Terry Marotta.

145   *the Sullivan sisters took Rosemary:* Invoice, Camp Fernwood, July 1940; and letter, Caroline Sullivan to RFK, August 16, 1940, private collection of Terry Marotta. See also Gail Cameron, *Rose:*

A Biography of Rose Fitzgerald Kennedy (New York: Putnam, 1971), 91.

Rosemary did not properly dispose: Terry Marotta, interview by author, April 2, 2013.

the Sullivans had had enough: Ibid.

Rose had inquired: Letter, Elizabeth Dunn to Caroline Sullivan, July 17, 1940, private collection of Terry Marotta.

146 *"left the final ordeal":* Postcard, Caroline Sullivan to Grace Sullivan, July 23–24, 1940, private collection of Terry Marotta.

"I see there is a $200 charge": Letter, RFK to Caroline Sullivan, April 7, 1941, private collection of Terry Marotta.

"Our charge is based": Letter, Caroline Sullivan to RFK, May 1, 1941, private collection of Terry Marotta.

147 *"lovable and well meaning":* Ibid.

Caroline Sullivan still bore lingering anger: Terry Marotta, interview by author, April 2, 2013.

148 *"better layout"* and following: "Rosemary Kennedy"; and letter, EM to RFK, June 7, 1940, RFKP, box 13.

Moore wrote to Joe in London: Letter, EM to RFK, June 7, 1940, RFKP, box 13.

Rose remained secluded: Letter, KK to JPK, August 6, 1940, JPKP, box 2.

She had left Fernwood: Letter, Caroline Sullivan to RFK, August 16, 1940, private collection of Terry Marotta.

149 *"I tried to get up":* Letter, RMK to Caroline and Grace Sullivan, July 25, 1940, private collection of Terry Marotta. See also Marotta, "Eunice and the 'Other Sister.'"

"I am going to work so hard": Letter, RMK to Caroline and Grace Sullivan, July 25, 1940, private collection of Terry Marotta.

"I am going to be a bit tired": Ibid.

"Write to me soon": Postcard, RMK to Caroline and Grace Sullivan, July 25, 1940, private collection of Terry Marotta.

150 *Rose sent inquiries:* Letter, Paul Murphy (secretary to Joe Kennedy) to Mother Ann Elizabeth, August 2, 1940; and receipts for books, radio, Miss Dunn, August 12, 1940. Mary Durkin was the tutor. Books were sent to Rosemary that summer as

well, indicating she was studying, not just boarding there. See also letter, Ellen Dalton to RFK, August 25, 1940; and letter, Mrs. Arthur Bastien (Alice Cahill) to RFK, August 2, 1940; both in JPKP, box 26.

"during the past ten or twelve years": Letter, V. Rev. Thomas J. Love to RFK, September 19, 1940, JPKP, box 26.

151 *"Dr. Waygood has had an abundance"*: Letter, Edward M. Day to RFK, September 20, 1940, JPKP, box 26.

"had begun to get sort of emotional": EKS, interview by Robert Coughlan, February 26, 1972, RFKP, box 10.

Rosemary was instead enrolled: Letter, Paul Murphy to Mother Superior, October 24, 1940, JPKP, box 26.

"went to see the President": "Visit to Washington, October 29, 1940," diary entry, RFKP, box 3.

152 *"enable the retarded child"*: Benedict Neenan, *Thomas Verner Moore: Psychiatrist, Educator, Monk* (Mahwah, N.J.: Paulist Press, 2000), 180.

"priest-psychiatrist": Ibid., ix.

153 *to "integrate a progressive world view"*: Ibid., 2–3.

Moore considered girls to be: Ibid., 165–66.

When Moore first began developing: Ibid., 175.

a "clear vision": Ibid., 166.

at the intersection of science and faith: Ibid., 2–3.

154 *"Get all the assistance you can"*: Ibid., 183.

He attracted student teachers: Ibid., 184–87.

"the treatment of emotional and behavior disorders": Katherine Keneally Stefic, "The Clinical Psychologist in the Reading Clinic," in *Survey of Clinical Practice in Psychology,* ed. Eli A. Rubinstein and Maurice Lorr (New York: International Universities, 1954), 326.

"disquieting symptoms": TTR, 244–45.

155 *"Many nights"*: Interview with Ann Gargan King in DKG, 643.

The nuns would bring her back: LL, *The Kennedy Women,* 319.

"Can you imagine": Interview with Ann Gargan King in DKG, 640.

"out of the {newspaper} columns": Smith, *Hostage to Fortune,* xv.

Even family members remain mostly in the dark: Anthony Shriver and Timothy Shriver, interviews by author, October 8, 2008, and November 2, 2010, respectively. Oral testimony of other Kennedy family members gathered by reporters and historians over the past fifty years all reveal the same information: they, too, have no idea what happened or whether any singular event occurred that precipitated Joseph Kennedy's ultimate decision to have his daughter lobotomized.

had looked into having Rosemary attend: Letter, JPK to William R. Hearst, June 21, 1941, JPKP, box 7.

156 *worried about "her welfare":* Letter, Dr. Thomas V. Moore to JPK, November 12, 1941, JPKP, box 230, in DN, 533.

"How is my old darling today?": Letter, JPK to RMK, October 10, 1941, JPKP, box 2.

"I trust that she will be able": Dr. Thomas V. Moore to JPK, November 12, 1941, JPKP, box 230, in DN, 533.

Joe had planned: Letter, JPK to Father Cavanaugh, October 28, 1941, JPKP, box 216.

157 *"a neurological disturbance":* TTR, 245.

7. NOVEMBER 1941

158 *Rosemary's behavior had now become:* Interview with John B. White in Lynne McTaggart, *Kathleen Kennedy, Her Life and Times* (New York: Dial Press, 1983), 98.

"was so afraid": Interview with Luella Hennessey Donovan in LL, *The Kennedy Men,* 169.

159 *the procedure was not performed there:* "The Strange and Curious History of Lobotomy," *BBC News Magazine,* November 8, 2011, http://www.bbc.com/news/magazine-15629160. See also Elliot S. Vallenstein, *Great and Desperate Cures: The Rise and Decline of Psychosurgery and Other Radical Treatments for Mental Illness* (Lexington, Ky.: Elliot S. Vallenstein, 2010), 172–73.

160 *"problems to their families":* Waldemar Kaempffert, "Turning the Mind Inside Out," *Saturday Evening Post,* May 24, 1941.

Rose, nevertheless, enlisted Kick's help: Interview with Kerry McCarthy in LL, *The Kennedy Women,* 319.

White later recalled: Interview with John White in LL, *The Kennedy Women,* 318–21. White also described the same story to author Lynne McTaggart. See McTaggart, *Kathleen Kennedy,* 98; and DKG, 640–43.

Saint Elizabeths did not allow: Jack El-Hai, *The Lobotomist: A Maverick Medical Genius and His Tragic Quest to Rid the World of Mental Illness* (Hoboken, N.J.: Wiley, 2005), 91, 123–24.

161   *"just not good":* Interview with John White in LL, *The Kennedy Women,* 318–19; see also McTaggart, *Kathleen Kennedy,* 98. White's article was never published.

"Oh, Mother, no": Interview with Kerry McCarthy in LL, *The Kennedy Women,* 319.

"Joe took matters": DKG, 640.

"I think he knew": Interview with Luella Hennessey Donovan in LL, *The Kennedy Women,* 321.

the feverish advocacy: "Front Brain 'Rules' Thoughts on Future," *New York Times,* April 8, 1939.

162   *"in spite of these improvements":* "Neurosurgical Treatment of Certain Abnormal Mental States Panel Discussion at Cleveland Session," *Journal of the American Medical Association* 117, no. 7 (August 16, 1941): 517.

"scientific knowledge": "Medical Men Warned Against 'Cutting Worry' Out of Brain," *Richmond (Va.) Times Dispatch,* August 15, 1941.

Though the prefrontal lobotomy: EKS, interview by Robert Coughlan, February 7, 1972, RFKP, box 10.

"The doctors told my father": Ibid.

"agitated depression": Interview with James Watts in Ronald Kessler, *The Sins of the Father: Joseph P. Kennedy and the Dynasty He Founded* (New York: Warner, 1996), 244.

163   *But the superintendent:* El-Hai, *The Lobotomist,* 123–24, 150.

By the time Joe was meeting: Vallenstein, *Great and Desperate Cures,* 164–65.

no certification process: George J. Annas and Leonard H. Glantz, "Psychosurgery: The Law's Response," *Boston University Law Review* 54, no. 2 (1974): 253.

164 *though claims by practitioners:* "Insanity Treated by Electric Shock," *New York Times,* July 6, 1940.

Doctors like Walter Freeman: Walter Freeman, James Watts, and Thelma Hunt, *Psychosurgery: Intelligence, Emotion, and Social Behavior Following Prefrontal Lobotomy for Mental Disorders* (London: Baillierre, Tindall & Cox, 1942), 284–94.

in the summer of 1941: "Frontal Lobotomy," *Journal of the American Medical Association* 117, no. 7 (August 16, 1941): 534.

"It is inconceivable": "Medical Association Issues Warning Against Operation," *Science News Letter,* September 6, 1941, 157. See also ibid.

165 *Women were most frequently institutionalized:* Annas and Glantz, "Psychosurgery," 249–67.

Freeman and Watts were using their patients and following: Jack D. Pressman, *Last Resort: Psychosurgery and the Limits of Medicine* (New York: Cambridge University Press, 1998), 147.

Shared views and following: Annas and Glantz, "Psychosurgery," 253; "Brain Surgery Fails to Cure Crime Tendency," *Saint Petersburg (Fla.) Independent,* April 19, 1950; "Women's Criminal Tendency May Be Cured by Operation," *Saint Petersburg (Fla.) Times,* December 7, 1946; "Surgery Found Quick Cure for Addiction," *Cape Girardeau Southeast Missourian,* May 4, 1948.

166 *"misfits":* Stephen Rose, review of *Lobotomy: The Last Resort,* by Jack D. Pressman, *New Scientist,* August 12, 1982, 440–41.

At McLean Hospital: Pressman, *Last Resort,* 443.

In hospitals across the country: El-Hai, *The Lobotomist,* 290–91.

167 *to "visit with my two youngsters":* Letter, JPK to Woodward, November 28, 1941, JPKP, box 237. In early December 1941, Rose wrote a letter to the entire family but excluded any mention of her eldest daughter: letter, RFK to "My Darlings," December 5, 1941, RFKP, box 55.

Rosemary would be one of twenty-eight patients: Freeman, Watts, and Hunt, *Psychosurgery,* 284–94.

"*exaggerated attention*": Ibid., 128.

168 "*panicky state*": Ibid., 108.

"*unnamed tortures*": Ibid., 109.

"*Apprehension becomes a little more marked*": Ibid., 108–9.

169 "*I made a surgical incision*": Interview with James Watts in Kessler, *Sins of the Father*, 243.

Through the openings: Freeman, Watts, and Hunt, *Psychosurgery,* 108.

Freeman asked Rosemary: Interview with James Watts in Kessler, *Sins of the Father*, 243–44.

"*painful intensity*": Freeman, Watts, and Hunt, *Psychosurgery,* 108.

she became incoherent: Interview with James Watts in Kessler, *Sins of the Father*, 243–44.

170 *The nurse who attended the operation:* Interview with the unidentified nurse in LL, *The Kennedy Men*, 170.

In the hours, days, and weeks: Freeman, Watts, and Hunt, *Psychosurgery,* 116–26.

"*They knew right away*": Interview with Ann Gargan King in DKG, 642.

Rosemary's was one of several dozen: Freeman, Watts, and Hunt, *Psychosurgery,* 294.

171 *According to their own records:* Ibid., 285–87.

"*Most of the patients*": Ibid., 294.

8. ROSEMARY GONE

174 *she "usually wrote"*: "Married Life," diary, RFKP, box 5.

Rose never referred to Rosemary: Rose F. Kennedy, "Correspondence, 1933–1947," digital identifier JFKPP-004-039, JFKPL, at http://www.jfklibrary.org/Asset-Viewer/Archives/JFKPP-004-039.aspx. See also JPKP, box 2; and letter, RFK to "My Darlings," December 5, 1941, RFKP, box 55.

"*except obliquely in surviving family letters*": See *Hostage to Fortune: The Letters of Joseph P. Kennedy,* ed. Amanda Smith (New York: Penguin, 2001), 514–15. The family letters located in the

JPKP and the RFKP from late 1941 through the next twenty years reveal a mere handful of references to Rosemary. None of the letters are addressed to Rosemary, nor are there any letters from her. See, for instance, letters, RFK to "Children" and to individual children by name: December 5, 1941; January 5, 1942; January 12, 1942; January 20, 1942; January 24, 1942; February 2, 1942; February 9, 1942; February 10, 1942; February 16, 1942; March 18, 1942; March 27, 1942; April 9, 1942; April 13, 1942; May 9, 1942; May 29, 1942; June 15, 1942; June 24, 1942; and October 19, 1942; all in JPKP, box 2. See also copies of these letters in RFKP, box 55.

He schemed: DN, 542.

175 *he had "stopped off to see Rosemary":* Letter, JPK to RFK, November 23, 1942, JPKP, box 2.

Joe's news about Rosemary: See "Family Correspondence," JPKP, boxes 2 and 3.

There is no record: Timothy Shriver, *Fully Alive: Discovering What Matters Most* (New York: Farrar, Straus & Giroux / Sarah Crichton Books, 2014), 49.

the lobotomy "was an absolute devastating thing": Interview with Ann Gargan King in DKG, 643.

an undisclosed type of neurosurgery: TTR, 245.

Rose bitterly explained: Interview with Rose Kennedy in DKG, 643.

176 *Youngest sister Jean:* Shriver, *Fully Alive,* 56.

Teddy feared: Interview with EMK in Burton Hersh, *Edward Kennedy: An Intimate Biography* (New York: Counterpoint, 2010), 522.

"Never violate people's privacy": Edward M. Kennedy, *True Compass* (New York: Twelve, 2009), 41.

Eunice's son Timothy noted: Shriver, *Fully Alive,* 49.

"That was the way things were going": Ibid., 56.

177 *"Dear Daddy":* Letter, KK to JPK, after March 25, 1942, RFKP, box 57.

she "did not have a good time": Interview with EKS in LL, *The Kennedy Women,* 327.

Rose was so concerned: Letter, JPK to RFK, November 23, 1942, JPKP, box 2. Rose followed Eunice to Stanford again for the 1942 fall semester; see also LL, *The Kennedy Women,* 335–36.

178   *Eunice later claimed:* LL, *The Kennedy Women,* 323.

Zelda Fitzgerald: Nancy Milford, *Zelda: A Biography* (New York: Perennial, 1970), 256–57, 286–88; and "Fonda's Wife, Ill, Commits Suicide," *New York Times,* April 15, 1950.

179   *There is evidence:* "Family Correspondence," JPKP, boxes 2 and 3.

Mary Moore saw her more frequently: DN, 628.

"private duty nurses": Ibid., 536.

These extra private benefits: "Rosemary Kennedy: Bills and Receipts, 1945, 1948," JPKP, box 26; and ibid.

mostly through his secretaries: "Rosemary Kennedy: Bills and Receipts, 1945, 1948," JPKP, box 26; DN, 536.

"getting along quite happily": Letter, JPK to JFK, July 6, 1942, JPKP, box 3; and letter, JPK to JFK, November 16, 1943, JPKP, box 2.

180   *"Rosemary is feeling quite well":* Letters, JPK to KK, February 21, 1944; JPK to JPKJR, February 21, 1944; and JPK to KK, March 8, 1944, all in JPKP, box 3.

Before they could be told: Lief Erikson, "Ex-Envoy Kennedy's Son Is Hero of PT-Boat Saga," *Boston Globe,* August 29, 1943; JFKPL, http://www.jfklibrary.org/JFK/JFK-in-History/John-F-Kennedy-and-PT109.aspx; and *TTR,* 251.

182   *"With your faith in God":* Lynne McTaggart, *Kathleen Kennedy, Her Life and Times* (New York: Dial Press, 1983), 160.

"too ill to discuss the marriage": Hank Searls, *The Lost Prince: Young Joe, the Forgotten Kennedy* (New York: Ballantine, 1969), 207.

Bobby lashed out: Ibid.

"horrified {and} heartbroken": McTaggart, *Kathleen Kennedy,* 163.

"What a blow": "Notes on My Reactions at Kick's Marriage," diary, undated (May 1944), RFKP, box 3. See also Smith, *Hostage to Fortune,* 584.

183   *"As far as what people will say":* Letter, JPKJR to RFK and JPK, May 8, 1944, JPKP, box 3.

"The Power of Silence": Cables, KK to JPK, May 5, 1944; JPKJR

to RFK, May 6, 1944; JPKJR to JPK, May 7, 1944; and letter, JPKJR to "Mother and Dad," May 8, 1944; all in JPKP, box 3.

she had "never met anyone": LL, *The Kennedy Women,* 380.

184 *Kick moved back to London:* McTaggart, *Kathleen Kennedy,* 198–206.

Kick became romantically involved: Ibid., 211–19; and LL, *The Kennedy Women,* 400–402.

185 *She threatened to cast Kick out:* Interview with Jackie Pierrepont, a friend of Kick's, in McTaggart, *Kathleen Kennedy,* 222–25.

Kick held out hope and following: McTaggart, *Kathleen Kennedy,* 231–36.

186 *Patient abuse:* See 1856.org, "Historical Overview" and "Social History," State Hospitals of Massachusetts, http://1856.org/.

187 *Joe consulted:* Letters, Sister Maureen to John J. Ford, December 21, 1948; and JPK to J. J. Ford, December 31, 1948; both in JPKP, box 220.

Joe . . . would donate more than $100,000: Letter, Sister Maureen to JPK, November 28, 1949, JPKP, box 220.

Within ten years: Cardinal Cushing Centers, "Intergenerational Communities, History," at http://www.coletta.org/CARDINAL/History/history.html.

188 *"it would be impossible":* DN, 628.

"Word has come": Letter, Sister Maureen to John J. Ford, December 21, 1948, JPKP, box 220.

"If you have time": Letter, JPK to John J. Ford, December 31, 1948, JPKP, box 220.

Sometime in the early summer: From Saint Coletta records, as reported in LL, *The Kennedy Women,* 412–13.

Over the next fifteen years: Letters, John J. Ford to JPK, February 26, 1960, and Unknown to John J. Ford, September 24, 1951, JPKP, box 220.

189 *Joe never saw Rosemary:* Shriver, *Fully Alive,* 49.

"for the residents": John Henry Ott, *Jefferson County, Wisconsin, and Its People: A Record of Settlement, Organization, Progress, and Achievement,* vol. 2 (Chicago: Clarke Publishing, 1921), 199. See also "The History of St. Coletta of Wisconsin," Saint Coletta

of Wisconsin website, http://www.stcolettawi.org/about-us/history.php.

Sister Margaret Ann . . . revealed: Interview with Sister Margaret Ann in LL, *The Kennedy Women,* 412–13. See also Joan Zyda, "The Kennedy No One Knows," *Chicago Tribune,* January 7, 1976.

Rosemary "was very uncontrollable": Interview with Sister Margaret Ann in LL, *The Kennedy Women,* 412–13.

Unhappy and feeling "inferior": Sister Sheila of Saint Coletta, quoted in Zyda, "The Kennedy No One Knows."

named the Kennedy Cottage: Zyda, "The Kennedy No One Knows."

190 *"A Mr. Rudy S. Holstein":* Letter, Sister Anastasia to JPK, May 21, 1958, JPKP, box 26.

"I do not know": Letter, JPK to Sister Anastasia, May 29, 1958, JPKP, box 26.

In 1958, Sister Anastasia . . . assured Ford: Letter, Sister Anastasia to JPK, May 21, 1958, JPKP, box 26.

"All you have to do": Letter, JPK to Sister Anastasia, May 29, 1958, JPKP, box 26.

191 *A car used by her caregivers:* "Rosemary Kennedy: Correspondence," JPKP, box 26.

"had to piece the story together": Interview with Ann Gargan King in DKG, 643.

"Because I did not know": Interviews with Ann Gargan King and Luella Hennessey Donovan in DKG, 643.

"eminent medical specialists": TTR, 245.

Her "whole life is wrapped up": Sister Sheila of Saint Coletta, quoted in Zyda, "The Kennedy No One Knows."

192 *One woman, Gloria:* Zyda, "The Kennedy No One Knows."

"the solution to Rosemary's problem": Letter, JPK to Sister Anastasia, May 29, 1958, JPKP, box 26.

9. ROSEMARY MADE THE DIFFERENCE

193 *Family weddings:* See, for example, "Those Kennedy Kids," *Sunday News,* March 11, 1954, "Clippings," RFKP, box 121; and

Harold H. Martin, "The Amazing Kennedys," *Saturday Evening Post,* September 7, 1957, 44.

194 *"We have tried"* and following: "Elizabeth M. Boggs, Oral History Interview—JFK#1," July 17, 1968, JFKPL.

"He didn't have to tell": Elizabeth Boggs, interview by Edward Shorter, February 24, 1993, in Edward Shorter, *The Kennedy Family and the Story of Mental Retardation* (Philadelphia: Temple University Press, 2000), 84.

195 *Jack experienced a transformed:* LL, *The Kennedy Men,* 280, based on Leamer's examination of institutional records and an interview with Bob Healey, a reporter for the *Boston Globe.*

Eunice approached her father: Shorter, *The Kennedy Family,* 67; "Robert E. Cooke, Oral History Interview—JFK #1," March 29, 1968, JFKPL; and "Robert E. Cooke, Oral History Interview—JFK #2," July 25, 1968, JFKPL.

196 *The hospital . . . "is doing so much":* Letter, EKS to JPK and RFK, August 27, 1958, RFKP, box 12.

They established: "Robert E. Cooke, Oral History Interview—JFK #2," July 25, 1968, JFKPL.

"as concerned with care": Shorter, *The Kennedy Family,* 7.

The Shrivers proposed: "Eunice Kennedy Shriver, Oral History Interview—JFK#1," May 7, 1968, JFKPL.

Other doctors and scientists: "Robert E. Cooke, Oral History Interview—JFK #1," March 29, 1968, JFKPL.

197 *the foundation had committed:* Shorter, *The Kennedy Family,* 42–45.

one of eleven senators: "U.S. Action Awaited on Key MR Legislation," *Children Limited,* May 1958; and Elizabeth M. Boggs, "Statement on S. 395, and Related Bills Concerning Advanced Professional Training in the Field of Education of the Mentally Retarded, 1958–1966" (unpublished manuscript), 9–10, Elizabeth M. Boggs Papers, JFKPL.

198 *"Rosemary, the eldest"* and following: "The Campaign: Pride of the Clan," *Time,* July 11, 1960.

"Rosemary is in a nursing home": Nan Robertson, "Kennedy Clan United on Coast as Senator Faces the Outsiders," *New York Times,* July 10, 1960.

"The story had just come out": "John Seigenthaler, Oral History Interview—JFK #1," July 22, 1964, JFKPL.

199   *"the President elect": Children Limited,* December 1960, Elizabeth M. Boggs Papers, box 1, JFKPL.

"No capital should be made": "Elizabeth M. Boggs, Oral History Interview—JFK#1," July 17, 1968, JFKPL.

200   *In the spring of 1961:* "Robert E. Cooke, Oral History Interview—JFK#2," July 25, 1968, JFKPL.

Focusing on the physical well-being: Shorter, *The Kennedy Family,* 111–15.

201   *"He is still very vital":* "1963: March–April, Europe," diaries, RFKP, box 4.

202   *"She was a beautiful child"* and following: Eunice Kennedy Shriver, "Hope for Retarded Children," *Saturday Evening Post,* September 22, 1962.

203   *The institute would focus:* The institute was renamed the Eunice Shriver National Institute of Child Health and Human Development by Congress in 2007. See the institute's page on the National Institutes of Health website, at https://www.nichd.nih.gov/about/Pages/index.aspx.

Five days later: Shorter, *The Kennedy Family,* 78–89.

204   *"Special Message":* "Papers of John F. Kennedy, Presidential Papers, President's Office Files, Legislative Files, Special Message on mental illness and mental retardation," February 5, 1963, http://www.jfklibrary.org/Asset-Viewer/Archives/JFKPOF-042-036.aspx.

The Maternal and Child . . . Amendments: These amendments are known as PL88-156; see National Institutes of Health, http://history.nih.gov/research/downloads/PL88-156.pdf.

Also, in October: This act is known as PL88-164; see National Institutes of Health, http://history.nih.gov/research/downloads/PL88-164.pdf.

In a joint venture and following: Shorter, *The Kennedy Family,* 129–40.

205   *The Special Olympics today:* See the Special Olympics website at http://www.specialolympics.org/.

"was nervous and uncomfortable": Rita Dallas and Jeanira Ratcliffe, *The Kennedy Case* (New York: Putnam, 1973), 143.

Though Eunice started visiting: Letter, RFK to Unknown, March 28, 1972, RFKP, box 57. Most of the correspondence between Rose and the staff at Saint Coletta in this collection regarding Rosemary and her care has been heavily redacted.

206 *"Rosemary showed disturbing signs"*: "The Tragic Story of . . . the Daughter JFK's Mother Had to Give Up," *National Enquirer,* November 5, 1967.

207 *"Thank you very much"*: "Condolence letters to others, 1969–1972," RFKP, box 73.

208 *Rose first visited Rosemary*: Historian Laurence Leamer believed that Rose visited Rosemary shortly after Rosemary was settled into Saint Coletta (LL, *The Kennedy Women,* 413); historian David Nasaw believed that Joe Sr. had not seen Rosemary for the twenty-five years before his own death, in 1969, and that Rose and Rosemary's siblings began to see Rosemary only sometime in the 1960s (DN, 630–31); and Doris Kearns Goodwin believed that Rose did not visit Rosemary until sometime after 1961, when Joe Sr. had had a stroke and could not stop her (DKG, 643).

"in the back of my mind": Interview with Sister Margaret Ann in LL, *The Kennedy Women,* 412–13.

"Sometime I should like": Letter, RFK to Thomas J. Walsh, February 27, 1969, RFKP, box 57.

209 *In March 1970*: "RFK Schedules, 1969–1972," November 30–December 1, 1970, RFKP, box 125.

"some little gifts": Letter, Diane Winter to Sister Caritas [*sic*], December 17, 1970, RFKP, box 57.

"I wish . . . you would send": Letter, RFK to "Children," December 17, 1970, RFKP, box 57.

"I am sure we are all very grateful": Letter, RFK to Sister Sheila, March 29, 1971, RFKP, box 57.

210 *"as you know"*: Letter, EKS to Sister Sheila, April 6, 1971, RFKP, box 57.

Dr. Raymond W. M. Chun: Letter, Sister Sheila to RFK, May 12, 1971, RFKP, box 57.

"*if {only} this could have been done*": Letter, Sister Charitas to RFK, April 25, 1971, RFKP, box 57.

"*It seems the longer she is off*": Letter, Sister Mary Charles to RFK, November 14, 1971, RFKP, box 57.

"*Because we feel*": Letter, Sister Sheila to RFK, May 12, 1971, RFKP, box 57.

211 "*My doctor . . . said*": Letter, Sister Charitas to RFK, April 25, 1971, RFKP, box 57.

"*a rather expensive frame*": Letter, Madeline Sulad to Sister Charitas, July 30, 1971, RFKP, box 57.

He "*sings his little heart out*": Letter, Sister Charitas to RFK, November 12, 1971, RFKP, box 57.

212 "*with all the indignation*": Letter, Sister Mary Charles to RFK, November 14, 1971, RFKP, box 57.

Rosemary was finding it "difficult": Letter, Sister Mary Charles to RFK, November 12, 1971, RFKP, box 57.

"*Many times the three of us*": Ibid.

"*I don't like*": Letter, Sister Paulus to RFK, November 14, 1971, RFKP, box 57.

"*I would like to emphasize again*": Letter, EKS to Sister Paula [*sic*], January 11, 1972, RFKP, box 57.

213 "*Mrs. Kennedy wanted you to know*": Letter, Madeline Sulad to Sister Paulus, January 19, 1972, RFKP, box 57.

"*Mrs. Kennedy is very involved*": Letter, Madeline Sulad to Sister Paulus, January 4, 1972, RFKP, box 57.

Days before Christmas 1971: Letter, Felice Lenz, R.N., to RFK, December 29, 1971, RFKP, box 57.

Rose may have felt: Letter, Madeline Sulad to Felice Lenz, R.N, January 5, 1972, RFKP, box 57.

"*Mrs. Shriver has followed*": Letter, RFK to Unknown, March 28, 1972, RFKP, box 57.

"*We understand*": Letter, Unknown to RFK, March 2, 1972, RFKP, box 57.

214 *"Her mind is gone completely":* RFK, interview by Robert Coughlan, January 14, 21, and 24, 1972, RFKP, box 10.
"Rose had an accident": Ibid.

215 *Within a month:* EKS, interview by Robert Coughlan, February 26, 1972, RFKP, box 10. See also Barbara A. Perry, *Rose
Kennedy: The Life and Times of a Political Matriarch* (New York:
Norton, 2013), 166. Perry discovered that the word *lobotomy*,
misspelled as "labadomy," had been redacted, so she made a formal request to the library to have the redaction removed, and it
complied.
the fact of the lobotomy: TTR, 244–45.
"And then I think sometimes" and following: RFK, interview by
Robert Coughlan, January 11, 1972, RFKP, box 10.

216 *"She was sure":* LL, *The Kennedy Women,* 674.
"I cannot understand": Letter, RFK to Sister Sheila, August 17,
1972, RFKP, box 57.
"buy presents for Rosemary": Letter, Madeline Sulad to Sister Paulus, August 30, 1972, RFKP, box 57.
Sister Paulus agreed: Letter, Sister Paulus to RFK, (early September 1972), RFKP, box 57.
Noting, first, her pleasure: Letter, RFK to Sister Paulus, December
28, 1972, RFKP, box 55.

217 *"do{ing} the little things":* Letter, Sister Mary Charles to RFK,
June 21, 1973, RFKP, box 57.
Rose told Coughlan in 1972: RFK, interview by Robert Coughlan,
January 7, 1972, RFKP, box 10.
"Bronxville" . . . *"European":* LL, *The Kennedy Women,* 682.

218 *"I was wondering":* Letter, RFK to Sister Sheila, July 19, 1974,
RFKP, box 57.
Assured that Rosemary would be fine: Letter, Sister Sheila to RFK,
July 23, 1974, RFKP, box 57.
Saint Coletta preferred: Barbara Gibson and Ted Schwarz, *Rose
Kennedy and Her Family: The Best and Worst of Their Lives and
Times* (New York: Birch Lane Press, 1995), 69–70.
"Of course, I would like": Letter, RFK to EKS, January 8, 1975,
RFKP, box 58.

"I don't have a favorite": Document dated 1971, "Rose Kennedy Personal Files, 1975–1977," RFKP, box 126.

Rose sent a letter to Pat: Letter, RFK to Patricia Kennedy Lawford, April 17, 1975, RFKP, box 58.

219   *they did not fulfill the obligation:* Letter, RFK to Patricia Kennedy Lawford and Jean Kennedy Smith, June 15, 1975, RFKP, box 58.

"With reference to Eunice": Letter, RFK to Jean Kennedy Smith, n.d., RFKP, box 59.

The next letter: Letter, RFK to Jean Kennedy Smith, n.d., RFKP, box 59.

Mother–daughter tension ran deep: LL, *The Kennedy Women,* 751.

Rosemary "came bouncing up": Interview with Jim Connor in ibid., 681.

Another family staff member and following: Interview with Bob Davidoff in LL, *The Kennedy Women,* 681.

"Arbarb": Gibson and Schwarz, *Rose Kennedy and Her Family,* 67.

220   *Rosemary . . . looked "straight ahead":* Ibid., 67–68.

"Rosie . . . Rosie": From a manuscript by niece Kerry McCarthy, quoted in LL, *The Kennedy Women,* 682.

She recalled Rose's instructions: Gibson and Schwarz, *Rose Kennedy and Her Family,* chap. 4 in particular.

221   *"President Kennedy's sister":* "Sister Gets News," *Milwaukee Sentinel,* November 23, 1963.

222   *Encounters between Rose and Rosemary:* Interview with Sister Margaret Ann Reckets in LL, *The Kennedy Women,* 413.

They had parties: LL, *The Kennedy Women,* 759.

223   *"Eunice has no compassion":* Gibson and Schwarz, *Rose Kennedy and Her Family,* 55.

"Damn Anthony": LL, *The Kennedy Women,* 683.

"If you know Rosemary": Joan Zyda, "The Kennedy No One Knows," *Chicago Tribune,* January 7, 1976.

"Are you looking for Eunice?": LL, *The Kennedy Women,* 682–83.

224   *Anthony Shriver became founder and chairman:* For more about Best Buddies International, see http://www.bestbuddies.org/best-buddies.

"A Kennedy through and through": Anthony Shriver, interview by author, October, 8, 2008.

Though her language was terribly limited: Timothy Shriver, interview by author, November 2, 2010.

225 *Tim believes:* Ibid.

"The interest {Rosemary} sparked": Letter, Anthony Shriver to author, February 17, 2009.

226 *"After watching the struggles"*: Jack McCallum, "Small Steps, Giant Strides," *Sports Illustrated,* December 8, 2008.

a "revolutionary": Ibid.

Rosemary . . . "sensitized": "A Tribute to Eunice Kennedy Shriver," November 16, 2007, 24–25, JFKPL.

"taught us the worth": EMK, at RMK funeral, January 10, 2005.

227 *"never doubted"*: Burton Hersh, *Edward Kennedy: An Intimate Biography* (New York: Counterpoint, 2010), 520.

"Many of us": Vincent Bzdek, *The Kennedy Legacy: Jack, Bobby, and Ted and a Family Dream Fulfilled* (New York: Palgrave Macmillan, 2009), 235.

Rosemary needed surgery: LL, *The Kennedy Women,* 759–60.

228 *"Rosemary's very cooperative"*: Interview with Sister Margaret Ann in ibid., 760.

"a magnetic personality": Ibid.

229 *"She knows her prayers"*: Ibid.

"There's a picture on the wall": Ibid., 761.

News of Rosemary's death: Martin Weil, "Rosemary Kennedy, 86, President Kennedy's Sister," *Washington Post,* January 8, 2005.

"I cannot attempt to judge": "'Times to Remember' Background Materials," RFKP, box 13.

230 *"my life {has been} lucky"*: "A Tribute to Eunice Kennedy Shriver," November 16, 2007, 24–25, JFKPL.

AUTHOR'S NOTE

236 *pink sheets marked "Withdrawal"*: See, for example, the withdrawal sheet in the file labeled "Rosemary Kennedy: Health, 1923–1949," JPK Papers #136, Series 1.2.5, JFKPL.

Index